Entertaining Made Easy

SUSAN WALTER
Writer

JANE HORN
Editor

KEVIN SANCHEZ
Photographer

SUSAN MASSEY-WEIL
Food Stylist

LIZ ROSS
Photographic Stylist

Susan Walter began her culinary career while working for a caterer during college. She has studied cooking in the United States and at Le Cordon Bleu in France, and has traveled extensively in Europe and Latin America studying the cuisines. She owns Susan Walter Catering and is the Catering Director at the Queen Anne Hotel in San Francisco, as well as a cooking teacher, event organizer, and author. She serves on the Board of Directors of the San Francisco Professional Food Society and is Treasurer of the Northern California chapter of the American Institute of Wine and Food, and is a member of the International Association of Cooking Professionals. Ms. Walter lives in San Francisco.

The California Culinary Academy In the forefront of American institutions leading the culinary renaissance in this country, the California Culinary Academy in San Francisco has gained a reputation as one of the most outstanding professional chef training schools in the world. With a teaching staff recruited from the best restaurants of Western Europe, the Academy educates students from around the world in the preparation of classical cuisine. The recipes in this book were created in consultation with the chefs of the Academy. For information about the Academy, write the Office of the Dean, California Culinary Academy, 625 Polk Street, San Francisco, CA 94102.

Front Cover
Sparkling with a shiny glaze, Fruit-Stuffed Squab (page 22) make wonderful party fare. Steamed Vegetables (page 75), which showcase the season, are deliciously sauced with herb butters (page 75). A beautiful cluster of hydrangeas enhances the buffet table.

Title Page: Beef Tenderloin Roll (see page 28) and Baked Potato Sticks (see page 31) would make an elegant and easy main course for your next dinner party.

Back Cover
Upper Left: Aromatic root vegetables such as leeks, carrots, and onions add depth of flavor to a basic meat stock.

Upper Right: Vanilla-Nutmeg Pound Cake (see page 35) pairs with Zinfandel Peaches (see page 37) for a grand, yet simple finale to any meal.

Lower Left: Every host needs a repertoire of quick and easy appetizers (see Effortless Appetizers, page 66).

Lower Right: Fish poached in gently simmering liquid is a classic preparation.

Special Thanks to
Paul Bauer; Biordi Art Imports; Claire's Antiques, Linens, and Gifts; Cookin'; Crate and Barrel; Cottage Tables; Peggy Fallon; Mark Felton; Lance Foster; Rebecca Johnson; Forrest Jones; Sue Fisher King; Patricia O'Brien; Rush Cutters; Charles Walter; Williams-Sonoma.

Contributors

Calligraphers
Keith Carlson, Chuck Wertman

Additional Photographers
Anthony Abuzeide, author, at left;
Laurie Black, at the Academy, pages 13, 50, 80, 92, and 104
Alan Copeland, at the Academy, pages 17, 34, 67, and 94
Michael Lamotte, back cover, upper left and lower right
Kit Morris, chefs, at left

Copy Chief
Melinda E. Levine

Copyeditor
Judith Dunham

Indexer
Elinor Lindheimer

Proofreader
Karen K. Johnson

Layout & pagination by
Tamara Mallory

Editorial Coordinator
Cass Dempsey

Composition Coordinator
Linda M. Bouchard

Systems Coordinator
Laurie Steele

Series format designed by
Linda Hinrichs and Carol Kramer

Production by
Studio 165

Separations by
Color Tech Corp.

Lithographed in the U.S.A. by
Webcrafters, Inc.

The California Culinary Academy series is produced by the staff of Ortho Information Services.

Publisher
Robert J. Dolezal

Editorial Director
Christine Robertson

Production Director
Ernie S. Tasaki

Series Managing Editor
Sally W. Smith

System Manager
Katherine L. Parker

Address all inquiries to
Ortho Information Services
Box 5047
San Ramon, CA 94583

1 2 3 4 5 6 7 8 9

89 90 91 92 93 94

ISBN 0-89721-190-1

Library of Congress Catalog
Card number 88-72343

Chevron Chemical Company
6001 Bollinger Canyon Road
San Ramon, CA 94583

Entertaining Made Easy

A well-planned party is easy on both host and guest, but it does require behind-the-scenes effort. Planning, practice, and a creative touch ensure success.

Planning Easy Parties

When the nineteenth-century French gastronome Brillat-Savarin wrote of the pleasures of the table, he was describing good food enjoyed in the company of good friends. This delightful form of social interaction is still the goal of all hosts. With this book you will learn how to entertain with style, confidence, and ease. Each chapter focuses on a particular type of entertaining— the classic dinner party, the impromptu gathering, the do-ahead meal, the large-scale event—and tells you how to prepare for it. The more than 175 recipes form a solid, creative, and foolproof collection that will become your entertaining signature.

PLANNING A PERFECT PARTY

Everyone is comfortable in the role of guest. However, when people assume the role of host, they may feel worried and apprehensive. Celebrating a special birthday or anniversary or inviting friends for dinner need not be an overwhelming challenge. Remember that the most important reason to entertain is to spend time with friends, and that sharing the occasion is more significant than what is served or how it is presented. By adopting a relaxed attitude, following some simple guidelines, and using a few special techniques, you can entertain easily and successfully. You will be able to enjoy your guests and your party from beginning to end—from the moment the invitation is issued to the last goodbye at the end of the evening.

CREATING CONFIDENCE

Entertaining is never effortless. Yet, with practice, planning, and mastery of basic techniques, you will develop or improve the skills needed to guide you through all types of party situations, a spur-of-the-moment dinner or an event planned weeks in advance, whether a small gathering for 8 or an open house for 30.

Perfect the dishes that you enjoy preparing and decide how you prefer to serve them. These dishes will become your signature. Practice them until you know they will go smoothly every time, with no unpleasant surprises to slow you down. By knowing what each recipe looks like at various stages, you won't panic when the dish appears to be wrong but really isn't. When you try a recipe for the first time, track preparation time and note it on the recipe for future reference. As you learn how long each dish takes to prepare, you will be better able to compose a menu matched to the amount of time available for a particular occasion.

Discover your style, the special method of entertaining that suits you best. Also determine the mood that makes you the most comfortable. If you enjoy formality, plan elegant dinner parties (small ones are most manageable) or stylish Champagne breakfasts. Remember that every party doesn't have to be a formal, sit-down dinner. A birthday brunch, a luncheon buffet, an easy-to-eat stand-up supper, an extravagant dessert buffet, or a midnight post-theater soup buffet are wonderful alternatives. Creating an event around a special occasion gives the cook, as well as the guests, a focus. A theme, event, or holiday can help suggest food, decor, and entertainment.

MAKING EASY MENUS

The menu is the foundation of a party. Create a comfort zone with proven recipes—some quick, some made ahead, and some created from a supply of pantry goods. To accommodate a busy schedule you may want to purchase carefully chosen prepared items. In relaxed moments, search out purveyors who offer high-quality ready-made foods that will complement homemade dishes.

When writing a menu, keep in mind your time, guests, budget, available space, tableware, and kitchen equipment. Hallmarks of a good menu include variety of color, texture, ingredients, and flavor. When harmonizing ingredients and seasonings, don't use the same flavor repetitively. Fresh seasonal fruits and vegetables bring vitality and color to all recipes, require little seasoning, and are a bargain, too.

GETTING ORGANIZED

Planning is essential. Make a shopping list based on your menu selections. Before the party, shop in stages; be aware of which foods can be prepared in advance and stored, and which must be purchased or prepared at the last minute. Some fresh ingredients, such as tomatoes or pears, need time to ripen and develop full flavor. Prepared dishes, such as some stews or marinated dishes, may need to rest for a day or two in the refrigerator to develop their flavors.

Next, list tasks in chronological order. Break recipes into small, manageable steps such as washing, slicing, dicing, or puréeing. For example, the preparation of a simple green salad includes making the dressing; washing the salad greens; cutting the accents such as tomatoes, cucumbers, or bell peppers; and tossing all ingredients together just before serving. Combining comparable tasks from several recipes will save time and effort. Wash all produce before proceeding, chop onions for two or three recipes at once, or toast nuts while the oven is being used for another baking job.

At cooking time, organize each dish using the traditional French method of *mise en place*—gathering measured amounts of ingredients together on a tray or baking sheet, ready to sauté, mix, or bake. When all the ingredients are at hand, you can proceed to prepare the recipe rapidly and efficiently without being interrupted by additional preparation or lack of an ingredient. With a task list, you will know which foods can be prepared ahead, and which must be organized for the dishes that are completed at the last minute.

For the actual party, draw up a timetable to help you keep track of which dishes cook in the oven, when to start simmering stovetop foods, when to cook vegetables or pasta, and what time to bring a chilled or frozen dessert to room temperature. Allow time for roasts to rest and wine to breathe. Combine procedures that begin and end at the same time, so that you reduce the amount of time spent in the kitchen. A good timetable leaves nothing to memory and helps to estimate cooking and serving requirements. By following such a plan, you will be better able to concentrate on guests, not on remembering your next move. For a sample timetable, see Working From Lists, opposite page.

WORKING FROM LISTS

Well-organized parties are successful parties. The best way to be organized is to create a specific and useful set of lists. Begin with a written menu and a shopping list. After shopping, create a task list and a timetable to enumerate specific tasks and the times they should be completed.

The preparation plans that accompany the menus throughout this book offer shopping suggestions and guide you through the planning and preparation of each meal. Refer to the plans when creating a shopping list, task list, and timetable. With practice, using these organizational tools will become second nature. The reward will be faster, more efficient preparation.

The following lists are based on the Afternoon Tea Buffet menu, page 11.

PANTRY LIST

Almonds
Almond extract
Baking powder
Baking soda
Black pepper
Butter
Cornstarch
Crackers
Currants (dried)
Curry powder
Eggs
Flour
Garlic
Ground white pepper
Onion
Orange-flavored liqueur
Orange juice
Salt
Semisweet chocolate
Strawberry preserves
Sugar (granulated and brown)
Tea
Unsweetened cocoa
Walnuts, pecans, or pine nuts
Whipping cream
White pepper
Whole almonds

SPECIAL PURCHASES

Allspice
Bourbon
Brillat-Savarin cheese
Buttermilk
Chicken livers
Cranberry juice
Dark corn syrup
Fresh basil, chives, parsley, or thyme
Sherry
Smithfield ham or other
  good-quality ham
Sparkling mineral water
Strawberries, grapes, or seasonal fruit
Sweet-hot mustard

TASK LIST

In advance:

Make and freeze Chocolate Truffles up to 1 month ahead.

Prepare and bake 2 recipes Butter Pastry (for Herbed Scrambled Egg Tart and Jim's Nut Tarts) up to 1 month ahead. Make a third recipe of pastry if serving Lemon Curd Tarts.

Prepare and bake nut tarts up to 1 month ahead; freeze in a rigid container with pieces of waxed paper separating tarts.

Make and freeze Hugh Duggan's Almond Crunch and Maggie's Best Biscotti up to several weeks ahead.

Make Marlene's Quick Curried Pâté up to 1 week ahead and refrigerate.

Shop for special ingredients 1 to 2 days before party.

Day of party:

Mix double recipe scone dough.

Wash fresh fruit, pat dry, and chill until needed.

Scramble eggs and keep warm over double boiler.

Make tea and prepare juices for spritzers.

TIMETABLE

9:00 a.m.   Mix double batch of scones; cut and arrange on baking sheets. Cover with dry towels. Arrange Hugh Duggan's Almond Crunch, Chocolate Truffles, and Maggie's Best Biscotti on a tray ready for afternoon tea. Make sure cups and saucers are ready and linens are pressed. Set table and plan where food will be placed. Do a trial arrangement with empty serving trays to make sure all will fit as planned. Put orange juice or cranberry juice in serving pitcher; chill until serving time.

1:45 p.m.   Arrange Brillat-Savarin cheese on a leaf-lined serving plate; wash fruit and store in refrigerator.

2:00 p.m.   Set out Jim's Nut Tarts on buffet (if frozen, refresh tarts in a 350° F oven for 5 minutes before serving). Fill empty tart shells with lemon curd (if using) and place on buffet.

2:30 p.m.   Place Marlene's Quick Curried Pâté on table. Arrange crackers in napkin-lined basket or around pâté on serving plate.

3:00 p.m.   Arrange fruit and crackers around cheese.

3:30 p.m.   Arrange Smithfield ham on a serving tray, leaving room for warm scones; near platter place a small container to hold mustard, or set out preserves (if using). Preheat oven for scones.

3:45 p.m.   Scramble eggs; reserve in double boiler until guests arrive. Bake scones and arrange around ham on tray.

4:00 p.m.   Party begins. Mix juice with chilled sparkling mineral water for spritzers. Serve juice spritzers and tea as guests arrive.

4:15 p.m.   Place eggs in 11-inch tart shell after guests arrive; place on buffet table immediately. Or, put eggs in 6 miniature tart shells at a time; pass immediately after filling. Repeat with all the egg tarts. If serving eggs in two 8-inch tart shells, fill 1 shell, then fill second shell when needed.

Basic fruits and vegetables

Apples, carrots, celery, lemons, lettuce, onions, oranges, garlic, shallots, fresh ginger, cabbage, potatoes, sweet potatoes, selection of seasonal vegetables and fruits

Cooking equipment

Food processor and blender; heavy-duty mixer with paddle, dough hook, and balloon whisk attachments; microwave oven; good knives including 4-inch paring, 8-inch chef's, 7-inch slicing; selection of 1-, 2-, and 3-quart casserole dishes that can go from stovetop to oven to table; 1½- and 2-quart soufflé dishes; a shallow gratin or baking dish; saucepans ranging from 1 to 8 quarts; skillets (8 and 12 inch); wok (14 inch) for quantity cooking and deep-frying; baking sheets and cooling racks; gadgets, including whisks (balloon and elongated sauce), slotted spoon, tongs, hot pads, metal and rubber spatulas. For large parties: several large (up to 12 quart) stainless steel mixing bowls, large baking and roasting pans (sized to fit your oven), and a variety (2-cup to 4-quart size) of food storage containers

Cupboard staples

Bread, dried beans and grains (long-grain rice, basmati rice, Arborio rice, lentils, wheat berries, bulgur and other favorite grains), dried Italian pasta and Asian noodles, granulated sugar, confectioners' sugar, brown sugar, honey, flour, cornmeal, rolled oats, vanilla extract, almond extract, unsweetened and semisweet chocolate, semisweet chocolate chips, unsweetened cocoa, baking powder, baking soda, cornstarch, apricot and raspberry jams, preserves, maple syrup, salt, pepper, dried herbs and spices, coffee, tea, canned plum tomatoes, tomato paste (in a tube), canned chicken and beef broth, Dijon-style mustard, olive oil, safflower oil, varietal-wine vinegars (cabernet, chardonnay, sherry) and fruit vinegars, dried apricots, dried currants, raisins, and dried pears

Special Feature

THE PARTY PANTRY

Pantry upkeep revolves around shopping bimonthly to restock basic ingredients and maintain a selection of prepared sauces, condiments, and other staples. Once or twice a week, you will need to add fresh meat, poultry, seafood, dairy products, fruit, and vegetables in moderate amounts to supplement the frozen and dry goods. Leftovers, a starting point for creative cooking, can be incorporated into pantry menus. Planned leftovers can reduce cooking time and allow you to prepare impromptu meals.

Cookware and tableware are also important components of the party pantry. Although closets full of cookware are unnecessary for preparing party food, a few carefully chosen pieces of equipment will make entertaining a pleasure rather than a chore. Select good-quality equipment that will be useful and durable. It is better to have a few items that last than many poor-quality pieces that need to be replaced often. As you work in the kitchen, decide which cookware and appliances to add in order to save time and effort and give the best results.

A supply of serving pieces and attractive tableware is essential. For versatility, choose tableware that has simple lines. Buy a large quantity of one size of glasses and dinner plates rather than the same number of dishes in an assortment of sizes. For example, 36 all-purpose glasses, holding 8 to 10 ounces, can be used for white wine, red wine, and non-alcoholic drinks as well as for fruit compotes and dessert mousses. Twenty-four white dinner plates can be dressed up with elegant accents or made festive with bright colors.

When all the components are at the ready, entertaining becomes easy. Polished silver, pressed linens, and sparkling crystal are almost as helpful as a well-stocked food pantry.

The following foods, equipment, and tableware are recommended as staples for a party pantry. Adapt these lists to suit your needs and style.

Fancy foods Dried mushrooms (*porcini*, *shiitake*), *amaretti* or other dry almond cookies, red and white wines, rum, brandy, liqueur (orange or coffee flavored), jars of roasted red peppers, soy sauce, Asian sesame oil, assorted canned beans (chick-pea, black, cannellini, kidney), canned gooseberries, tins of anchovies, canned oysters and clams, canned tuna, chutneys, sun-dried tomatoes, *cornichons* or dill pickles, olives (black, Niçoise, Greek, oil-cured, green), capers, and crackers

Freezer staples Corn, cherries, peas, peaches, blueberries, blackberries, strawberries, raspberries, good-quality tortellini, ice cream, active dry yeast, puff pastry, filo dough, Parmesan cheese, bread crumbs, spinach, stock (chicken, beef, and fish), butter, nuts (almonds, hazelnuts, pecans, pine nuts, walnuts), sausages, bacon, duck and chicken breasts, chops (veal, pork, and lamb), flank steak, pesto sauce, orange juice, cranberry juice

Refrigerator staples Blue cheese, goat cheese, Cheddar cheese, Swiss cheese, cream cheese, Monterey jack cheese, butter, cream, milk, sour cream, plain yogurt, eggs, parsley and other fresh herbs, bacon, smoked chicken or smoked turkey, fresh meat (or poultry or seafood), corn or flour tortillas

Tableware A selection of tablecloths; at least 12 matching napkins; candles (votive and tapers); one size of basic glasses and large dinner plates; casserole dishes and platters in a variety of styles to complement simple dishes and glassware; chafing dish (for buffet main courses or side dishes, or to use in place of an extra burner in the kitchen) chosen to harmonize with the tableware; an abundant supply of cocktail napkins, serving trays, toothpicks, and bamboo skewers; vases for cut flowers, and bowls and baskets for arrangements of vegetables, herbs, and fruit; dried and silk flowers, paper and polyester leaves, attractive pots, and paper doilies

FINDING THE RIGHT APPROACH

Different entertaining situations call for different solutions. Each chapter offers creative, practical solutions to common entertaining challenges. The second chapter contains a wealth of recipes designed to form a foolproof foundation for easy entertaining. With practice, they will allow you to entertain comfortably in any situation because you know that your recipes are proven winners.

The important Party Pantry, at left, is used in the third chapter to form the backbone of easy entertaining. Foods—including leftovers—that store well in the cupboard, freezer, or refrigerator are always on hand to be turned into great meals, facilitating menu planning and saving time.

When you are pressed for time or must entertain on short notice, there are still lots of choices for party food. A repertoire of quick and easy dishes—found in the fourth chapter—allows you to issue an invitation late in the workday or to see friends during a busy week. That chapter also shows you how a quick stop at the market for fresh ingredients, plus a skillful use of the pantry, can make this kind of entertaining realistic and enjoyable.

When you have some breathing room because a special event is weeks away, you can shop in advance, cook at leisure, store the food, and finish cooking on the day of the party. The fifth chapter focuses on such do-ahead recipes, which many cooks consider the most convenient way to entertain.

Menus for grand occasions always need more time and organization. The last chapter provides time-saving tips, techniques, and recipes for large gatherings, including a suggestion for a weekend of parties that use the same foods in different ways.

Tips

... ON MASTERING RELAXED ENTERTAINING

Once you've decided to issue an invitation, whether formal, handwritten, or telephoned, keep the following thoughts in mind throughout the planning and execution of the party.

☐ Guests will come to a party because they want to be there. They enjoy your company and home as is, so do not worry about having the perfect dishes or decor.

☐ The goal of a party is to have fun; this applies to you, the host, as much as to the guests. The host should be a participant in the party, not a slave to the kitchen.

☐ Don't do too much. Making too much food, too elaborate a menu, or too fussy a centerpiece will cause you to be tired and nervous and the guests to be uneasy. The surest way to create a disaster is by trying too hard to impress company.

☐ Stick with recipes and ideas that suit your abilities and interests and the amount of time you have available.

☐ Draft complete shopping and preparation lists. Forgetting items at the store or starting to cook a dish late will cause needless anxiety.

☐ Organize equipment and serving pieces well in advance, so that the meal is your only concern on the day of the party.

☐ Set your table the night before the event, and arrange your centerpiece, if possible. Some floral arrangements look better if the flowers have a day or so to open.

This charming Afternoon Tea Buffet is easy to organize because much of the food can be prepared ahead of time.

AFTERNOON TEA BUFFET

Marlene's Quick Curried Pâté

Herbed Scrambled Egg Tart

Jim's Nut Tarts

*Lemon Curd Tarts
(optional; see page 47)*

Maggie's Best Biscotti

Chocolate Truffles

Hugh Duggan's Almond Crunch

*Currant Scones, With Country Ham
And Sweet-Hot Mustard or
Strawberry Preserves*

*Brillat-Savarin Cheese, Garnished
With Strawberries and Grapes*

*Orange or Cranberry
Spritzers and Tea*

This sweet and savory tea buffet can be adapted to suit your entertaining requirement, whether it be for a morning coffee klatch or a post-theater dessert party. Simply match the beverages to the time of day: Serve a robust coffee in the morning, juice spritzers and tea in the afternoon, and wine or Champagne in the evening. This menu serves 12.

Preparation Plan

Make and freeze Chocolate Truffles up to one month ahead. If you are serving Lemon Curd Tarts, the curd can be prepared up to three weeks ahead and stored, tightly covered, in the refrigerator. Hugh Duggan's Almond Crunch and Maggie's Best Biscotti can be prepared up to several weeks ahead and frozen. Make Marlene's Quick Curried Pâté up to one week before the party and store in the refrigerator. Make 2 recipes Butter Pastry: one recipe for Herbed Scrambled Egg Tart and one recipe for Jim's Nut Tarts. The single, 11-inch scrambled egg tart makes an outstanding presentation. Slice it into thin wedges and serve on small plates. If you prefer to serve the scrambled eggs in two 8-inch tarts or in 3-inch individual tarts, bake preferred size of shell "blind" (unfilled) and place the scrambled egg mixture (reserved in the double boiler until needed) into the tart shells as guests arrive. The nut tarts can be made up to one month ahead and frozen. Refresh frozen tarts in oven for 5 minutes before serving. Blind-bake a third recipe of pastry if serving Lemon Curd Tarts. Fill with Lemon Curd just before setting out on the table.

Mix a double recipe of the scone dough up to 8 hours before party, cut, cover with dry towel, and let rest on baking sheets until 20 minutes before guests arrive. Arrange 1 pound thinly sliced, cooked Smithfield ham on a serving tray, leaving room for scones.

Garnish Brillat-Savarin cheese (a triple cream cheese from Normandy, France) with strawberries or grapes. Place crackers for cheese and pâté in napkin-lined basket. Scramble eggs 30 minutes before party and keep warm over double boiler. Prepare spritzers: Mix juice with sparkling mineral water. Set pitcher out on table. Fill prepared tart shells after guests arrive.

MARLENE'S QUICK CURRIED PÂTÉ

Nothing could be simpler to prepare than a savory pâté of chicken liver. It should be refrigerated at least one day in advance of serving to let the flavors blend. The pâté will keep about 10 days in the refrigerator. Serve with homemade Country Loaf (see page 23), good-quality crackers, or purchased baguettes.

> 4 *tablespoons unsalted butter*
> 1 *small onion, diced*
> 1 *clove garlic, minced*
> 2 *teaspoons curry powder*
> 1½ *tablespoons flour*
> ½ *pound chicken livers*
> ¼ *cup sherry*
> ½ *teaspoon salt*
> ¼ *teaspoon freshly ground pepper*
> ¼ *teaspoon allspice*
> 1 *egg*
> *Crackers or baguette slices, for accompaniment*

1. Preheat oven to 350° F. In a 12-inch skillet over medium heat, melt butter. Stir in onion and sauté until softened (3 to 4 minutes). Add garlic and curry powder and cook until garlic is softened (2 to 3 minutes). Stir in flour and cook until mixture is slightly thickened (3 to 4 minutes). Add chicken livers, sherry, salt, pepper, and allspice. Reduce heat to low, cover, and simmer until livers are barely cooked and no longer pink in the center (about 15 minutes).

2. Purée liver mixture in a blender or food processor until smooth. Add egg and mix in thoroughly. Place mixture in an ovenproof, 2-cup soufflé dish. Cover tightly with aluminum foil and set in a shallow pan filled with 1 inch of hot water. Bake until top of pâté appears set and firm to the touch (about 35 minutes). Cool and refrigerate for at least 24 hours for flavors to develop.

3. To serve, remove aluminum foil and place on a serving dish surrounded by crackers.

Makes 1½ cups, 20 servings as an appetizer.

HERBED SCRAMBLED EGG TART

This light egg tart can be garnished with minced chives or salmon caviar for a colorful, glamorous presentation. To fill one 11-inch tart shell or two 8-inch tart shells, prepare a double recipe of the scrambled eggs.

12 eggs, beaten
¼ cup minced fresh basil, chives, parsley, or thyme
1 teaspoon salt
½ teaspoon white pepper
3 tablespoons unsalted butter
½ cup whipping cream

Butter Pastry

1½ cups flour
1 teaspoon sugar
½ teaspoon salt
½ cup unsalted butter, chilled and cut into ½-inch cubes
1 egg
2 tablespoons cold water

1. In a 3-quart bowl beat eggs with basil, salt, and pepper. In a double boiler over barely simmering water, melt butter; add eggs, stirring constantly. Reduce heat to medium-low.

2. Cook eggs, stirring to keep them from sticking to pan, until soft curds begin to form (about 20 minutes); stir in cream and continue cooking until soft curds reappear but eggs are still moist (about 10 minutes). Scoop into baked tart shell(s) and serve immediately.

Serves 14.

Butter Pastry

1. Place flour, sugar, and salt in a 3-quart mixing bowl or in work bowl of a food processor. Cut butter into flour using a pastry blender or 2 knives, or with quick on-and-off bursts if using food processor. Beat together egg and the water. When flour mixture resembles coarse crumbs, stir in egg-water mixture; mix only until dough begins to hold together.

2. Press dough into tart pan(s). Refrigerate for 1 hour or wrap carefully and freeze for up to 1 month.

3. Before baking, preheat oven to 400° F. Bake "blind" (unfilled): Line tart shell(s) with aluminum foil, fill with dried beans, and bake 12 minutes. Lift out foil and beans and bake 10 minutes more.

Makes one 11-inch tart shell, two 8-inch tart shells, or fourteen 3-inch miniature tart shells.

JIM'S NUT TARTS

Only one mixing bowl is required to prepare these rich individual walnut, almond, pine nut, or pecan pies, so cleanup is a cinch. Use the Butter Pastry recipe (at left) to line 14 shallow, 3-inch-diameter tart tins. Or, use to line an 11-inch tart pan; bake 1 hour at 350° F.

¾ cup firmly packed brown sugar
¼ cup cornstarch
3 large eggs
½ cup butter, melted
½ cup dark corn syrup
¼ cup bourbon
1 cup coarsely chopped walnuts, almonds, pine nuts, or pecans
14 unbaked 3-inch shells Butter Pastry (at left)

1. Preheat oven to 350° F. In a 2-quart bowl mix together sugar and cornstarch. Beat in eggs. Stir in butter, corn syrup, and bourbon; mix thoroughly. Stir in nuts.

2. Divide filling among tart shells (about ¼ cup per shell) and bake until top of tarts appears dry and a knife inserted in center comes out clean (about 30 minutes). Cool about 30 minutes before serving.

Serves 14.

Chocolate Chip Nut Tarts Stir
½ cup semisweet chocolate chips into filling before baking. Bake as directed.

MAGGIE'S BEST BISCOTTI

Biscotti store well in an airtight tin, ready for a brunch treat, tea party, or dessert accompaniment. A heavy-duty mixer will ease the job of mixing this very stiff dough.

2 cups flour
1¼ cups sugar
2½ teaspoons baking powder
½ teaspoon baking soda
¾ teaspoon salt
2 whole eggs, plus 1 egg, separated
1 teaspoon almond extract
1½ cups whole almonds, coarsely chopped

1. Preheat oven to 350° F. Line 2 baking sheets with parchment paper.

2. Sift together flour, sugar, baking powder, baking soda, and salt. Add 2 whole eggs and 1 egg yolk, almond extract, and almonds. Mix thoroughly until dough holds together. Add half of reserved egg white, if necessary, to make a cohesive dough.

3. With wet hands shape dough into 6 logs, each 1¾ inches in diameter and 6 inches long. Place 3 to 4 inches apart on prepared baking sheets. Bake on middle rack of oven until logs are light golden brown and spring back when touched (about 24 minutes). Cool 15 minutes.

4. Lower oven to 275° F. Slice logs diagonally into ½-inch-thick slices. Return to oven and bake until completely dry and crisp throughout (about 40 minutes). Cool.

Makes about 5 dozen cookies.

Breakfast Biscotti Replace
1 cup flour with 1 cup whole wheat flour, ½ teaspoon cinnamon, and ¼ teaspoon nutmeg. Replace ¾ cup granulated sugar with ½ cup firmly packed light brown sugar.

CHOCOLATE TRUFFLES

Rich and creamy, truffles are an easy way to impart a touch of elegance to any party. They are best made ahead and frozen. Make a double or triple recipe and defrost, as needed, in the refrigerator six to eight hours before serving.

- ½ cup whipping cream
- 10 ounces semisweet chocolate, finely chopped
- 2 egg yolks
- 2 tablespoons orange-flavored liqueur
  Unsweetened cocoa, for dusting

1. In a 1-quart saucepan bring cream to a boil. Remove from heat and stir in chocolate. Pour into a small bowl and whisk in egg yolks and liqueur. Chill 2 to 48 hours.

2. Sprinkle a baking sheet or small plate with cocoa. Scoop up a teaspoonful of chocolate mixture and shape into a ball. Roll in cocoa. Repeat. Freeze if not serving immediately.

Makes 26 truffles.

HUGH DUGGAN'S ALMOND CRUNCH

This simple candy stores well and should be a staple to have on hand when guests drop by unexpectedly or to serve after dinner with a sip of almond-flavored liqueur.

- 9 tablespoons unsalted butter
- 1 cup sugar
- ¼ cup water
- ½ cup coarsely chopped toasted almonds
- 4 ounces semisweet chocolate, melted

1. Evenly grease a baking sheet with 1 tablespoon butter; reserve. In a 2-quart saucepan over medium-high heat, place remaining butter, sugar, and the water. Cover pan and bring to a boil.

2. Uncover and stir in ¼ cup almonds. Cook, stirring, over medium-high heat until honey-colored (about 20 minutes; 280° F on a candy thermometer). For a thick candy, pour mixture onto prepared baking sheet; do not spread. For a thinner version, pour onto baking sheet and spread with a metal spoon or wooden spatula to within 1 inch of edges.

3. When cool cover nut mixture with melted chocolate and then sprinkle with remaining almonds. Chill until chocolate is firm. Break into bite-sized pieces.

Makes 2 dozen bite-sized pieces, about 1 pound.

CURRANT SCONES

Mix the scone dough, cut, and place on a baking sheet early in the day (up to eight hours ahead). Store, loosely covered with a clean towel, and bake just before serving time. Serve with a good-quality country ham (such as Smithfield), accompanied by a Dijon-style mustard or a sweet-hot mustard, or serve with strawberry preserves or lemon curd. For one dozen scones, you will need about ½ pound ham. For this menu, prepare a double recipe of scones and buy 1 pound sliced, cooked ham.

- 2 cups flour, plus flour for dusting
- 2 tablespoons sugar (optional)
- 4 teaspoons baking powder
- ½ teaspoon salt
- ½ cup butter, chilled, plus 2 tablespoons butter, melted
- ¾ cup buttermilk
- ¼ cup dried currants

1. Preheat oven to 425° F. In a 3-quart bowl, sift together flour, sugar (if used), baking powder, and salt. Dice the ½ cup butter into ½-inch cubes and, using 2 knives or a pastry blender, cut into flour mixture until mixture resembles small, coarse crumbs.

2. Make a depression in center of flour-butter mixture and gently stir in buttermilk and currants, taking care not to overmix dough. Mix only until dry ingredients are moistened.

3. Lightly dust a work surface with flour. Place dough on work surface and pat into a 1½-inch-thick rectangle. Cut out biscuits with a round cutter or cut into squares with a knife. Place on an ungreased baking sheet. Brush with melted butter and bake until light, golden brown (about 15 minutes).

4. To serve, split scones horizontally; serve immediately.

Makes 1 dozen scones.

Make-Ahead Tip Scones are best freshly baked, but can be baked ahead, cooled, and frozen. Refresh by placing in a 350° F oven for 5 minutes (if defrosted) or 20 minutes (if still frozen).

Establish your entertaining style,
be it classic, contemporary, or
a bit of both, with foods
and table decor that reflect
your personal taste.

Entertaining With Confidence

Success breeds confidence, and nowhere more so than in the kitchen. All will go smoothly if the meal is one you can execute flawlessly because it's a repeat performance, rather than the opening night. The recipes in this chapter are guaranteed to garner rave reviews from your guests. You will also find step-by-step instructions for risotto (see page 31), a festive Italian rice dish; all you need to know about homemade mayonnaise and vinaigrette sauces (see pages 20 and 21); plus tips and recipes for simple yeast breads for all occasions (see page 23). The two menus (see pages 24 and 33) are examples of easy-to-organize dinner parties—one an informal supper and the other a somewhat dressier meal.

Full of garden-fresh flavor, Vegetable Soup Printanier is inviting when served from a pretty tureen at the table. For a more informal party, let guests help themselves from a stockpot kept warm on the stove.

PRACTICE PRODUCES A PERFECT REPAST

Entertaining can generate some anxious moments. Will the food taste the way it was planned? Will it look as good as in the photograph? Will everything be ready at the right time? Will the pie come out of the pan easily? Will guests enjoy themselves? Good planning, practice, and timing matched to your own pace will give you the confidence to answer "yes" to all these questions.

Calm will replace frantic haste if you cook with practiced moves. This means planning a menu around delicious and reliable dishes that you can serve with ease and style because you've made them often. You will actually move faster and more efficiently in the kitchen when the meal is a repeat performance. Most importantly, you will enjoy the party along with your guests when you know that the food will taste superb. When the kitchen is under control, everyone is more comfortable and relaxed and the fun can begin.

A FOUNDATION OF FAMILIAR FAVORITES

Let the recipes in this chapter form the foolproof foundation for your repertoire. They are not the bland basics of the first-time cook. Rather, they are an exciting, failure-free collection guaranteed to be successful whether you are a novice or a pro. Rehearse them at weeknight meals or at casual gatherings until you can prepare them—even on the spur of the moment—with little or no stress. Some are simple; others will take more time. But, with practice, all will become familiar favorites and will enable you to entertain serenely and successfully.

Mastering Techniques

Entertaining will be easier and more pleasant when you've mastered some basic techniques. Steaming, broiling, sautéing, and baking are some quick and easy methods of cooking. As you prepare these foundation recipes, you will improve your cooking skills and gain experience with techniques that will prove useful throughout the book. Your skills will create a comfort zone as the recipes become second nature to you. With repetition, you will gain the same assurance as a chef in a four-star restaurant.

Signature Recipes

Once you've mastered the techniques and become familiar with the recipes, you can modify the dishes so that they become your own creations. They may even become signature dishes, the dishes that you are known for and that build your reputation for successful entertaining. For example, Nora's Potato Gratin (see page 30) is transformed when layered with sautéed leeks or steamed artichoke bottoms. The wonderful Zinfandel Pears (see page 37) changes dramatically when peaches are substituted for the pears.

If you have a talent for grilling, plan meals around the barbecue. Mediterranean Leg of Lamb (see page 29) and Salmon Steaks With Green Onion-Dill Butter (see page 34) both adapt well to the grill. If you love desserts, make the last course the showcase of the meal and keep the rest of the menu simple. Try extravagantly rich Chocolatte (see page 26) or fragrant Frangipane Fruit Tart (see page 34).

Planning a Menu

With the recipes in this chapter, a simple menu, precisely prepared, is an attainable goal for any cook. Meals should not be overorchestrated or both you and your guests may become ill at ease. If the menu is too ambitious, recipes are too difficult or time-consuming, or there is more food than guests want or need, entertaining becomes too much work and too little fun. Guests will feel uncomfortable with a host who is constantly running back and forth between kitchen and dining room to attend to an overwhelming number of preparation details.

APPETIZERS AND FIRST COURSES

Appetizers set the stage. Blanched vegetables, arranged like a bouquet of flowers, can be served with Aioli or Rémoulade Sauce (see page 20). Beef or chicken cubes can be marinated, skewered, grilled, and served at room temperature with an Italian Salsa Verde (see page 21) or spicy Romesco Sauce (see page 20). A basic chicken stock is the foundation for both Creamy Carrot Soup (at right) and refreshing Vegetable Soup Printanier (see below). Remember that appetizers stimulate, rather than satiate, the appetite, so plan moderate quantities of light foods.

VEGETABLE SOUP PRINTANIER

To make this refreshing soup throughout the year, use whatever vegetables are in season. If using canned broth, for a homemade taste use 2½ cups broth and an equal amount of water.

4 tablespoons butter
2 medium white onions, finely diced
14 baby turnips, trimmed and halved lengthwise
14 baby carrots, peeled and cut in 1-inch lengths
1 pound fresh peas, shelled, or about 2 cups frozen peas
6 green onions, sliced diagonally into 1-inch lengths
5 cups Chicken Stock (see page 56)
½ cup julienned fresh basil
½ teaspoon salt
¼ teaspoon white pepper

1. In a 3-quart saucepan over medium heat, melt butter. Stir in white onion and cook until softened and translucent (about 10 minutes).

2. Add turnips and carrots and cook 10 minutes more. Add peas, green onions, and Chicken Stock. Over medium-high heat bring soup to a boil; then reduce heat to medium-low and simmer 10 minutes. Stir in basil, salt, and pepper. Serve immediately.

Makes 7 cups, 6 servings.

CREAMY CARROT SOUP

This quick soup can be frozen for one month. Vary by substituting cauliflower or broccoli for the carrots.

1 pound carrots, peeled and coarsely chopped
1 medium potato, peeled and coarsely chopped
½ cup unsalted butter
1 teaspoon salt
¼ teaspoon freshly ground pepper
3 cups Chicken Stock (see page 56)
¼ cup sour cream, for garnish
4 to 6 sprigs fresh oregano, for garnish

1. In a 2-quart saucepan over medium-low heat, place carrots and potatoes and add water to cover; simmer until vegetables are easily pierced with a sharp knife (about 25 minutes).

2. Purée carrots and potato in a blender or food processor with butter, salt, and pepper. Return to saucepan and stir in Chicken Stock. Place over medium heat and cook until warm. Serve immediately. Garnish each serving with a tablespoon of sour cream and a sprig of fresh oregano.

Makes 5 cups, 4 to 6 servings.

Smoked Chicken Salad is an elegant first course that can be quickly assembled with one market stop during a busy day. A piquant dressing made with raspberry vinegar enhances the flavor of the fresh raspberries in the salad.

SMOKED CHICKEN SALAD

Use smoked turkey or smoked ham for tasty variations on this quick and beautiful first-course salad.

- 2 small bunches (about 8 oz) baby curly endive (frisée), shredded
- ½ pound smoked chicken breast, shredded
- 2 small peaches
- 16 fresh raspberries, for garnish

Raspberry Vinaigrette

- 2 tablespoons raspberry vinegar
- 4 tablespoons safflower oil
- ½ cup julienned fresh basil
- ⅛ teaspoon salt
  Freshly ground pepper, to taste

Divide curly endive and chicken among 4 salad plates. Slice peaches and arrange on salad plates. Dot with fresh raspberries. Drizzle with vinaigrette and serve immediately.

Serves 4.

Raspberry Vinaigrette   In a 2-cup bowl, whisk together vinegar, oil, basil, salt, and pepper.

Makes about ¾ cup.

ARTICHOKE SALAD

Wine-based salad dressings accent, rather than clash with, the wines served with dinner. Steam artichokes the day before serving this salad. Toasting the hazelnuts enhances their natural flavor. Place them on a baking sheet and toast in a preheated 325° F oven 6 to 8 minutes. Wrap in a kitchen towel and rub together gently to remove some of the slightly bitter skin.

- 4 artichokes
  Wine Vinaigrette (see page 21)
- 8 cups salad greens, washed, dried and torn into bite-sized pieces
- 1 cup hazelnuts, toasted and coarsely chopped

1. Trim sharp, pointed tips from artichoke leaves with scissors. If stem end appears dry, trim away about ½ inch. Remaining part of stem is edible. *To boil artichokes:* In a 6-quart Dutch oven bring 5 quarts water to a boil. Place artichokes in water, reduce heat to medium, and boil until tender (about 35 minutes; a knife will easily pierce stem end). *To steam artichokes:* Place artichokes in a steamer basket fitted into a 6-quart Dutch oven filled with 2 inches of water. Cover and steam until tender (about 35 minutes; a knife will easily pierce stem end). Remove artichoke leaves and reserve for another use (leaves are delicious dipped in Homemade Mayonnaise, see page 20). Scrape away furry center (the choke) of each artichoke and discard. What remains is the artichoke bottom.

2. Slice artichoke bottoms ¼ inch thick. Toss with Wine Vinaigrette. Place salad greens in large salad bowl, add artichoke bottoms and vinaigrette, and toss together. Sprinkle with hazelnuts. Serve immediately.

Serves 6 to 8.

MAIN COURSES

With these fundamental, unpretentious main courses in your recipe file, you will never be at a loss when planning a party menu. Practice these dishes until you know them well.

LASAGNE CON TRE FORMAGGI

Lasagne with three cheeses makes a fine accompaniment to a baked ham for a simple buffet, or it can be served by itself as a main course for a family supper.

      4   tablespoons olive oil
      2   shallots, minced
      1   bunch spinach, washed and
          shredded
      ¾   pound fresh lasagne noodles
          (4 noodles, about 5 in. by
          10 in.) or 6 ounces dried
          lasagne noodles
      3   pounds ricotta cheese
      2   large tomatoes, sliced
      1   pound mozzarella or
          provolone cheese, sliced
      1   cup parsley, minced

Parmesan Sauce

      4   tablespoons butter
      5   tablespoons flour
      2   cups milk
      1   teaspoon salt
      ¼   teaspoon ground white pepper
      ⅛   teaspoon ground nutmeg
      ½   cup freshly grated
          Parmesan cheese

1. Prepare Parmesan Sauce and reserve. Grease an 8- by 12-inch baking dish with 2 tablespoons of the olive oil. Preheat oven to 350° F. In a 12-inch skillet over low heat, heat remaining olive oil. Sauté shallots and spinach together until spinach is wilted (about 8 minutes).

2. Place ½ cup Parmesan Sauce in baking dish. Place one lasagne noodle on sauce. For first layer: Spread 1 pound ricotta on noodle, cover with one half the tomato, then ½ cup Parmesan Sauce, and finally another lasagne noodle. For second layer: Spread 1 pound ricotta cheese on noodle, cover with all of spinach mixture, one half of the mozzarella, another ½ cup Parmesan Sauce, and

top with another noodle. For the final layer: Spread on remaining ricotta, remaining tomato, remaining mozzarella, ½ cup Parmesan Sauce, and remaining noodle. Top with remaining Parmesan Sauce and sprinkle with parsley.

3. Bake until lightly browned on top and bubbly around edges (about 35 minutes). Cool 10 minutes before serving.

Serves 8.

Parmesan Sauce   In a 2-quart saucepan over low heat, melt butter. Whisk in flour and cook until golden brown (4 to 5 minutes). Slowly add milk, whisking until smooth and slightly thickened. Add salt, pepper, nutmeg, and Parmesan. Reserve.

Makes about 2½ cups.

Make-Ahead Tip   Tightly cover unbaked lasagne casserole with aluminum foil and place in a plastic bag from which air has been pressed. Freeze up to 3 months. Bake frozen casserole, covered with foil, in a 350° F oven 1 hour; remove foil and cook until heated through and slightly golden brown on top (another 15 minutes).

Lasagne con Tre Formaggi is a delicious way to use leftovers such as chicken, beef, sausage, broccoli, leeks, Swiss chard, or zucchini—simply add a layer of leftovers to the dish.

MARVELOUS MAYONNAISE

Making mayonnaise is so simple and the result so superior in flavor and texture to commercial versions that you will wonder why you don't make your own all the time. Begin with egg yolks, and whisk by hand or whirl in a blender or food processor until light in color. Slowly add oil in a thin stream to make a thick, smooth emulsion. Then stir in seasonings.

Match the mayonnaise to your palate and your recipe by varying the oil and the vinegar, or by adding tomato paste, minced or dried herbs, garlic, or citrus juice. Add diced jalapeño chiles to make a spicy mayonnaise dressing for chicken or steak, or season with minced parsley, watercress, green onion, and capers to drizzle over romaine lettuce. Use walnut oil instead of vegetable oil and toss with apples, walnuts, and celery for a new twist on Waldorf salad. The choice is up to you.

HOMEMADE MAYONNAISE

Once you become comfortable with this recipe, you will find it easier to prepare mayonnaise yourself than to take the time to drive to the market to buy it ready-made. For a south-of-France flavor, substitute olive oil for the vegetable oil. Or add 1 cup fresh minced herbs and use as a sandwich spread or vegetable dip.

> *2 egg yolks*
> *1 teaspoon Dijon-style mustard*
> *1 cup vegetable oil*
> *1½ tablespoons white wine vinegar*
> *Juice of ½ lemon*
> *¾ teaspoon salt*
> *¼ teaspoon ground white pepper*

1. In a 1½-quart bowl or in a food processor or blender, beat egg yolks with mustard until color of mixture has lightened to pale yellow.

2. Add oil by the teaspoonful, or in a thin stream if pouring through feed tube of processor (with machine running), until it is incorporated and mayonnaise has thickened. Add vinegar, lemon juice, salt, and pepper; stir to combine.

Makes 1 cup.

Aioli (Garlic Mayonnaise)
Finely mince 3 cloves garlic and stir into Homemade Mayonnaise.

RÉMOULADE SAUCE

A classic mayonnaise-based sauce, rémoulade complements many foods—fish, meat, and poultry. Vary its flavor by adding minced jalapeño chile and serve with the Cornmeal-Crusted Orange Roughy (see opposite page) or Red Pepper Terrine (see page 83).

> *½ cup small dill pickles, minced*
> *Juice of ½ lemon*
> *1 tablespoon capers*
> *2 cloves garlic, finely minced*
> *⅓ cup finely minced parsley*
> *2 green onions, minced*
> *2 tablespoons tomato paste*
> *1½ cups Homemade Mayonnaise (at left)*

In a small bowl stir pickles, lemon juice, capers, garlic, parsley, green onions, and tomato paste into Homemade Mayonnaise.

Makes about 2 cups.

Jalapeño Rémoulade Stir 1 minced jalapeño chile into Rémoulade Sauce.

ROMESCO SAUCE

This sauce is a staple of *tapas,* the snacks found all over Spain. Often served spread on toasted garlic bread, it is equally good with baguette slices, as a dip for meat or seafood, swirled in a creamy soup, or as a spread for turkey sandwiches. Store in the refrigerator for up to two weeks.

> *1 red bell pepper or 1 jar (7 oz) roasted red peppers*
> *1 tablespoon tomato paste*
> *3 cloves garlic, peeled*
> *1 teaspoon minced dried red chile*
> *1 tablespoon red wine vinegar*
> *4 tablespoons olive oil*
> *½ cup blanched almonds, finely ground*
> *½ teaspoon salt*
> *¼ teaspoon freshly ground pepper*
> *¼ cup Homemade Mayonnaise (at left)*

1. Roast bell pepper by placing on a rack over a direct flame or under a preheated broiler, about 3 inches from heat source. Turn frequently to roast all sides. When skin is blistered, remove from flame and immediately place in a plastic bag. Seal and let steam for 20 minutes. Remove bell pepper from bag and peel away charred skin under running water. Pat dry. Pepper should be cut into 4 to 6 pieces to purée more easily.

2. Place bell pepper, tomato paste, garlic, chile, vinegar, oil, almonds, salt, and pepper in a blender or food processor; purée until almost smooth (leave some small chunks). Stir in mayonnaise. Serve sauce at room temperature.

Makes about 1¾ cups.

CORNMEAL-CRUSTED ORANGE ROUGHY

Orange roughy, a New Zealand fish, is now readily available in the fish market. Other firm-fleshed fish, such as sole, can be substituted. Simply remember to sauté the fish for 10 minutes per inch of thickness. The fish can be coated up to 8 hours ahead of cooking and stored in the refrigerator. Toast almonds on a baking sheet in a 350° F oven 6 to 8 minutes. If you make this recipe often, toast and chop the almonds when you have spare time, and store them in the freezer until needed.

    ¼ cup cornmeal
    ½ cup finely chopped toasted
       almonds
    ½ teaspoon salt
    ½ teaspoon dried thyme
    ¼ teaspoon freshly ground
       pepper
    6 fillets (about ¼ lb each)
       orange roughy
    3 tablespoons unsalted butter
       Lemon wedges and parsley
       sprigs, for garnish
       Jalapeño Rémoulade
       (see opposite page),
       for accompaniment

1. In a shallow mixing bowl or pie plate, stir together cornmeal, almonds, salt, thyme, and pepper. Coat fillets in cornmeal mixture.

2. In a 14-inch skillet melt butter over medium heat. Sauté fillets on one side until golden brown (about 6 minutes). Turn and cook second side until done (about 4 minutes). Serve with lemon wedges, parsley sprigs, and Jalapeño Rémoulade.

Serves 6.

VERSATILE VINAIGRETTE

Vinaigrettes not only make salads shine but can be used to marinate seafood, poultry, and meat. Just as with mayonnaise, the flavor of a vinaigrette can change dramatically with different combinations of oils and vinegars. Mild spring and summer lettuces are enhanced by light, fresh-tasting Lemon Vinaigrette (see below). Hearty winter greens, such as romaine lettuce, curly chicory, Belgian endive, and watercress, support intensely flavored vinaigrettes made with olive, walnut, or hazelnut oils and pungent vinegars such as balsamic or varietal-wine vinegars.

LEMON VINAIGRETTE

A dressing sparked with fresh lemon juice invigorates baby greens and other mild-flavored greens. Fresh peas, cherry tomatoes, and asparagus spears can bolster a simple salad.

    ½ cup fresh lemon juice
    ½ cup vegetable oil
    1½ teaspoons salt
       Freshly ground pepper

Whisk together all ingredients.

Makes ⅔ cup.

Dijon Vinaigrette Substitute 1½ tablespoons red wine vinegar for the lemon juice. Add 1 tablespoon Dijon-style mustard. Whisk together with oil, salt, and pepper.

Wine Vinaigrette Substitute ¼ cup good-quality red or white wine and 2 tablespoons wine vinegar for the lemon juice. Use ½ cup olive oil instead of vegetable oil. Whisk together with salt and pepper.

ITALIAN SALSA VERDE

Italian green salsa, made without chiles, is basically a vinaigrette colored and flavored with the bright green tint and fresh taste of parsley. It can be used to dress up grilled meat and seafood. Serve on the side with Mediterranean Leg of Lamb (see page 29), grilled chicken legs, or broiled swordfish.

    ½ cup olive oil
    2 tablespoons red wine vinegar
    1 tablespoon capers
    1 teaspoon anchovy paste
    1 bunch parsley, finely chopped
    1 clove garlic, finely minced

In a small bowl, stir together all ingredients.

Makes 1½ cups.

FRUIT-STUFFED SQUAB

Squab, Cornish game hens, and baby chickens (poussins) make great dinner party food because each bird is a single serving. With food precisely measured, the cooking and serving are simplified. Although the birds must be stuffed just before roasting, the filling and glaze can be prepared ahead. To toast almonds, bake until lightly browned (6 to 8 minutes) in a preheated 350° F oven.

½ cup dried apricots, diced
6 tablespoons dried currants
2 tablespoons toasted slivered almonds
4 green onions, diced
1 cup cooked long-grain white rice
1½ teaspoons salt
1 teaspoon curry powder
4 tablespoons sour cream or plain yogurt
¼ cup Chicken Stock (see page 56)
6 squab, Cornish game hens, or poussins (12 to 16 oz each)
¼ teaspoon freshly ground pepper

Honey Glaze

¼ cup honey
2 tablespoons soy sauce
2 tablespoons Chicken Stock (see page 56)

1. Preheat oven to 375° F. In a 2-quart bowl, stir together apricots, currants, almonds, onions, cooked rice, 1 teaspoon of the salt, curry powder, sour cream, and stock. Rinse squab and pat dry. Sprinkle squab cavities with remaining salt and pepper. Place ½ cup filling in each squab. Arrange squab snugly in a roasting pan just big enough to hold birds. Brush each with Honey Glaze.

2. Bake until birds are a rich brown and internal temperature is 170° F on an instant-read thermometer (about 40 minutes). Baste once. Serve immediately.

Serves 6.

Honey Glaze   In a small bowl combine all ingredients.

Makes ½ cup.

TERIYAKI PRAWNS

You can also use this sauce as a marinade for boneless chicken breasts; marinate the chicken for 30 minutes to several hours before broiling. There is enough marinade for four chicken breast halves. The marinade recipe can be doubled and the remainder stored in the refrigerator to use as a last-minute marinade. Toast sesame seed in a dry skillet over medium heat for 3 to 5 minutes until lightly browned.

1 tablespoon grated fresh ginger
2 cloves garlic, minced
2 green onions, chopped
¼ cup soy sauce
2 tablespoons honey
1 tablespoon rice wine vinegar or apple cider vinegar
½ tablespoon Asian sesame oil
1 pound (about 24) prawns, shelled and deveined
1 tablespoon vegetable oil
½ teaspoon cornstarch
1 tablespoon water
2 tablespoons sesame seed, toasted, for garnish
Steamed rice, for accompaniment

1. In a 2-quart bowl stir together ginger, garlic, onions, soy sauce, honey, vinegar, and sesame oil. Reserve half of this marinade mixture in another bowl. Place prawns in first bowl and toss with marinade. Marinate 30 minutes to 4 hours in refrigerator.

2. In a wok or 14-inch skillet over medium-high heat, warm vegetable oil. Sauté prawns on one side until bright pink (2 to 3 minutes). Toss and cook second side until done (about 2 minutes). Remove to a dish and reserve.

3. Combine cornstarch and the water in a small bowl. Pour reserved marinade into skillet, bring to boil over medium-high heat, and stir in cornstarch mixture. Stir until sauce thickens (about 1 minute). Add prawns, stirring to coat with sauce.

4. To serve, place prawns on a serving dish, sprinkle with toasted sesame seed, and accompany with steamed rice.

Serves 4.

PARTY PIZZA

Bake dough early in the day and set aside at room temperature. At party time, arrange choices of toppings and let guests create their own pizzas.

1 recipe Basic Bread Dough (see opposite page) Cornmeal, for dusting
3 tablespoons olive oil
3 cups Spicy Tomato Sauce (see page 47)
1 pound teleme or mozzarella cheese, chilled and sliced
1 cup sliced green bell pepper
8 slices smoked bacon, diced
1 pound mild Italian sausage, cooked and drained
24 Kalamata or Niçoise olives, halved and pitted
1 cup Marinated Onions (see page 46)
4 tablespoons chopped fresh herbs (basil, thyme, oregano, parsley)

1. Complete Basic Bread Dough through step 3. Then let dough rise 1 hour; punch down. Divide into 6 equal pieces and flatten each piece into a 7-inch circle. Place on a cornmeal-sprinkled baking sheet. Cover loosely with plastic wrap; let rise 30 minutes. Preheat oven to 450° F.

2. Brush edges of dough circles with olive oil. Bake 7 minutes. Remove from oven. If dough has puffed up, flatten by pressing with a pot holder (pot holder will prevent you from being burned by steam released from dough as it is flattened).

3. On each baked dough circle evenly spread ½ cup Spicy Tomato Sauce. Top with cheese, peppers, bacon, sausage, olives, onions, and herbs, as desired. Bake until cheese melts (8 to 10 minutes). Remove from oven and cut each pizza into 4 pieces. Serve immediately.

Serves 4 to 6.

EASY YEAST BREADS

Yeast doughs are fairly hardy. Their preparation can be spread over a period of hours or even overnight, so that cooks who are away from home during the day can offer family and guests the special treat of home-baked breads. Bread dough can rest, covered and with room to rise, in a cool location for up to 8 hours; it can be shaped and placed in baking pans to rise in the refrigerator for up to 24 hours. Unbaked dough can be frozen, and, of course, the baked loaves will keep in the freezer as well.

Doughs can be mixed by hand in a large bowl. A heavy-duty mixer, however, will simplify preparation and cleanup. In the bowl of the mixer, the yeast can proof, the ingredients can be added and kneaded with the aid of a dough hook, and the dough can be left to rise.

Making bread dough in a food processor saves time, is neat and tidy, and produces a delicious result. In the processor the dough is mixed and kneaded quickly. For smaller capacity machines, cut the recipe in half. Dissolve yeast in a mixing bowl as described in the basic recipe. Place dry ingredients in the food processor and turn on and off to combine. Add liquid ingredients, then yeast mixture, and process until dough forms a ball. If dough is sticky, gradually add more flour until a soft, malleable dough is formed. Cover and let rise as directed in the basic recipe.

Loaves of bread, dinner rolls, bread sticks, and pizza bases freeze best after baking and cooling completely. Ice crystals and freezer burn can be prevented by wrapping breads airtight: Wrap first with aluminum foil pressed tightly against loaf, then place loaf in a plastic bag; press out air from bag. Thaw breads in the refrigerator to prevent moisture from clinging to surface of loaf. To freshen bread, reheat unthawed in a 350° F oven for 15 to 30 minutes, depending on size of baked good. If loaf has been defrosted, reheat for 15 to 20 minutes.

BASIC BREAD DOUGH

Master one quick, versatile yeast dough and shape it many ways. Each of the following shapes has a specific baking time. A substantial, homey loaf and individual bread sticks complement hearty casseroles, stews, and soups. Individual dinner rolls dress up a luncheon or form the base for sandwiches. *Focaccia* is an appealing dinner bread, whether served with an Italian meal or a family supper. Leftover focaccia, sliced horizontally and filled with cheese and mortadella, makes great picnic fare.

> 1½ cups warm (105° to
>   115° F) water
> 1 teaspoon sugar
> 1 package active dry yeast
> 2 tablespoons olive oil
> 1 tablespoon salt
> 3½ to 4 cups unbleached flour

1. In a 4-quart mixing bowl, combine ½ cup of the water, sugar, and yeast and stir until solids are dissolved. Stir in the remaining water, olive oil, and salt. Add 3 cups flour to form a soft dough. If making dough by hand, when the dough becomes too stiff to stir, remove from mixing bowl and place on a lightly floured work surface.

2. Knead dough by hand until smooth on the floured work surface or in a heavy-duty mixer for 5 to 7 minutes, adding the remaining flour as needed if dough is too sticky, to make a soft easily shaped dough.

3. Shape dough into a ball and place in lightly oiled bowl; cover with plastic wrap and let rise at room temperature until doubled in bulk (at least 1 hour), or place dough in refrigerator, covered with plastic wrap, for up to 24 hours.

4. After first rising, punch down dough, set on lightly floured surface, and shape as desired (see variations at end of recipe). Let rise again until doubled in bulk (time varies with shape), then bake in a 375° F oven as directed in individual recipes.

Country Loaf Let Basic Bread Dough rise 1 hour; punch down, shape into a round loaf, and place on a cornmeal-sprinkled baking sheet. Cover loosely with a towel and let rise 1 hour. Brush loaf with olive oil and bake until loaf is golden brown and sounds hollow when tapped on bottom (about 1 hour). Cool on wire rack 30 minutes before serving.

Makes 1 round loaf.

Dinner Rolls Let Basic Bread Dough rise 1 hour; punch down and divide into 12 equal pieces; roll each piece into a small ball. Place dough balls on buttered baking sheet or in buttered muffin cups. Cover loosely with a towel and let rise 45 minutes. Brush with melted butter; bake until lightly browned (about 35 minutes).

Makes 12 rolls.

Salt-Crusted Bread Sticks Let Basic Bread Dough rise 1 hour; punch down and divide into 24 equal pieces. Roll each piece into an 8-inch-long rope. Brush 2 baking sheets with olive oil. Brush bread sticks with olive oil and sprinkle with coarse salt. Cover loosely with a towel and let rise 30 minutes. Bake until light golden brown (22 to 24 minutes).

Makes 24 bread sticks.

Pesto Focaccia Let Basic Bread Dough rise 1 hour; punch down and divide in half. Roll each piece into an 8- by 12-inch rectangle. Place on a cornmeal-sprinkled baking sheet. Cover loosely with a towel; let rise 30 minutes. Preheat oven to 450° F. Brush each rectangle with ½ cup olive oil, top with 8 cloves garlic, cut in slivers, and spread with 1¼ cups Pesto Sauce (see page 47). Bake until crisp and browned on the edges (about 24 minutes). Cool on a rack 10 minutes.

Serves 8.

A FEAST FOR FRIENDS

Cider Pork Loin

Tomato and Mixed Greens Salad

Pepper Bruschetta

Chocolatte

Zinfandel and Champagne

Invite guests for Sunday supper at 5 p.m. The timetable at right will allow you to assemble a festive meal at a leisurely pace without feeling rushed or burdened. Enjoying the company of friends is one of life's greatest pleasures. To make sure that you are with your guests, not confined to the kitchen, planning is crucial and smooth execution the key to success. You will feel more at ease if you use familiar recipes. And if help is offered, learn to say "yes" comfortably. This menu serves 8.

Preparation Plan

Prepare this easy menu in stages, part on Saturday and the rest on Sunday. Place the Cider Pork Loin on the stove to simmer at 3:45 p.m. (2:45 p.m. if using pork leg) Sunday afternoon. This will give you about thirty minutes with guests for conversation and a glass of wine, and will provide a grace period for late arrivals. Offer toasted nuts, black olives, or a small wedge of cheese, if desired.

Some of the dishes in this menu will let your guests participate in their preparation. Be organized enough to have some simple tasks you can assign to willing hands, such as arranging the salad or assembling the bruschetta. A skilled carver could be drafted to slice the boneless pork loin. Opening the wine and putting the finishing touches to the table—lighting the candles or giving the flowers a final arranging—are also good jobs to delegate.

The day before the party, wash salad greens, pat dry with paper towels, and refrigerate. Slice tomatoes, cover with plastic wrap, and refrigerate. Make Chocolatte, and score top into 8 portions to simplify serving; store, covered, overnight at room temperature. Make Raspberry Purée and refrigerate.

The day of the party, make Wine Vinaigrette and let sit at room temperature, ready to drizzle on washed greens and sliced tomatoes. Slice bread for bruschetta, brush with oil, and place on baking sheet. At serving time broil, placing cheese and pepper topping nearby for last-minute finishing. Coat dessert plates with Raspberry Purée and place a slice of Chocolatte on each; top with whipped cream. Offer Champagne to celebrate your successful party.

CIDER PORK LOIN

When strained and degreased, the liquid from the braised pork makes a delicious sauce. If a leg of pork is used instead of the loin, increase the cooking time to 2½ hours.

> 1 pork loin (about 3 lb) or leg (4 to 6 lb), boned and tied
> Salt, to taste
> Freshly ground pepper, to taste
> ¼ cup vegetable oil
> 2 onions, quartered
> 2 carrots, peeled and cut in 2-inch pieces
> 2 teaspoons dried thyme
> 2 cinnamon sticks
> 2½ cups apple cider
> 4 apples, halved and cored
> 1 cup whipping cream

1. Pat pork dry and season with 1 teaspoon salt and ½ teaspoon pepper. In an 8-quart ovenproof casserole or Dutch oven over medium heat, lightly brown pork in oil on all sides (about 5 minutes per side).

2. Arrange onions and carrots around pork and add thyme and cinnamon sticks. Pour apple cider over pork; cover, reduce heat to low, and simmer about 1½ hours for loin or 2½ hours for leg. Arrange apple halves around meat and cook until internal temperature of pork is 165° F on an instant-read thermometer (about 15 minutes more).

3. Remove meat to a carving board. Discard onions and cinnamon sticks. Reserve apple halves and carrots. Strain cooking juices into a 1-quart saucepan; skim away fat from juices with a large, shallow metal spoon. Bring pan juices to a boil over medium heat and cook until reduced by half (about 5 minutes). Stir in cream, whisk until smooth, and season with salt and pepper.

4. Slice pork and pour cider-cream sauce over meat. Garnish with apple halves and carrots.

Serves 8.

Share this Sunday supper of apple-infused pork loin, salad, pepper-topped grilled bread, and an extravagant chocolate cake with good friends.

TOMATO AND MIXED GREENS SALAD

Choose salad greens with a pungent flavor to complement the creamy smoothness of the Cider Pork Loin—oakleaf lettuce, arugula, baby curly endive (*frisée*), green leaf lettuce, baby spinach, and watercress are all good choices.

    8 cups mixed greens, torn into
       bite-sized pieces
    4 medium, ripe tomatoes, sliced
       ¼ inch thick
       Wine Vinaigrette
       (see page 21)

Arrange greens in center of a large serving plate. Place tomato slices around outside edge of plate. Pour dressing over greens and tomatoes. Serve immediately.

Serves 8.

PEPPER BRUSCHETTA

To have a ready supply of garlic-infused oil, store peeled cloves of garlic in olive oil. As the garlic steeps, it imparts its flavor to the oil. Use 6 to 8 cloves garlic per cup of oil.

    1 loaf Italian bread
    1 cup olive oil, preferably
       garlic-infused
    ¼ cup freshly grated
       Parmesan cheese
    1 jar (7 oz) roasted red peppers,
       cut in strips

Preheat grill or broiler. Slice bread about ¾ inch thick (you should have about 16 slices). Place slices on baking sheet. Brush 2 teaspoons oil on each side of each slice of bread. Toast bread on grill or under broiler until lightly browned (about 1 minute per side). Sprinkle one side with Parmesan cheese and top cheese with a strip of roasted red pepper. Serve immediately.

Serves 8.

CHOCOLATTE

A rich chocolate cake is impossible to resist. It can be made early in the day or even the day before up through step 5. Crème Anglaise (see page 37), either the basic version or the orange-flavored variation, is a simple and delicious alternative to the Raspberry Purée.

    1 cup butter, plus butter for
       greasing pan
    ¼ cup flour, plus flour for
       dusting
   10 ounces semisweet chocolate,
       chopped
    2 ounces unsweetened chocolate,
       chopped
    6 eggs, separated
    ¾ cup sugar
    ½ teaspoon vanilla extract
    ⅛ teaspoon cream of tartar
    1 cup whipping cream
    2 tablespoons confectioners'
       sugar
       Raspberry Purée (see page 37)

Chocolate Glaze

    ½ cup whipping cream
    4 ounces semisweet chocolate,
       chopped

1. Butter bottom of a 9-inch springform pan, line bottom with aluminum foil or parchment paper, then butter and flour paper and pan sides. Preheat oven to 350° F.

2. Place chopped chocolate and the 1 cup butter in a 4-quart stainless steel mixing bowl. Fill a 10-inch skillet with 1 inch of water and bring to a boil over medium heat. Remove from heat and place mixing bowl of chocolate in skillet of warm water. Stir until chocolate melts. In a separate bowl, beat together egg yolks and sugar until light and fluffy. Fold in vanilla extract and chocolate mixture. Sift the ¼ cup flour into mixture and fold in gently.

3. In a large, nonaluminum bowl beat egg whites with cream of tartar to soft peaks. Stir one third of egg whites into chocolate mixture thoroughly. Set remaining whites on chocolate mixture and gently fold into chocolate mixture, taking care not to overwork (small bits of white will be left unincorporated).

4. Pour into prepared pan and bake until toothpick inserted 2 inches from edge comes out dry, but center still appears moist (about 35 minutes). Cool completely in pan on a wire rack. Cake will deflate in the center as it cools. To remove from pan, loosen edges with a knife and remove pan sides. Lay a wire rack on top of cake, invert cake, and remove pan bottom and parchment paper.

5. To glaze, set cooled cake (still on the wire cooling rack) over another pan or a large sheet of aluminum foil or parchment paper. Pour glaze over cake to cover.

6. Whip cream with confectioners' sugar. To serve, cut cake into 8 to 10 wedges. Place about 3 tablespoons Raspberry Purée on each serving plate and place a wedge of Chocolatte in center of purée. Garnish with a rosette of whipped cream.

Serves 8 to 10.

Chocolate Glaze   In a 1-quart saucepan set over a pan of simmering water, heat cream. Stir chocolate into hot cream until it melts and mixture is smooth. Cool until slightly thickened (20 to 30 minutes). If glaze gets too thick to pour, simply reheat and cool again.

Makes ¾ cup.

Almond Chocolatte   Prepare Chocolatte, substituting almond extract for the vanilla extract and ⅓ cup ground toasted almonds for the ¼ cup flour.

GRANDMOTHER'S PANFRIED CHICKEN

Double the recipe and plan a picnic around leftovers of this crunchy buttermilk chicken. Make mouth-watering Mom's Buttermilk Biscuits (see page 94) if enough buttermilk is left in the carton.

    1   chicken (3½ lb), cut into
         6 pieces
    2   cups buttermilk
 1¼ cups flour
    2   tablespoons paprika
    1   tablespoon dried thyme
    1   tablespoon dried basil
 1½ teaspoons salt
    ½   teaspoon freshly ground
         black pepper
    ¼   teaspoon cayenne pepper
    ¼   cup butter
    ¼   cup vegetable oil

Creamy Chicken Gravy

    4   tablespoons butter
    3   tablespoons flour
    3   cups Chicken Stock
         (see page 56)
    ½   cup half-and-half
         Salt and freshly ground
         pepper, to taste

1. Place chicken pieces in 3-quart mixing bowl. Pour buttermilk over chicken. Toss chicken in buttermilk to coat; cover and set aside at least 40 minutes or up to 8 hours in refrigerator. While chicken is marinating, stir together flour, paprika, thyme, basil, salt, pepper, and cayenne in a shallow bowl.

2. Remove chicken pieces from buttermilk and place in flour mixture. Thickly pat seasoned flour over chicken. At this point chicken can be held for up to 8 hours, loosely covered, in refrigerator.

3. In a 14-inch skillet over medium-high heat, heat butter and oil. When butter is melted, place chicken legs and thighs skin side down in skillet; cook 10 minutes. Add chicken breasts

and cook all chicken until golden brown on one side (20 minutes more). Turn chicken pieces and cook until done (about 15 minutes).

4. Make Creamy Chicken Gravy while chicken is cooking; keep gravy warm over low heat until ready to serve. Serve chicken pieces drizzled with Creamy Chicken Gravy.

Serves 6.

Creamy Chicken Gravy   In a 2-quart saucepan, melt butter. Whisk in flour and cook, stirring constantly, 3 to 4 minutes. Add Chicken Stock gradually, whisking to maintain a smooth, creamy texture. Stir in half-and-half and season with salt and pepper as needed.

Makes about 3½ cups.

Bread Grandmother's Panfried Chicken early in the day and put on to cook as guests arrive. Serve it piping hot with freshly baked Mom's Buttermilk Biscuits (see page 94), also easily assembled earlier and baked at the dinner hour.

Roast the Beef Tenderloin Roll and Baked Potato Sticks (page 31) while you and your guests enjoy cocktails. When the roast is sliced, the spiral pattern of the filling shows nicely.

BEEF TENDERLOIN ROLL

Bake the Baked Potato Sticks alongside this tenderloin of beef. The tenderloin can be served hot from the oven or prepared early in the day and served at room temperature.

- 1 beef tenderloin (3½ lb), trimmed of fat
- 4 strips bacon, diced
- 1 bunch spinach, washed and dried
- 2 tablespoons Dijon-style mustard
- 2 tablespoons brandy
- 2 tablespoons olive oil
  Baked Potato Sticks (see page 31) or Nora's Potato Gratin (see page 30), for accompaniment

1. To make a flat ¾-inch-thick piece of beef, butterfly tenderloin by cutting, from top to bottom, through center to within ¾ inch of bottom; open like a book and press to flatten. Cut horizontally, starting at the center of each half, to within ¾ inch of each side. Open and flatten tenderloin slightly with a meat pounder or side of a meat cleaver or Chinese cleaver so that whole piece is about the same thickness.

2. In a 12- to 14-inch skillet over medium heat, sauté diced bacon until golden brown. When fat is rendered and bacon is crisp, add spinach and cook until wilted (about 6 minutes). Place spinach-bacon mixture over tenderloin. Roll up tenderloin, jelly-roll fashion. Tie with kitchen twine in 4 places to fasten tightly.

3. In a small bowl mix together mustard and brandy. Rub over tenderloin. At this point, meat can be refrigerated for about 8 hours, if desired; 1 hour before cooking, bring meat to room temperature.

4. Preheat oven to 425°F. Return skillet to medium heat, add olive oil, and place tenderloin, seam side down, in skillet; brown on all sides (5 minutes per side). Place tenderloin in oven; roast until medium-rare (about 40 minutes, or until internal temperature is 125° F on an instant-read thermometer). Let tenderloin rest 12 to 15 minutes, loosely covered with aluminum foil, before slicing. Slice into 6 pieces across the grain of the meat, and serve immediately with Baked Potato Sticks.

Serves 6.

MEDITERRANEAN LEG OF LAMB

Lamb is wonderful when marinated, then roasted in the oven. It is also delicious grilled. To grill, prepare a fire in the barbecue and brush rack lightly with vegetable oil. Drain marinade from lamb and reserve. Place lamb on rack and grill 10 minutes, baste with marinade, turn and grill 10 minutes, baste again, and turn and cook 10 minutes more. Repeat until internal temperature reaches 135° F (about 15 minutes more). Leftover lamb can be made into sandwiches and paired with Aioli (see page 20) or used in salads.

4 cloves garlic, minced
2 teaspoons minced fresh or dried rosemary
1 cup olive oil
½ cup red wine vinegar
1 teaspoon salt
½ teaspoon freshly ground pepper
1 leg of lamb (about 3½ lb), butterflied

1. In a 3-quart glass, ceramic, or stainless steel bowl, whisk together garlic, rosemary, oil, vinegar, salt, and pepper. Place lamb in marinade, turning to coat thoroughly. Marinate 2 to 24 hours.

2. Preheat oven to 425° F. Drain marinade from lamb and discard marinade. Place lamb in a 9- by 12-inch roasting pan. Roast in oven until medium-rare (about 45 minutes, or until internal temperature is 135° F on an instant-read thermometer). Let lamb rest 15 minutes before serving. Carve across grain into ½-inch-thick slices.

Serves 6.

Variation Marinate 4 lamb sirloin steaks (about ¾ pound each) in one half of the marinade; sauté steaks in 4 tablespoons olive oil, 3 minutes on each side.

ACCOMPANIMENTS

Plan to serve side dishes that complement not only the flavor of the main course but also its method of cooking. If the main course is baked, choose a side dish that can share the oven rack—such as Nora's Potato Gratin (see page 30). If you want a side dish that cooks on top of the stove, consider Braised Seasonal Vegetables (at right) or Broccoli and Snow Pea Pasta (see page 30).

Often side dishes can be transformed into more substantial fare by the addition of more ingredients. Braised Seasonal Vegetables tossed with Lemon Vinaigrette (see page 21) and cooked chicken breast makes a superb luncheon salad. Rabat Rice Pilaf (see page 30) is transformed into a simple first-course salad when dressed with Dijon Vinaigrette (see page 21) and mixed with cherry tomatoes and fresh parsley. Let these accompaniments inspire you to develop your own combinations.

CARROT AND BOURBON TIMBALES

This side dish is delicious served with grilled lamb chops, roast chicken, or broiled steak. You can substitute cream cheese when goat cheese is unavailable, but the dish won't have the same pungency.

3 tablespoons butter, for greasing
2 medium carrots, shredded
6 tablespoons (about 3 oz) fresh goat cheese
1 cup half-and-half
4 eggs
½ teaspoon salt
½ teaspoon ground white pepper
1 clove garlic, finely minced
3 tablespoons cornmeal
2 tablespoons bourbon

1. Heavily grease six ½-cup timbale molds or ramekins with butter. Preheat oven to 325° F.

2. In a 1-quart bowl, combine carrots, goat cheese, half-and-half, eggs, salt, pepper, garlic, cornmeal, and bourbon. Divide mixture between the 6 timbale molds.

3. Place molds in a shallow pan filled with 1 inch of hot water. Bake until timbales appear dry on top and a knife inserted halfway between center and edge comes out clean (50 to 55 minutes). Let timbales rest 5 minutes before serving. To unmold run a knife between timbale and mold and invert onto individual plates.

Serves 6.

Red Pepper and Corn Timbales
Replace carrot with 1¼ cups corn kernels and ½ red bell pepper, diced; replace goat cheese with ½ cup freshly grated Parmesan cheese. Increase salt to 1 teaspoon and pepper to ¾ teaspoon; add ½ teaspoon ground nutmeg and ½ cup minced chives. Omit bourbon. Mix as directed above. Pour into 6 prepared molds and swirl ½ teaspoon Pesto Sauce (see page 47) on top of each timbale. Bake as directed above, until timbales are firm and a knife inserted in center comes out clean (about 35 minutes).

BRAISED SEASONAL VEGETABLES

Substitute any vegetables in season for the Brussels sprouts. The dish is a good, basic preparation that you will use often.

2 tablespoons vegetable oil
1 large onion, sliced
2 cloves garlic, minced
1 pound Brussels sprouts, trimmed
¼ cup Chicken Stock (see page 56)
1 red bell pepper, sliced
1 teaspoon salt
½ teaspoon freshly ground pepper

1. In a 14-inch skillet over medium heat, heat oil. Sauté onion until translucent (about 3 minutes). Add garlic and cook for 2 minutes.

2. Stir in Brussels sprouts and Chicken Stock; reduce heat and simmer, uncovered, for 15 minutes. Add bell pepper, salt, and pepper; simmer 5 minutes. Serve immediately.

Serves 6 to 8.

RABAT RICE PILAF

Toasted nuts, dried currants, diced dried apricots, shredded carrots, or minced fresh herbs will add variety to this basic pilaf. If serving beef or lamb, substitute Beef Stock (see page 56) for the Chicken Stock.

    2 tablespoons butter
    1 onion, minced
    1 carrot, finely diced
    2½ cups long-grain white rice
    4½ cups Chicken Stock
       (see page 56)
    ½ tablespoon salt
    ¼ teaspoon freshly ground
       pepper

In a heavy, 2-quart saucepan over medium heat melt butter. Sauté onion and carrot until softened but not browned (about 6 minutes). Add rice, stock, salt, and pepper. Stir to combine. Cover and cook over medium to low heat until liquid is absorbed (about 25 minutes). Serve warm.

Serves 8.

Multigrain Pilaf   Use 1 cup long-grain white rice; 1 cup wheat berries, rye berries, triticale berries, or barley; and ½ cup wild rice. Increase Chicken Stock to 5 cups. Cook pilaf for 40 minutes.

BROCCOLI AND SNOW PEA PASTA

Use this one-pot technique for any pasta tossed with vegetables; blanching the vegetables in the same pot used later for the pasta will save cleanup time.

    3 shallots, minced
    3 tablespoons butter
    1 bunch broccoli, cut into florets
    ½ pound snow peas
    1 pound dried fusilli pasta
    1 cup (5 oz) grated Asiago
       cheese
    ½ teaspoon hot-pepper flakes
       Freshly ground black pepper

1. In a 4-quart saucepan over medium heat, sauté shallots in butter until softened (about 3 minutes); remove from pan and reserve.

2. In same pan bring water to a boil. Boil broccoli until tender (3 to 4 minutes). Remove with a slotted spoon and reserve. Blanch snow peas in boiling water until bright green (about 30 seconds); remove with a slotted spoon and reserve. Return water to a boil and stir in pasta. Boil until pasta is al dente (about 12 minutes). Drain in colander.

3. In a serving bowl, combine pasta, broccoli, snow peas, and reserved shallots. Toss with ½ cup of the Asiago cheese and hot-pepper flakes. Transfer to a serving bowl. Sprinkle with remaining cheese and pepper.

Serves 6 to 8.

NORA'S POTATO GRATIN

Early in the day, prepare potato gratin up to the point of baking. Store in refrigerator until ready to bake; add an extra 10 minutes to baking time if chilled. To keep potatoes from darkening while the dish is held, press plastic wrap on surface of gratin to submerge potatoes in liquid.

    2 tablespoons butter, for
       greasing
    2½ pounds (about 4 large)
       baking potatoes
    2 cups half-and-half
    1 cup milk
    2 cloves garlic, minced
    1½ teaspoons salt
    ½ teaspoon freshly ground
       pepper

1. Preheat oven to 350° F. Grease a 10- by 15-inch baking dish with butter. Peel potatoes; slice about ⅛ inch thick. In a 2-quart bowl whisk together half-and-half, milk, garlic, salt, and pepper.

2. Layer one third of sliced potatoes in buttered baking dish. Pour in one third of milk mixture. Place another third of potatoes into baking dish. Pour in another third of milk mixture. Finish with remaining potatoes and milk mixture. Bake until browned slightly on top and tender when pierced with a knife (about 1 hour). Serve immediately.

Serves 8 to 12.

Potato and Artichoke Gratin
Prepare 4 artichoke bottoms as described in Artichoke Salad (see page 18). Follow directions for Potato Gratin, layering as follows: Place one third of potatoes in gratin dish. Layer one half of sliced artichoke bottoms over potatoes, then cover with one third milk mixture. Place another third of potatoes over artichokes; then place remaining sliced artichoke bottoms over potatoes. Cover with another third of milk mixture. Finish with remaining potatoes and milk mixture. Bake as directed above.

Potato and Leek Gratin   Clean and dice 4 leeks. Sauté them slowly in 4 tablespoons butter until tender and wilted (about 20 minutes). Follow directions for Potato and Artichoke Gratin, substituting leeks for artichoke bottoms.

SAFFRON RISOTTO

Risotto, made with Arborio rice, a short, plump Italian rice, is as popular in the north of Italy as pasta is in the south. It is traditionally served as a first course, accompanied by grated cheese, sautéed spring vegetables, or rehydrated dried mushrooms. This recipe also includes cream, an addition suggested by an Italian chef.

    5 to 6 cups Chicken Stock
       (see page 56)
    ¼ gram (½ teaspoon) saffron
       threads
    6 tablespoons butter
    1 onion, minced
    2 cloves garlic, minced
    2 cups Arborio rice
    ½ cup freshly grated Parmesan
       cheese
    ½ cup whipping cream
       Salt and freshly ground
       pepper, to taste

1. In a 2-quart saucepan over medium heat, bring stock to a boil. Reduce heat to simmer. Remove ½ cup stock to a small bowl. Steep saffron threads in the ½ cup of stock 15 minutes. Reserve.

2. In a 3-quart saucepan over medium heat, melt butter. Sauté onion and garlic until onion is softened but not browned (6 to 8 minutes). Add rice and stir to coat with butter. Add 1 cup hot stock and stir to cover rice. Reduce heat to low. Let rice cook, uncovered, about 5 minutes. As rice absorbs liquid add a second cup of stock, stirring carefully to make sure that rice is not sticking and liquid is evenly distributed.

3. Continue to add more liquid as previous quantity is absorbed, stirring from time to time as it cooks. Stir in reserved saffron-infused stock with last addition of stock. When all liquid is added, risotto will appear creamy and its texture will be slightly chewy (al dente). Stir in Parmesan and cream just before serving. Season with salt and pepper.

Serves 6 to 8.

Corn and Wild Mushroom Risotto Omit saffron. Sauté ¾ pound sliced wild mushrooms (shiitake, porcini, chanterelles, hedgehog, oyster, or a combination) with minced onion. Add 2½ cups corn kernels with Arborio rice. Toss ¼ cup fresh julienned basil into risotto with Parmesan cheese.

BAKED POTATO STICKS

For an easy oven dinner, bake potatoes on the rack along with Mediterranean Leg of Lamb (see page 29) or Beef Tenderloin Roll (see page 28).

> 6 *medium baking potatoes*
> 9 *tablespoons butter*
> 1½ *teaspoons salt*
> 1 *teaspoon freshly ground pepper*

1. Preheat oven to 400° F. Scrub and quarter potatoes. Melt butter in a 9- by 12-inch ovenproof baking dish in oven.

2. Place potato quarters in dish and turn to coat with melted butter; arrange potatoes cut side down and sprinkle with salt and pepper. Bake until tender when pierced with a sharp knife (30 to 35 minutes).

Serves 6.

Step·by·Step

RISOTTO

Arborio rice (traditionally used for risottos) will absorb up to five times its weight in liquid (usually stock), while remaining tender and creamy. Unlike a pilaf, a risotto is stirred continuously over low heat until it is al dente or possesses just a little bite. Risotto needs constant attention during the 20 or so minutes it takes to cook and should be served as soon as it is finished. Therefore the rest of the meal should be fairly simple. The following photographs illustrate the preparation of Saffron Risotto (see opposite page).

1. In a heavy saucepan melt butter. Sauté minced onion and garlic until translucent (about 6 minutes).

2. Add Arborio rice and stir to thoroughly coat grains with butter.

3. Add 1 cup hot stock, stirring occasionally until stock is absorbed. Continue adding stock gradually, waiting until each addition has been absorbed before adding the next. Stir occasionally to keep the rice from sticking.

4. When all hot stock is absorbed (20 to 25 minutes), rice will be tender and creamy but still somewhat chewy (al dente).

5. Stir in flavoring, here freshly grated Parmesan cheese and cream. Season to taste with salt and pepper. Serve immediately.

Sophisticated salmon adds a touch of glamour to any dinner party. Carrot Purée, Spinach Sauté, and Frangipane Fruit Tart share star billing.

A SAVORY SALMON DINNER

Fettuccine Alfredo

Salmon Steaks With Green Onion–Dill Butter

Carrot Purée

Spinach Sauté

Frangipane Fruit Tart

Chardonnay or White Burgundy

A main course of salmon transforms any dinner— even one as simple to orchestrate as is this one— into a special occasion. The setting for this company meal can be dressed up or down as needed. For an honored guest, serve in the dining room at a table set with crystal, china, and silver. A more casual gathering for close friends could be enjoyed in the kitchen. This menu serves 6.

Preparation Plan

Learning to compose a menu is a challenging but pleasant task. The goal is to create a balance of flavor, textures, and colors, at the same time selecting dishes sufficiently unde-manding that the cook can leave the kitchen. The courses of this salmon dinner fulfill all of these require-ments. However, the dinner isn't ef-fortless; its smooth execution requires organization and planning. A fool-proof plan is one that reflects well-thought-out moves. The following tasks can be spread out over several days. Shopping can be done two days in advance and the table can be set and serving dishes collected a day ahead—perhaps while the Frangi-pane Fruit Tart is baking.

To simplify preparation, Carrot Purée can be made ahead and frozen for two months or stored for four days in the refrigerator. Make the Green Onion–Dill Butter ahead and freeze (it will keep well-wrapped up to two months). Prepare the Butter Pastry for the tart four to five days ahead, shape the tart shell, and re-frigerate. Twenty-four hours before serving, mix the frangipane filling, pour into the tart shell, and bake. Wash the spinach for Spinach Sauté and dry thoroughly; store between paper towels in a plastic bag in the refrigerator.

Place the Carrot Purée in a double boiler over simmering water to re-heat. If using a barbecue, start the fire thirty minutes before serving salmon. If using a broiler, preheat it while enjoying the pasta. Put the salmon under the broiler when you clear the first-course plates. Prepare the Spinach Sauté. Turn the salmon to broil the second side, and arrange the dinner plates in the kitchen. Cut the Frangipane Fruit Tart into eight wedges, place on dessert plates, and garnish each serving with a sprig of fresh mint.

FETTUCCINE ALFREDO

Alfredo sauce, a classic of northern Italian cuisine, is one of the simplest and quickest sauces to prepare. It also lends itself to additions of cooked ham or chicken, fresh herbs, or vegetables. This recipe is very effi-cient: The pasta is cooked with the sauce in the same pan and at the same time. To substitute dried pasta, increase the milk to 6 cups and cook 12 ounces dried fettuccine pasta for 20 minutes, following the directions for fresh pasta.

> 2 tablespoons butter
> 1 tablespoon olive oil
> 3 shallots, minced
> 3 cups milk
> 12 ounces fresh fettuccine
> 1 cup (5 oz) freshly grated Parmesan cheese, plus grated Parmesan for garnish
> ¼ teaspoon white pepper
> 1 tablespoon chopped parsley, for garnish

1. In a 3-quart heavy saucepan over medium heat, melt butter with olive oil. Sauté shallots until softened, but not browned (about 5 minutes). Add milk, increase heat to medium-high, and bring to a boil.

2. Stir in fettuccine, reduce heat to medium-low, and simmer, stirring constantly, until pasta is tender (3 to 4 minutes). Toss with the 1 cup Parmesan cheese and season with pepper. Serve immediately, sprinkled with additional cheese and parsley.

Serves 4 to 6 as a first course.

Fettuccine Alfredo With Clams and Garlic Follow main recipe. Cook 3 cloves minced garlic with shallots. Stir 8 ounces chopped, cooked, canned clams into sauce with fettuccine; cook until clams are heated through.

SALMON STEAKS WITH GREEN ONION–DILL BUTTER

Compound butters are a boon to the busy cook. Blend softened butter with your favorite herbs well in advance of the dinner. At serving time, lay a pat of butter on broiled meats, poultry, or fish. For a special presentation, press flavored butter into purchased molds or roll ½ inch thick between sheets of waxed paper and cut into shapes with cookie cutters.

> 6 salmon steaks (about
>   8 oz each)
> 3 tablespoons butter, melted
>   Green Onion–Dill Butter
>   (see page 75)

Preheat broiler. Arrange salmon steaks on broiler pan. Brush with melted butter. Broil 6 minutes about 4 inches from heat; turn and broil until flesh is opaque when flaked with a fork (about 4 minutes). Set 1 salmon steak on each plate and place 1 tablespoon Green Onion–Dill Butter on each steak.

Serves 6.

Note Fatty fish such as salmon, sea bass, and halibut also benefit from being grilled: Baste fish with oil to reduce charring, prepare fire in barbecue (about 30 minutes before grilling), and brush grill rack lightly with vegetable oil. Grill fish for 5 minutes, brush other side with oil, turn, and grill 5 to 8 minutes more depending on the thickness. The rule of thumb for cooking any fish, by any method, is to cook it 10 minutes per inch of thickness.

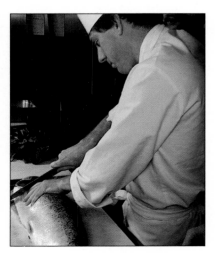

CARROT PURÉE

Prepare this dish hours (or days) ahead of serving, reserve in the refrigerator, and reheat in a double boiler at serving time.

> 1 pound carrots, peeled and
>   coarsely chopped
> 1 medium potato, peeled and
>   coarsely chopped
> ½ cup unsalted butter
> 1 teaspoon salt
> ¼ teaspoon freshly ground
>   pepper

In a 2-quart saucepan, cover carrots and potato with water and simmer over medium-low heat until soft (about 25 minutes). Purée carrots and potato in blender or food processor with butter, salt, and pepper.

Makes 2½ cups, about 6 servings.

SPINACH SAUTÉ

Spinach, one of the tastiest of vegetables, is an especially delicious winter treat when lightly sprinkled with fragrant nutmeg.

> 2 tablespoons unsalted butter
> 2 bunches spinach, washed,
>   tough stems removed, and
>   chopped coarsely
> 4 cloves garlic, minced
> ¼ teaspoon salt
> ⅛ teaspoon white pepper
> ⅛ teaspoon ground nutmeg

In a 14-inch skillet over medium heat, melt butter. Sauté spinach and garlic until spinach is wilted (about 10 minutes). Season with salt, pepper, and nutmeg.

Serves 6.

FRANGIPANE FRUIT TART

The beauty of the Frangipane Filling in this tart, other than its delicate almond flavor, is that it acts as a barrier to keep the crust from getting soggy. You can assemble the tart hours in advance and not worry that the fruit filling will soak into the crust. Toast almonds as directed in Cornmeal-Crusted Orange Roughy (see page 21).

> 1 unbaked 11-inch shell Butter
>   Pastry (see page 12)
> ¼ cup apricot jam
> 2 tablespoons water
> 3 kiwifruit, peeled and sliced
>   ¼ inch thick
> 1 cup raspberries
> ¼ cup toasted slivered almonds

Frangipane Filling

> 2 tubes (7 oz each)
>   almond paste
> 4 tablespoons unsalted butter
> ⅔ cup confectioners' sugar
> 2 eggs
> 1 tablespoon dark rum
> ½ teaspoon almond extract

1. Preheat oven to 350° F. Spread Frangipane Filling in unbaked tart shell. Bake until top of filling looks dry (about 40 minutes); let cool.

2. Heat apricot jam and the water over low heat. Strain and brush one half of the mixture over almond filling. Arrange kiwifruit slices around perimeter of filling. Arrange raspberries next to kiwifruit. Fill center with toasted almonds. Brush fruit with remaining apricot jam.

Serves 8 to 10.

Frangipane Filling With an electric mixer or food processor, cream almond paste and butter until smooth. Add confectioners' sugar, eggs, rum, and almond extract; beat well until smooth.

Makes about 1 cup.

Make-Ahead Tip Tart may be prepared completely ahead of serving. Reserve, covered, at cool room temperature for 6 to 8 hours; refrigerate if held longer.

DESSERTS

Desserts are an opportunity for the cook to make a grand statement with relatively little effort. Most desserts can be prepared ahead of serving time and held without problem until the moment of serving.

VANILLA-NUTMEG POUND CAKE

This versatile vanilla pound cake can be dressed up with Chocolate Fudge Sauce (see page 37) or Zinfandel Peaches (see page 37). For a slightly more dramatic presentation, sprinkle the top layer with Nutty Walnut Streusel (see Blackberry and Peach Crisp, page 36) before baking, then slice into three layers and fill with Lemon Curd (see page 47).

> Butter and flour, for coating
> 4 cups cake flour
> 2 teaspoons baking soda
> 1 teaspoon salt
> 1 teaspoon ground nutmeg
> 1 cup unsalted butter, softened
> 2 cups granulated sugar
> 2 eggs
> 1 tablespoon vanilla extract
> 2 cups buttermilk or sour cream
> Confectioners' sugar, for dusting

1. Butter and flour a 12-cup tube pan. Preheat oven to 350° F. Sift flour, baking soda, salt, and nutmeg together on aluminum foil, waxed paper, or baking parchment.

2. Cream butter and sugar until light and fluffy. Add eggs, one at a time, beating well after each egg is added. Stir in vanilla.

3. Stir half of the sifted flour mixture into the butter-sugar mixture. Add 1 cup of the buttermilk. Add the other half of the flour mixture, then the remaining buttermilk.

4. Pour batter into prepared tube pan and bake until a toothpick inserted 2 inches from edge comes out clean (about 1 hour and 5 minutes). Cool cake in pan 10 to 15 minutes; invert

onto a cooling rack, remove pan, and cool completely before serving. Transfer to a serving plate. Dust with confectioners' sugar.

Serves 12.

Citrus-Pecan Pound Cake
Substitute almond extract for vanilla extract and add rind of 1 lemon and 1 orange with extract. Reduce amount of flour to 2 cups and sift with dry ingredients; stir in as directed. Fold in 2 cups finely ground pecans after flour mixture.

Hazelnut Pound Cake   Substitute
½ cup ground, toasted hazelnuts (for toasting directions, see Artichoke Salad recipe, page 18) for ½ cup of the flour in the recipe.

Vanilla-Nutmeg Pound Cake topped with Zinfandel Peaches presents a stylish yet simple finale to almost any meal. Use pears, apples, or figs when peaches are out of season.

MILK SPONGE ROLL WITH JAM FILLING

Vary the sponge roll by filling with Chocolate Mousse (at right) and a dusting of unsweetened cocoa, or use Lemon Curd or Orange Curd (see page 47) for a quick, refreshingly tart jelly-roll filling. Garnish with Chocolate Fudge Sauce, Crème Anglaise, or Raspberry Purée (all on opposite page) for an even grander finale.

    4 eggs
    1 cup confectioners' sugar
    2 tablespoons milk
    4 tablespoons butter
    1 teaspoon vanilla extract
    ½ cup flour
    1 teaspoon baking powder
    ½ teaspoon salt
    Confectioners' sugar,
        for dusting
    2 cups blackberry or raspberry
        jam, for filling
    ½ cup granulated or
        confectioners' sugar,
        for garnish

1. Preheat oven to 350° F. Line an 11- by 17- by 1-inch baking pan with parchment paper (or butter and flour pan). In a small saucepan over medium-low heat, place milk and butter and heat until butter is melted. Remove from heat and cool until tepid; stir in vanilla; reserve.

2. In a 4-quart bowl beat eggs and confectioners' sugar together with a wire whisk until mixture is pale yellow and thickened to consistency of mayonnaise.

3. Sift together flour, baking powder, and salt. Using a rubber spatula, gently fold flour mixture into eggs.

4. Scoop 1 cup batter into a small mixing bowl and whisk together with milk-butter mixture. Fold mixture into batter. This will enable the heavy milk-butter mixture to be easily and completely folded into the light, airy batter without deflating it. Pour batter into prepared pan and bake until cake is pale golden brown and dry on top, and springs back when gently pressed with finger (20 to 22 minutes).

5. Cool 2 to 3 minutes in pan. Loosen edges of cake from pan with a small knife. Dust a tea towel with confectioners' sugar. Invert cake onto sugar-dusted towel; carefully peel away parchment paper from cake roll. Roll up jelly-roll fashion with towel or parchment paper. Cool completely.

6. When cool, unroll cake and remove tea towel. Spread cake with jam and roll again. Finish with a dusting of granulated sugar. Cover loosely with plastic wrap and chill if not serving immediately.

Serves 8 to 12.

CHOCOLATE MOUSSE

Use this rich mousse to fill a Milk Sponge Roll (at left) or baked tart shells (see Butter Pastry, page 12), or mound in wineglasses.

    10 ounces semisweet chocolate,
        chopped
    ½ cup sugar
    4 eggs, separated
    1 teaspoon vanilla extract
    1 cup whipping cream

1. In a 4-quart stainless steel mixing bowl, place chopped chocolate. Fill a 10-inch skillet with 1 inch of water and bring to a boil over medium heat. Remove from heat and place mixing bowl of chopped chocolate in skillet of warm water. Stir until chocolate melts.

2. Whisk ¼ cup sugar, egg yolks, and vanilla into melted chocolate.

3. In a clean 3-quart bowl, beat egg whites until frothy. Beat in remaining sugar and continue beating until soft peaks form. Partially fold beaten egg whites into chocolate mixture, leaving some egg white showing. In same 3-quart bowl, add whipping cream and beat to soft peaks. Fold whipped cream into chocolate mixture carefully but thoroughly, leaving no egg white or cream showing.

4. To serve, spoon into wineglasses, spread in the Milk Sponge Roll, or pipe with a pastry bag into tart shells. Chill until serving time.

Serves 8.

BLACKBERRY AND PEACH CRISP

Nutty streusel topping over fresh seasonal fruit produces this lovely baked dessert. The streusel can be stored for up to three months in the freezer.

    9 tablespoons butter, melted
    3 peaches, peeled and sliced,
        or 1 pound frozen
        unsweetened peach slices
    ½ cup firmly packed
        brown sugar
    1 tablespoon ground cinnamon
    ½ teaspoon ground nutmeg
    ¼ teaspoon salt
        Juice of 1 lemon
    3 cups blackberries or
        1 pound frozen
        unsweetened blackberries
    1 cup whipping cream,
        for garnish

Nutty Walnut Streusel

    1 cup butter, softened
    ½ cup firmly packed brown
        sugar
    1½ cups flour
    ½ tablespoon ground cinnamon
    ½ teaspoon baking powder
    ¼ teaspoon salt
    1 cup toasted walnuts, chopped
        coarsely

1. Preheat oven to 350° F. Brush a 9- by 12-inch baking dish with 1 tablespoon of the butter. In a 3-quart bowl toss together remaining butter, peaches, brown sugar, cinnamon, nutmeg, salt, and lemon juice. Gently mix in blackberries and place mixture in prepared pan.

2. Sprinkle Nutty Walnut Streusel over mixture in baking dish. Bake until streusel is crisp and lightly browned (about 1¼ hours).

3. Whip cream to soft peaks. Serve dessert while still warm with a dollop of cream.

Serves 6 to 8.

Nutty Walnut Streusel   In a 3-quart bowl cream butter and brown sugar until fluffy. Sift together flour, cinnamon, baking powder, and salt; cut into butter-sugar mixture. Stir in walnuts and mix until crumbly.

Makes 3 cups.

ZINFANDEL PEARS

Pears, peaches, apples, and quince are among the many fruits that taste sensational when poached in red wine. Serve warm with a scoop of vanilla ice cream melting over the fruit; chilled in a wineglass; as the filling of a fruit tart; or with warm Chocolate Fudge Sauce (at right). Mint is in the same herb family as basil and may be substituted for the basil in the recipe.

> 6 pears
> 1 small bunch fresh basil, plus basil leaves for garnish
> 2 cups zinfandel wine
> ½ cup sugar

1. Peel pears. Core pears by cutting a cone-shaped wedge from the bottom of each. Leave stems intact. Discard seeds and cores. Wash and julienne bunch of basil.

2. Place wine and sugar in a non-aluminum 2-quart saucepan. Add julienned basil and bring mixture to a boil over medium-high heat. Place pears upright in poaching liquid, reduce heat, and simmer until pears are tender and do not offer resistance when pierced with a sharp knife (about 20 minutes).

3. Remove fruit with a slotted spoon to a serving dish. Return syrup to a boil and reduce by half to about 1 cup (about 10 minutes). Pour syrup over pears and cool for 3 hours in refrigerator.

4. To serve, place pears in stemmed glasses, spooning some of the cooking juices over each fruit. Garnish with basil leaves.

Serves 6.

Zinfandel Peaches Follow recipe for Zinfandel Pears; substitute 6 peaches for pears. Peel peaches with a sharp knife, or dip in a pan of boiling water for about 1 minute to loosen skin then peel by hand. Halve and remove pit. Place in poaching liquid and cook until tender (15 to 20 minutes). Proceed with recipe.

DESSERT SAUCES

A great sauce will dress up a plain dessert. Chocolate Fudge Sauce (at right) can be the finish on Vanilla-Nutmeg Pound Cake (see page 35). The Orange Crème Anglaise sauce (at right) emphasizes the orange rind in Citrus-Pecan Pound Cake (see page 35). Quick Caramel Sauce (see below) adds richness to Apple and Walnut Strudel (see page 119), and Raspberry Purée (see below) gives fruit flavor to Mom's Double Dutch Chocolate Cake (see page 119).

QUICK CARAMEL SAUCE

This delicious sauce can be easily prepared at the last minute to crown a dish of coffee ice cream.

> 1½ cups whipping cream
> ½ cup firmly packed brown sugar
> 2 tablespoons dark corn syrup
> 2 tablespoons molasses
> 2 tablespoons unsalted butter
> 1½ teaspoons vanilla extract

In a 1-quart saucepan over medium heat, warm cream. Whisk in brown sugar, corn syrup, molasses, and butter and stir until sugar is dissolved. Remove from heat and stir in vanilla. Serve warm.

Makes 2 cups.

RASPBERRY PURÉE

Drizzled over Vanilla-Nutmeg Pound Cake (see page 35), swirled in Crème Anglaise (at right), or added to a wine spritzer, Raspberry Purée has style and elegance. If using frozen berries in syrup, eliminate the sugar.

> ½ pint fresh raspberries or 1 package (10 oz) frozen berries in syrup or 8 ounces unsweetened frozen berries
> ¼ cup confectioners' sugar
> 1 tablespoon orange-flavored liqueur (optional)

In a food processor or blender, purée raspberries with sugar. Strain into a jar and add liqueur (if used). Store in refrigerator up to 5 days or in freezer up to 1 month.

Makes about ¾ cup.

CRÈME ANGLAISE

This rich custard sauce can make a simple dessert into a four-star dining experience. Lightly coat a dessert plate with the sauce, swirl in a teaspoonful of Raspberry Purée (at left) for color, and place a poached pear on top. Crème Anglaise will keep about 10 days in the refrigerator.

> 4 egg yolks
> ½ cup sugar
> 1 cup whipping cream
> ½ cup milk
> 1 teaspoon vanilla extract

1. In a 2-quart bowl whisk egg yolks and sugar until blended. In a 1-quart saucepan over low heat, heat cream and milk until small bubbles form at edge of pan; whisk cream mixture into egg mixture.

2. Return mixture to saucepan. Cook over low heat, stirring constantly, until slightly thickened (3 to 5 minutes; the mixture will coat a spoon). Strain into a clean bowl. Stir in vanilla. Cover surface of custard with plastic wrap and chill for 4 hours.

Makes about 2 cups.

Orange Crème Anglaise
Substitute ¼ cup orange juice for ¼ cup of the milk; add 1 tablespoon orange rind to cream-milk mixture when heated.

CHOCOLATE FUDGE SAUCE

Every cook should have a recipe for a fabulous chocolate sauce. This is it. Spoon into tiny tart shells and top with a rosette of whipped cream and a sprinkling of toasted pistachio nuts.

> 1 cup whipping cream
> 8 ounces semisweet chocolate, chopped
> 4 tablespoons unsalted butter
> ¼ cup firmly packed brown sugar
> 2 tablespoons light corn syrup

In a 1-quart saucepan heat cream over medium heat. Stir in chocolate, butter, brown sugar, and corn syrup. Cool slightly before serving.

Makes about 2 cups.

A carefully planned, well-stocked pantry keeps you thoroughly prepared for every aspect of entertaining: food, equipment, and decor.

Pulled From the Pantry

When your pantry is carefully and completely stocked with basic food, equipment, and table accessories, you can entertain very stylishly on short notice and with little or no shopping. The recipes in this chapter feature pantry staples (including leftovers) in many creative combinations. You will also learn how to put up your own fancy sauces, curds, and condiments (see page 46); how to stock up on homemade stocks (see page 56); and how to transform unassuming ingredients such as pasta, tortillas, and eggs into party fare (see page 42). With a delicious menu for a spur-of-the-moment supper (see page 52), based on the party pantry, you'll never hesitate to extend that last-minute invitation.

SOCIAL SECURITY

A carefully planned and stocked pantry is a form of social security. It will enable you to put together a satisfying meal for just about any entertaining situation without stepping outside the kitchen door. Pulling out a delectable homemade treasure or a carefully chosen purchase can be a time-saver and sometimes even a party-saver. A practical pantry is useful in a number of situations: cooking accidents or food failures, extra or last-minute guests, a sudden inspiration to have a party, or the need for a bread-and-butter gift when you are the guest.

The well-stocked pantry can also give you the courage to invite guests on the spur of the moment and allow you the pleasure of seeing friends without the need for elaborate preparations. And because the atmosphere is less formal, guests can be drafted to help or can be invited to keep you company in the kitchen while the meal is being prepared. Already prepared or quickly assembled appetizers, such as Spicy Pecans (see page 46) or Blue Cheese Crostini (see page 54), help pass the time and stave off hunger pangs. The pantry can also help with more formal meals by reducing the amount of shopping required.

Refreshing homemade Lemon Curd (see page 47) can be waiting in the pantry to top tarts for a last-minute dessert or to wrap in crêpes for a festive finale. A supply of Fresh Tomato Sauce (see page 47) in the refrigerator or freezer is handy for tossing with pasta, pouring on pizza, or serving over grilled pork chops.

TODAY'S PANTRY

The word *pantry* evokes images of old-fashioned home-canned foods, cured meats, and out-of-season produce stacked in storage bins and cellars—but today the reality is different. Modern pantries tend to be smaller than those of two generations ago. The advent of supermarkets, with their long shopping hours, has made extensive stocking unnecessary.

However, the pantry, now defined to include the refrigerator and the freezer as well as a dry goods cupboard, is still one of a cook's most important assets.

A pantry (from the French *paneterie*, a wooden wall-hung storage cupboard with lattice doors, used to store bread) can be as small as two shelves, a tiny freezer, and a section of the refrigerator. It can also be the traditional room separate from the kitchen. The size of a pantry is less important than what it should contain—a carefully chosen selection of purchased and homemade staples. Your pantry should be designed to allow you the flexibility to entertain as often as desired and as comfortably as possible. The key to pantry cooking is to choose staples that will be used regularly, to replenish them when necessary, and to have fun in the process.

STOCKING YOUR PANTRY

The usual pantry items—flour, sugar, and butter—can be expanded to include favorite foods stashed in the cupboard, freezer, and refrigerator, ready to turn into last-minute meals. Auxiliary ingredients allow the cook to feel relaxed when unusual entertaining situations occur.

Stocking a pantry doesn't mean overpurchasing items to cover every appetite or to anticipate every crisis. It does mean taking into consideration your palate and entertaining style. When you buy foods that you enjoy eating, the pantry will work for you. Start with the basic lists suggested in the first chapter (see page 8), then personalize the food choices.

Choose High-Quality, Versatile Ingredients

Purchase versatile and high-quality ingredients. Sun-dried tomatoes, for example, make a fine addition to an omelet or a sauce for chicken breasts, an impressive topping for pizza, or a tasty layer in a cheese *torta* appetizer. The ubiquitous can of tuna flavors a veal or pasta sauce, or becomes part of a Niçoise salad. Cans of cooked shell beans are a great time-saver

and can be seasoned with sausage or ham, diced vegetables, or Dijon Vinaigrette (see page 21) for a simple salad. Take time to sample the high-quality prepared foods that can be purchased from delicatessens and specialty stores. Also look for brands of purchased foods that, whether used alone or with additional seasonings, will not compromise your standards.

Incorporate Leftovers and Perishables

Leftover foods, whether half a roast chicken or a cup of steamed broccoli, should be considered assets. They can be added to pasta, eggs, tortillas, rice, stock, or tossed with salad greens. A small amount of leftover blanched carrots can be tossed in Dijon Vinaigrette (see page 21) to garnish salad greens, or diced and added at the last minute to Vegetable Soup Printanier (see page 17). This is the best way to use foods that will not stretch to serve the number of people on your guest list, but can be combined with other ingredients.

A well-planned pantry can also extend fresh foods. Ripe, red tomatoes or fresh asparagus can be tossed with pasta for a quick first course. A large roast can often be marinated for dinner, and its leftovers used for a main-course salad the next night, and become meat pies for a weekend lunch. Some ingredients, such as onions, cabbage, kale, potatoes, pumpkins, and other winter squash, although perishable, will keep for several weeks if properly stored. Dry goods can be enhanced by fresh tomatoes, herbs, green onions, peaches, raspberries, and other seasonal perishables that appear in the marketplace.

With a carefully selected pantry and a working knowledge of favorite, successful recipes, you will be able to handle drop-in guests and to extend spur-of-the-moment invitations. As further rewards, cooking will become creative as well as fun, and there will be more time to enjoy the company of friends.

Pantry staples such as canned tomatoes and tortillas pair with meat leftovers to make hearty Chihuahua Chilaquiles (see page 58).

VERSATILE STAPLES: EGGS, PASTA, AND TORTILLAS

A practical pantry should include eggs, dried pasta, and corn and flour tortillas. Eggs, the critical ingredient in soufflés, omelets, crêpes, and many baked goods, give every pantry limitless possibilities. They fit well into any menu, are easily stored, and can be prepared at the last minute. Pasta, one of the most versatile pantry foods, is delicious simply tossed with butter and cheese or as part of a do-ahead lasagne. Dried pasta stores well in the pantry for up to one year. Fresh pasta, available in many supermarkets or from specialty stores, can be held in the freezer ready to use as part of a speedy and savory supper. In most recipes use 50 percent more fresh pasta when substituting fresh for dried (12 ounces fresh pasta for 8 ounces dried, for example). Tortillas, both flour and corn, are a great foundation for snack, lunch, and supper casseroles.

ROASTED PEPPER AND BACON OMELET

Omelets are the exception to the rule that eggs should be cooked slowly to keep them soft and tender. A perfect omelet is a slightly scrambled egg that cooks in about 1 minute. Omelets are best made in one- or two-portion servings; if served to a large group, they can be cooked assembly-line style, one after the other. Using a pan of the proper size is critical to the speed of cooking: The egg should coat the bottom of the pan to a depth of about ¼ to ½ inch. Too much egg in the pan and the omelet will start to overcook in some spots and undercook in others. The method for this Roasted Pepper and Bacon Omelet may be used for a variety of fillings, such as cheese, mushroom, ham, or spinach.

12 eggs
½ teaspoon salt
¼ teaspoon freshly ground black pepper
4 tablespoons unsalted butter

Roasted Pepper and Bacon Filling

6 slices bacon (about 8 oz)
1 medium onion, sliced
2 cloves garlic, minced
1 jar (7 oz) roasted red peppers, diced
1 teaspoon dried oregano
¼ teaspoon freshly ground black pepper

1. Prepare filling. Beat eggs with salt and pepper in a 1-quart bowl. In a 12-inch skillet over high heat, melt 2 tablespoons butter and swirl to coat bottom and sides of pan.

2. Pour one half of the egg mixture into pan. Grasp handle of pan with one hand and gently shake pan to keep omelet from sticking. With other hand, lightly scramble top of eggs with a fork, taking care to let bottom set slightly so that bottom surface is cooked and top stays moist. Cook about 1 minute (omelet should still be moist).

3. Place one half of filling in a thin line down center of omelet at right angle to pan handle. Using a spatula or fork, fold third of omelet nearest handle over filling. Lifting handle of omelet pan, place edge of pan on a serving plate. Push omelet over onto itself and gently roll it onto serving plate (underside of omelet will be on top). Cut omelet in half and serve immediately. Repeat with remaining egg mixture.

Serves 4.

Roasted Pepper and Bacon

Filling Slice bacon into ½-inch-long pieces. Set an 8-inch skillet over medium heat, add bacon pieces, and cook until bacon starts to brown (about 3 minutes). Stir in onion and garlic; sauté about 2 minutes. Add red peppers, oregano, and black pepper; stir to mix; cook over low heat for about 2 minutes. Keep warm over low heat while omelet cooks.

Makes about 2 cups.

Cheese and Bacon Omelet
Grate 6 ounces Monterey jack cheese. Place 3 ounces of cheese in center of each omelet on top of bacon mixture before folding.

Dessert Omelet   Omit ground pepper in egg mixture. Stir 4 tablespoons sugar and 2 tablespoons dark rum into beaten eggs. Omit filling. Proceed as directed. Dust finished omelet with confectioners' sugar.

PASTA PUTTANESCA

Onions, canned tomatoes, olives, and dried herbs—all from the pantry—combine to make this simple pasta sauce. Vary it with additions of salami, cooked chicken breast, or kidney beans, or add fresh seasonal produce such as asparagus, broccoli, sugar snap peas, or bell peppers.

2 onions, diced
4 tablespoons olive oil
4 cloves garlic, minced
1 can (28 oz) whole plum tomatoes, drained and diced
24 black olives, pitted and halved
1 teaspoon hot-pepper flakes
1 teaspoon dried oregano
1 teaspoon dried basil
1 teaspoon salt
¼ teaspoon freshly ground black pepper
12 ounces dried fusilli or other dried pasta
½ cup (2½ oz) freshly grated Asiago or Parmesan cheese (optional), for garnish

1. In a 3-quart saucepan or large skillet over medium heat, sauté onions in oil until translucent (about 4 minutes). Add garlic and cook 3 minutes. Stir in tomatoes, olives, hot-pepper flakes, oregano, basil, salt, and pepper; reduce heat to medium-low and simmer 15 minutes.

2. In a 4½-quart saucepan bring 4 quarts water to a boil. Cook pasta until tender, but slightly resistant to the bite (al dente; about 12 minutes, or according to package instructions). Drain thoroughly and toss with sauce. Serve immediately, sprinkled with Asiago cheese (if desired).

Serves 6 as a main course.

QUESADILLAS

A quesadilla is a south-of-the-border grilled cheese sandwich. When prepared with Cheddar, Monterey jack, goat cheese, or Brie layered between two flour tortillas, quesadillas make an appealing hors d'oeuvre or accompaniment to soup or salad.

1 cup (5 oz) grated Cheddar cheese
1 cup (5 oz) grated Monterey jack cheese
12 medium-sized flour tortillas
6 green onions, diced
12 sprigs cilantro (optional)
3 tablespoons vegetable oil
Fresh Pineapple Salsa (see page 89) or purchased hot salsa

1. In a small bowl combine cheeses. Sprinkle one sixth of the cheese mixture on 1 flour tortilla. Dot with diced green onions and 2 sprigs cilantro (if used). Cover with a second tortilla. Repeat with remaining tortillas.

2. In a 10-inch skillet over medium-high heat, heat 1 teaspoon oil. Cook stuffed tortillas, one at a time, until very lightly browned and crispy (about 3 minutes). Turn and cook second side until lightly browned and cheese is melted (about 2 minutes).

3. Remove from pan and reserve in a warm oven until all quesadillas are done. Cut each in 6 pieces at serving time and serve with salsa.

Serves 12 as an hors d'oeuvre, 6 as a sandwich, or 6 as an accompaniment.

Sophisticated Smoked Salmon Roulade is a perfect main course to serve for a romantic, spur-of-the-moment Champagne supper.

APPETIZERS AND FIRST COURSES

A well-stocked pantry provides many options for the enterprising host. If your dinner party for 10 has mush-roomed to 14, and you need to stretch the menu, the pantry can come to the rescue. Add a first-course pantry pasta, crêpe torte, or flavorful soup to extend the menu. When there is no time to shop or a favorite ingredient is out of season, substitute pantry ingredients for their unavailable counterparts. Nutritious canned shell beans, which don't need to soak and simmer, provide short-order variety for a menu: Toss them in salads or add to vegetable soups for punch. Your imagination and the pantry will help you become an unruffled host.

SMOKED SALMON ROULADE

A roulade is a rolled, filled soufflé that makes a simple yet elegant do-ahead dish and is a clever way to extend expensive ingredients such as the smoked salmon used in this rec-ipe. It is a versatile dish that is appropriate at any time of day: for brunch, lunch, a light supper, or as a first course of a multicourse dinner.

　5　tablespoons butter
　½　cup freshly grated Parmesan cheese
　4　tablespoons flour
　1　cup milk
　½　teaspoon salt
　¼　teaspoon ground white pepper
　⅛　teaspoon cayenne pepper
　⅛　teaspoon ground nutmeg
　1　cup (about 5 oz) grated Swiss cheese
　4　eggs, separated
　2　packages (10 oz each) frozen spinach, kale, or Swiss chard, thawed and thoroughly drained
　⅛　teaspoon cream of tartar
　8　ounces smoked salmon pieces
　　　Lemon wedges and watercress, for garnish

Dill-Cheese Filling

　12　ounces cream cheese, at room temperature
　1　cup sour cream
　1½　teaspoons dill
　4　green onions, diced
　½　teaspoon salt
　½　teaspoon ground white pepper

1. Preheat oven to 375° F. Line bottom of an 11- by 17- by ½-inch baking pan with parchment paper or aluminum foil. Grease paper and sides of pan with 2 tablespoons of the butter and sprinkle with ¼ cup of the Parmesan cheese; set aside.

2. In a 2-quart saucepan over medium heat, melt the remaining butter. Whisk in the flour and cook until butter and flour blend and thicken (3 to 4 minutes). Whisk in milk, salt, white pepper, cayenne, and nutmeg, whisking continuously until small bubbles appear around edges of pan and mixture has thickened (2 to 3 minutes). Remove pan from heat and stir in Swiss cheese, the remaining Parmesan cheese, and egg yolks.

3. Beat egg whites until foamy; add cream of tartar and beat to stiff peaks. Thoroughly fold thawed spinach into cheese sauce, then fold in beaten egg whites. Spread in the prepared pan.

4. Bake until soufflé appears dry on top and is lightly browned (24 to 25 minutes). Loosen edges with a metal spatula. Invert soufflé onto a dry towel or sheet of parchment paper. Any parchment paper or foil that has adhered to soufflé should be peeled away. Roll up soufflé, jelly-roll fashion, in the towel. Cool completely.

5. Unroll cooled soufflé and spread with Dill-Cheese Filling. Place smoked salmon pieces on filling. Reroll the soufflé tightly, cover loosely with a towel, and refrigerate at least 1 hour. Cut into 12 slices, approximately 1¼ inch thick each. Serve two slices per person, and garnish with lemon wedges and watercress.

Serves 6.

Dill-Cheese Filling   In a 2-quart bowl, beat together the cream cheese, sour cream, dill, green onions, salt, and white pepper.

Make-Ahead Tip   The soufflé base can be prepared through step 2 early in the day. If preparing ahead, transfer from 2-quart saucepan to a 1-quart bowl; cover surface with plastic wrap and refrigerate if letting sit over 4 hours. Bring to room temperature, fold in spinach and beaten egg whites, spread in pan, and continue with step 4. Or, prepare soufflé ahead through step 4. At least 1 hour before serving, unroll, fill, reroll, and chill until ready to serve.

KUMI'S MUSHROOM SOUP

A clear, rich beef stock can almost stand alone as a first-course soup. A few tasty additions—fresh peas, carrot slivers, diced green onions, fresh herbs—cook in less than ten minutes to create an elegant starter.

  5 *cups Beef Stock (see page 56)*
1½ *cups thinly sliced*
     mushrooms
  1 *cup bean sprouts*
 ½ *cup thinly sliced*
     green onions
  3 *tablespoons soy sauce*

In a 3-quart saucepan over high heat, bring Beef Stock to a boil. Reduce heat to low and stir in mushrooms, bean sprouts, green onions, and soy sauce. Simmer, uncovered, until heated through (5 to 8 minutes). Serve immediately.

Makes 6 cups, 6 servings.

Flavorful homemade stock is the base for fast and faultless soups. Kumi's Mushroom Soup cooks in about 8 minutes. When accompanied by Quick Hunan Pancakes (see page 67), the soup becomes a complete meal.

PUT UP A PARTY PANTRY

Personalize your entertaining style by spending a few pleasant hours putting up homemade specialty foods. A selection of flavored nuts, relishes, sauces, and curds will embellish your cooking and add sparkle to meals. Packaged in pretty containers, Spicy Pecans, Pesto Sauce, and Lemon Curd also make welcome gifts.

These fancy foods are costly to buy ready-made. When you prepare them yourself, you will be able to stock a pantry with premium products at a more affordable price.

SPICY PECANS

Pecans with a sweet and peppery coating make a spicy cocktail snack or a delicious garnish for a salad of winter greens dressed with Dijon Vinaigrette (see page 21). Also try using almonds, walnuts, hazelnuts, or a combination.

    4 tablespoons unsalted butter
    3 tablespoons sugar
 1½ tablespoons salt
    ½ teaspoon cayenne pepper
    ¼ teaspoon white pepper
    4 cups pecan halves

1. In a large skillet melt butter and stir in sugar, salt, cayenne, and white pepper; mix well. Add nuts and coat thoroughly. Drain nuts on a paper-towel–lined tray.

2. Store in refrigerator for up to 2 weeks or place in a plastic freezer bag, press out air, seal tightly, and freeze for up to 2 months.

Makes 4 cups.

MARINATED ONIONS

Store these piquant onion slices in the refrigerator ready to toss in a salad, place on a pizza, or garnish a hamburger.

    1 large red onion, thinly sliced
    ⅓ cup red wine vinegar
    ½ cup water
    1 tablespoon sugar
    ½ teaspoon salt
    5 or 6 peppercorns
    1 teaspoon dried oregano
    1 teaspoon dried basil

1. In a 3-quart saucepan bring onion, vinegar, the water, sugar, salt, peppercorns, oregano, and basil to a boil. Reduce heat to low and simmer, uncovered, until onion is tender (about 8 minutes).

2. Chill onion in the cooking liquid 2 to 12 hours. Store, covered, in refrigerator up to 1 week.

Makes about 2 cups.

SOUTH-OF-THE-BORDER SALSA

This versatile sauce can serve as a dip for crisp tortilla chips or as a spicy marinade for poultry or fish. Stir the salsa into a soup to spice up a light lunch, or top a burrito with the avocado variation. Avocado Salsa is a delicious condiment that can be used in the same way as guacamole. Since avocados are perishable, prepare the variation no more than one day ahead.

    3   large tomatoes, coarsely
        chopped
    1   small onion, finely diced
    2   cloves garlic, minced
        Juice of 2 limes
    1   jalapeño chile, minced
    1   teaspoon salt
    1   bunch cilantro, minced

In a medium bowl, stir together tomatoes, onion, garlic, lime juice, chile, salt, and cilantro. Let rest for at least 30 minutes before serving.

Makes 3½ cups.

Avocado Salsa   Follow South-of-the-Border Salsa recipe, but substitute 3 large, ripe (but not soft), coarsely chopped avocados and 3 fresh tomatillos (papery husks removed, fruit washed, dried, and diced) for the tomatoes.

Makes 4 cups.

PESTO SAUCE

Use this sauce for Pesto Focaccia (see page 23), toss with buttered fresh pasta, rub on chicken breasts before broiling, or add in a thin layer to Nora's Potato Gratin (see page 30). For variety try Pesto With Sun-Dried Tomatoes, below.

    2   cups fresh basil leaves
    4   cloves garlic
    1¼ cups olive oil
    ½   teaspoon salt
    1   cup freshly grated Parmesan
        cheese
    ¼   cup pine nuts or walnuts

In a blender or food processor, purée basil and garlic with olive oil. Blend in salt, cheese, and nuts. Seal tightly in one or two airtight containers. Store in the refrigerator up to 3 weeks and in the freezer up to 6 months.

Makes 2 cups.

Pesto With Sun-Dried Tomatoes
Follow Pesto Sauce recipe, but substitute 1 ounce sun-dried tomatoes for 1 cup of the basil leaves. To reconstitute tomatoes, cover with boiling water and let rest for 30 minutes. Drain, pat dry, and purée as directed.

LEMON CURD

Lemon Curd can be used as a filling for tartlets, as a tangy layer between a pair of Cream Cheese Cookies (see page 96), or as a spread to accompany scones. To make a dessert mousse, fold Lemon Curd into 1½ cups whipped cream and serve in elegant stemmed glasses or a pastry shell. Versatile enough to become a refrigerator staple, Lemon Curd keeps about 3 weeks when tightly covered.

        Grated rind and juice
        of 3 lemons
    3   eggs
    ½   cup sugar
    6   tablespoons butter, at room
        temperature

1. In a 1-quart saucepan stir together rind, juice, eggs, and sugar. Place over low heat, stirring constantly until thickened (10 to 12 minutes).

2. Pour into a ceramic, glass, or stainless steel bowl (not aluminum) and stir in butter. Cover with plastic wrap and chill.

Makes 1½ cups.

Orange Curd   Substitute juice and grated rind from 2 medium oranges for lemon juice and rind, and reduce sugar to ⅓ cup. Prepare as directed for Lemon Curd.

Makes 1½ cups.

FRESH TOMATO SAUCE

Fresh herbs enhance the flavor of this sauce but, in a pinch, dried herbs can also be substituted. Canned tomatoes are often superior in flavor to tomatoes out of season. They are also convenient, allowing last-minute preparation.

    2   pounds fresh tomatoes or
        1 can (28 oz) whole plum
        tomatoes
    2   tablespoons olive oil
    1   medium onion, diced
    3   cloves garlic, minced
    4   tablespoons chopped fresh
        parsley or 2 teaspoons dried
        parsley
    2   tablespoons chopped fresh
        basil or 1 teaspoon dried basil
    1   tablespoon chopped fresh
        oregano or 1 teaspoon dried
        oregano
    ½   teaspoon sugar
    1   teaspoon salt
    ½   teaspoon freshly ground
        pepper

1. To peel tomatoes, make an *X* in the blossom end of each tomato; drop in boiling water about 1 minute; remove with a slotted spoon, drain, and let cool. Remove skin and cut out core. Seed by halving tomatoes across their circumference, holding halves over sink, and gently squeezing out seeds. Chop tomatoes into medium dice. If using canned tomatoes, drain, discard juice, and dice.

2. In a 2½-quart saucepan over medium heat, heat oil and sauté onion 5 minutes. Add garlic and sauté 5 minutes more. Stir in tomatoes, parsley, basil, oregano, sugar, salt, and pepper. Simmer 20 minutes. Use immediately or store, tightly covered, in the refrigerator for 1 week or in an airtight container in the freezer for 1 month.

Makes about 2 cups.

Spicy Tomato Sauce   Add ½ teaspoon ground dried chiles to sauce.

Makes about 2 cups.

CLASSY CRÊPES

Basic crêpes *Pour crêpe batter in hot pan, swirling to coat bottom of pan with batter.*

Crêpes Suzette *Smear crêpes with sweetened, flavored butter and fold each into quarters; heat in oven in buttered ovenproof dish (see opposite page).*

Crêpe torte *Spread crêpe with filling (see Crepazes, at right); top with a second crêpe. Repeat layers, ending with a crêpe.*

CREPAZES

These ham and cheese crêpe tortes are easily prepared ahead for a dinner party, then baked at serving time. They also make a beautiful buffet presentation. The recipe makes two tortes, enough for eight servings, but the recipe can be halved to serve four. Fresh herbs can be added to the crêpe batter as well as the cheese filling, if desired.

     4 tablespoons butter, for
        greasing
     3 tablespoons butter
     3 tablespoons flour
    1¼ cups milk
     ½ teaspoon salt
     ¼ teaspoon ground white pepper
     ⅛ teaspoon cayenne pepper
     ⅛ teaspoon ground nutmeg
     1 cup (4 oz) grated Swiss cheese
     4 green onions, diced
    12 black olives, pitted and diced
     1 tablespoon dried dill
     8 ounces ham, diced
     1 recipe Basic Crêpes
        (see opposite page)

1. Preheat oven to 400° F. Heavily butter 2 soufflé or charlotte molds (1½ quarts each) with the 4 tablespoons butter.

2. *To prepare filling:* In a 2-quart saucepan over medium heat, melt the 3 tablespoons butter. Whisk in flour and cook 3 to 4 minutes. Whisk in milk, salt, pepper, cayenne, and nutmeg, mixing continuously until small bubbles appear around edges of pan and mixture has thickened (2 to 3 minutes).

3. Remove saucepan from heat and add Swiss cheese, stirring until melted. Stir in green onions, black olives, dill, and ham.

4. Place 1 crêpe in buttered dish. Spread crêpe with ¾ cup cheese-ham mixture (see Crêpe torte photograph, at left). Top with another crêpe and spread with another ¾ cup filling; repeat, using half of the crêpes. Using second dish, repeat the steps. Place filled dishes on a baking sheet and bake until golden brown on top (about 25 minutes).

5. Unmold by loosening edges with a knife. Invert a serving plate over mold and turn plate and mold over together; torte will slip onto plate. Repeat for second torte. Cut in quarters to serve.

Serves 8 as a first course, 4 as a main course.

PANZANELLA

This robust salad is a great way to use slightly stale French or Italian bread. Substitute crunchy red bell peppers when tomatoes are out of season.

    20 slices (about 1 lb) slightly
        stale French or Italian bread
     1 cup olive oil
     3 ripe tomatoes
     2 green bell peppers
     1 red onion, chopped
     2 cloves garlic, minced
     1 cup (6 oz) black olives, pitted
     ¼ cup vinegar
     1 tablespoon salt
     2 teaspoons dried basil
     ½ teaspoon freshly ground
        pepper

1. Preheat oven to 350° F. Brush bread with ½ cup of the olive oil. Place on a baking sheet and toast in oven until crisp and lightly browned (about 10 minutes).

2. Dice tomatoes and bell peppers into 1-inch cubes. In a 4-quart bowl toss together tomatoes, bell peppers, remaining olive oil, red onion, garlic, black olives, vinegar, salt, basil, and pepper.

3. Cover with plastic wrap and set aside to marinate 30 minutes at room temperature or up to 3 hours in the refrigerator. Bring to room temperature to serve.

4. About 1 hour before serving, break toasted bread into roughly 1-inch cubes. Toss with marinated vegetables. Transfer to a serving bowl; set aside until ready to serve.

Serves 8.

MINT POTATO SALAD

Sweet potatoes add a lovely taste and texture, plus a significant amount of vitamin A, to this dish, but the recipe can also be made entirely with white boiling potatoes. This salad is a delicious accompaniment to grilled ham, fried chicken, or smoked salmon.

    2 pounds sweet potatoes
    2 pounds white boiling
        potatoes
    1½ pounds tart red apples
        Shredded red cabbage,
        for garnish

Mint Salad Dressing

    4 cups fresh mint, julienned
        or 2 cups dried mint
    2 tablespoons boiling water
    ½ cup apple cider vinegar
    1 teaspoon sugar
    2 teaspoons salt
    ½ teaspoon ground white pepper
    1 cup Homemade Mayonnaise
        (see page 20)

1. Peel and cut potatoes into 1-inch cubes. Place potatoes in a 4-quart pan, cover with water, and bring to a boil over high heat. Reduce heat to medium and simmer until tender (10 to 12 minutes). Remove potatoes to a large bowl and cool for 15 minutes.

2. While potatoes are cooling, core and cut apples into 1-inch cubes. Prepare Mint Salad Dressing. Toss potatoes and apples with dressing. Refrigerate salad for 30 minutes before serving.

3. To serve, make a bed of shredded red cabbage on each salad plate and top with potato salad.

Serves 8 to 10.

Mint Salad Dressing   In a 3-quart bowl stir together ingredients.

Makes about 1¾ cups.

ELEGANT, APPETIZING CRÊPES

Crêpes make an appetizing package for leftovers and pantry foods.

BASIC CRÊPES

Vary the flavor of the crêpes by adding fresh or dried herbs or by substituting chicken stock for milk. To sweeten a dessert crêpe, add 2 tablespoons sugar to the batter. Always let the batter rest for about 30 minutes, which allows the flour to absorb the liquid and the batter to thicken to the consistency of whipping cream.

    ¾ cup milk
    ¾ cup water
    4 eggs
    ⅛ teaspoon salt
    ¼ cup butter, melted
    1 cup flour
    ¼ cup clarified butter (see Note)
        or vegetable oil, for cooking

1. In 2-quart bowl or a blender, thoroughly combine milk, the water, eggs, salt, and melted butter. Blend in flour to form a smooth batter. Let rest 30 minutes.

2. Heat a 6-inch-diameter steel crêpe pan or heavy skillet over medium-high heat until smoking. Lower heat slightly and brush interior surface of pan with clarified butter. Spoon about 3 tablespoons batter into pan, quickly swirling batter to coat bottom of pan. Pour any excess batter back into bowl.

3. Cook until crêpe is dry and slightly browned (1 minute). Turn crêpe over and cook second side 30 seconds. Remove to a plate to cool completely.

4. Repeat procedure with remaining batter. Brush pan with clarified butter as needed. Crêpes will keep a few days in the refrigerator or several weeks in the freezer; to store, layer cooled crêpes between pieces of parchment or waxed paper and wrap with aluminum foil. Bring crêpes to room temperature before using.

Makes 20 to 22 crêpes.

Herbed Crêpes   Stir ¼ cup minced fresh herbs into batter.

Crêpes Suzette   Prepare Basic Crêpes; set aside. Make Orange Butter by thoroughly blending 14 tablespoons butter, 5 tablespoons confectioners' sugar, juice and rind of 2 oranges, and 3 tablespoons orange-flavored liqueur. Preheat oven to 375° F. Spread each crêpe with 1½ teaspoons Orange Butter; fold in half, then in half again as shown in Crêpes Suzette photograph (opposite page). Place 2 tablespoons Orange Butter in a gratin dish or other shallow baking dish. Cover with folded, filled crêpes. Cover dish with aluminum foil and bake until butter has melted and crêpes are warm (about 12 minutes). Remove foil and bake 3 minutes more. Serve immediately. Place 2 crêpes on each dessert plate, spooning some of the sauce over each.

Serves 8 to 10.

<u>Note</u>   To clarify butter, melt butter over low heat in a shallow skillet. Remove from heat and skim white foam from surface. Carefully pour clear butter into a bowl and discard milk solids in bottom of skillet. Store in the refrigerator up to 2 weeks if not using immediately.

MAIN COURSES

Main courses made from ingredients in the pantry provide for occasions when the larder lacks perishable foods but is well stocked with root vegetables, frozen foods, dry goods, and leftovers. Always consider leftovers as part of the pantry inventory. Every home has some food on hand from a previous meal—whether a chunk of roast beef, cubes of cooked chicken, a small amount of Italian sausage, slices of ham, or pieces of smoked salmon. The trick is to manage leftovers so they can be used in another meal.

If cooked turkey, Cornish game hen, or duck is available, substitute it for the chicken in Thai Noodle Salad (at right). Make the Chihuahua Chilaquiles (see page 58) with leftover pork roast rather than the beef suggested. A lamb steak (purchased especially to have leftovers) can be used instead of the beef in Ginger Beef (see page 57).

These main courses do not preclude shopping. Whenever possible, fresh foods, chosen from what is seasonal and easily available, should be worked into the menu.

CHRIS'S MUSHROOM-STUFFED CHICKEN

Stuffing a chicken between the skin and the meat not only adds flavor but keeps the meat moist. It can also be done early in the day because the food won't spoil—stuffing under the skin does not have the risk of botulism that stuffing the bird's cavity does. Use this filling to stuff chicken breasts in the same way.

　　1　ounce dried porcini
　　　　mushrooms
　　2　tablespoons vegetable oil,
　　　　for greasing
　　2　tablespoons butter
　　2　cloves garlic, minced
　　2　shallots, minced
　　1　teaspoon salt
　　½　teaspoon pepper
　　¼　teaspoon dried thyme
　　¼　teaspoon dried sage
　　¼　teaspoon dried oregano
　　¼　teaspoon dried basil
　　1　chicken (3 to 3½ lb)
　　4　cloves garlic
　　1　bay leaf
　　3　tablespoons butter, melted
　　　　Fennel Roasted Potatoes
　　　　(see page 59) or Soubise
　　　　Casserole (see page 59),
　　　　for accompaniment

1. Reconstitute dried mushrooms by placing in a small bowl and covering with boiling water; let sit 30 minutes. Preheat oven to 350° F. Coat an 8- by 12-inch baking dish with oil.

2. In a 10-inch skillet over medium heat, melt the 2 tablespoons butter. Sauté the minced garlic and shallots until softened but not browned (3 to 4 minutes). Stir in salt, pepper, thyme, sage, oregano, and basil. Drain mushrooms, then mince and stir into garlic mixture.

3. Loosen skin covering chicken breasts and thighs by slipping an index finger between skin and meat, taking care not to tear skin. Place one fourth of mushroom filling between skin and meat of one thigh and leg; repeat with other thigh and leg. Place one fourth of the mixture between skin and meat of one breast; repeat with other breast. Stuff cavity with the 4 cloves garlic and bay leaf.

Place chicken in baking dish; brush chicken with melted butter.

4. Bake until lightly browned (about 1 hour and 10 minutes; internal temperature of 165° F on an instant-read thermometer). To serve, carve chicken into 6 or 8 pieces and accompany with Fennel Roasted Potatoes.

Serves 6 to 8.

THAI NOODLE SALAD

For a spicier salad, increase the amount of hot-pepper flakes. Asian sesame oil, made from toasted sesame seeds, contributes a characteristic flavor to the salad. It is available at Asian markets, specialty markets, and well-stocked supermarkets, as are the dried egg noodles.

　　1　pound Chinese dried egg
　　　　noodles or linguine
　　4　cooked chicken breast halves
　　　　Cilantro sprigs, mint leaves,
　　　　and chopped peanuts, for
　　　　garnish

Sesame-Soy Dressing

　　¾　cup soy sauce
　　¾　cup Chicken Stock (see
　　　　page 56) or water
　　½　cup coarsely chopped peanuts
　　¼　cup smooth peanut butter
　　¼　cup firmly packed brown
　　　　sugar
　　¼　cup white wine vinegar
　　¼　cup Asian sesame oil
　　2　tablespoons vegetable oil
　1½　cups minced fresh mint
　　½　cup minced cilantro
　　2　cloves garlic, minced
　　2　cups shredded carrots
　　4　green onions, minced
　　1　teaspoon hot-pepper flakes

1. In a 4½-quart saucepan bring 4 quarts water to a boil. Add noodles, stir to separate, and reduce heat to medium. Cook noodles until tender but still firm (about 18 minutes). Remove from heat and drain.

2. While noodles are cooking prepare the dressing. Toss warm noodles with dressing to coat thoroughly.

3. Tear each chicken breast half into 8 or 10 medium-sized pieces; add to noodles. Stir to coat chicken with sauce and to mix with noodles. Garnish with cilantro sprigs, mint leaves, and chopped peanuts, and serve.

Serves 8.

Sesame-Soy Dressing In a 4-quart bowl thoroughly combine all ingredients.

Makes about 2¾ cups.

SAUTÉED DUCK BREAST IN GOOSEBERRY SAUCE

The gooseberry resembles a Thompson seedless grape in size and color, but is closely related to the kiwifruit and has the same tart-sweet flavor. Its tartness contrasts with the richness of duck breast. Buying whole ducks and removing the breasts is the least expensive way to purchase duck breasts; reserve duck legs to braise in a slow-cooking stew. Bone and wrap several duck breasts to freeze for this dish. To bone a breast, place a small sharp knife flat against breastbone, run knife along length of breast, and pull meat away from breastbone. If you prefer not to bone the breasts yourself, ask the butcher to bone them for you. Duck breast is more tender when not overcooked.

> 2 *shallots, minced*
> 2 *cloves garlic, minced*
> 2 *tablespoons red wine vinegar*
> 2 *tablespoons olive oil*
> 1 *orange*
> 6 *boneless duck breasts*
> 2 *tablespoons vegetable oil*
> 1 *can (15 oz) gooseberries*
>   *Salt and freshly ground*
>   *pepper, to taste*

1. In a 2-quart bowl combine shallots, garlic, red wine vinegar, and olive oil. Grate rind from orange, taking care not to remove any bitter white membrane with the rind; add rind to marinade. Coat duck breasts with marinade and let marinate 30 minutes to 4 hours, uncovered, in refrigerator.

2. In a 12-inch skillet over medium heat, heat the vegetable oil until hot, but not smoking. Remove duck breasts from marinade and add to skillet. Sauté until lightly browned (about 5 minutes on first side, about 2 minutes on other side for medium and 4 minutes for well done). Duck breast dries out very rapidly; be careful not to overcook.

3. While duck cooks, purée gooseberries with their liquid in a food processor or blender. When duck is done, remove from skillet and reserve on a cutting board loosely covered with aluminum foil. Pour puréed gooseberries into skillet and mix with browned bits of duck breast remaining in pan. Season to taste with salt and pepper; remove from heat.

4. Slice duck breasts across the grain (with knife at 45-degree angle to the meat) into 4 to 6 pieces, each about ¼ inch thick. To serve, pour a small amount of sauce over each portion. Serve remaining sauce on the side.

Serves 4 to 6.

The tart-sweet flavor of exotic gooseberries complements the rich, meaty appeal of sautéed duck breast. With a well-stocked pantry, this impressive main course is quick to put together.

PUTTING THE PANTRY TO WORK

Blue Cheese Crostini

Tortellini in Brodo

Broccoli and Chicken Strudels

Mediterranean Green Salad

*Ice Cream and Amaretti
Cookies or Homemade Cookies
(see Quick Cookies, page 96)*

Fresh Fruit

Soave or Sauvignon Blanc

---

*If you run into friends while
shopping or leaving a movie,
you could go to a noisy
coffeehouse to visit. But, if
you have a well-stocked
pantry, you can invite them
back to your house for a
simple supper. This type
of spur-of-the-moment
invitation is the epitome of
relaxed entertaining. A
working pantry puts the
cook at ease and encourages
impromptu entertaining
without the need for
a mad shopping spree.
This menu serves 6.*

Preparation Plan

Set frozen filo dough and cookies (if frozen) out to thaw at room temperature as soon as you get home. The filo dough needs an hour to defrost. Let Roquefort and cream cheeses soften at room temperature for *crostini*. Start to hard-cook the eggs for the salad. Offer guests a glass of wine and let them join you in the kitchen while you prepare the filling for the Broccoli and Chicken Strudels. Remove hard-cooked eggs from pan and cool under running water. Preheat oven for crostini. Briefly chill the filling for the Broccoli and Chicken Strudels. Wash salad greens, make Dijon Vinaigrette. Peel hard-cooked eggs and cut each egg into quarters. Mix crostini spread in food processor or electric mixer. Slice baguettes and spread with seasoned cheese-nut mixture.

Place crostini in the oven about 10 minutes before the strudel starts to bake. Cook tortellini; assemble Broccoli and Chicken Strudels while soup is cooking. Let guests each roll their own strudel under your tutelage. Bake strudels. Offer crostini while dishing out soup; put remaining crostini on each plate of Tortellini in Brodo and let each guest carry the first course to the table. Any extra crostini can be offered with the main course. After clearing soup plates, toss green salad with vinaigrette and arrange on dinner plates. Take strudels from oven, slice on diagonal, and arrange on dinner plates.

Start coffee or tea while scooping ice cream into dessert dishes, and arrange cookies and fresh fruit on a serving platter.

Let guests enjoy Tortellini in Brodo and the crostini while the strudels bake. For extra-hungry guests, make enough crostini to accompany the main course.

BLUE CHEESE CROSTINI

Whirl cheese, brandy, and pecans in a food processor or mixer for a smoother spread. Bringing the cheese to room temperature will allow it to blend more easily with the other ingredients.

> 4 ounces Roquefort cheese, at room temperature
> 4 ounces cream cheese, at room temperature
> ½ tablespoon brandy
> ¼ cup pecans, coarsely chopped
> 12 slices baguette

1. Preheat oven to 425° F. Thoroughly mix Roquefort and cream cheese. Stir in brandy and pecans.

2. Arrange bread slices on a baking sheet. Spread cheese mixture over bread slices. Bake until cheese is lightly browned (about 10 minutes). Serve immediately.

Serves 6.

TORTELLINI IN BRODO

Tortellini can be simmered in stock for this savory soup; tossed with cheese, butter, or a sauce for a substantial first course or main dish; or skewered on bamboo picks for a delightful appetizer dipped in Jane's Pesto-Crème Fraîche (see page 66). Stir leftover bits of beef or vegetables into this soup for variety. If purchased beef broth is used, make it resemble homemade by mixing 3 cups broth with 3 cups water.

> 6 cups Beef Stock (see page 56)
> 1 tablespoon dried basil or 3 tablespoons chopped fresh basil
> 10 ounces frozen tortellini
> 2 tablespoons freshly grated Parmesan cheese

Bring Beef Stock to a boil over medium-high heat; add basil and tortellini. Return soup to a boil, reduce heat to simmer, and cook until tortellini are tender (about 10 minutes, or according to package instructions). Divide among 6 shallow soup bowls, sprinkling each with 1 teaspoon Parmesan cheese.

Makes 6½ cups, 6 servings.

BROCCOLI AND CHICKEN STRUDELS

Main-dish strudels utilize leftover cooked chicken, turkey, beef, or even sturdy fish (salmon, halibut, or sea bass) in a delicate, delicious manner. This same filling makes a tasty deep-dish pie: Fill a buttered baking dish with the chicken mixture and place a piece of commercially prepared puff pastry over the top; bake in a 400° F oven 30 to 35 minutes.

> 1 pound broccoli, cut into florets
> 4 tablespoons butter
> 1 onion, diced
> 2 cloves garlic, minced
> 4 tablespoons flour
> 2 cups Chicken Stock (see page 56) or milk
> 1½ teaspoons salt
> ½ teaspoon freshly ground pepper
> 1½ teaspoons dried thyme
> ⅛ teaspoon ground nutmeg
> 1 jar (4 oz) roasted red peppers, diced
> 3 cooked chicken breast halves, shredded
> 18 sheets (about 1 lb) filo dough, thawed according to package directions
> ½ pound butter, melted

1. In a 4½-quart saucepan bring 4 quarts water to a boil. Blanch broccoli florets in boiling water until bright green (3 minutes). Drain in a colander and drop into ice water to stop cooking and set color. Pat dry and reserve.

2. In a 3-quart saucepan over medium heat, melt butter. Sauté onion and garlic until onion is translucent but not browned (3 to 4 minutes). Whisk in flour and cook until mixture thickens and starts to turn golden

brown (about 2 minutes). Whisk in Chicken Stock and cook, stirring constantly, until thickened (about 3 minutes). Season with salt, pepper, thyme, and nutmeg. Stir in reserved broccoli, roasted peppers, and shredded chicken.

3. Preheat oven to 400° F. Place one sheet of filo dough on work surface. Brush filo dough with some of the melted butter. Cover with another sheet of filo dough and brush with melted butter. Repeat with a third sheet of filo dough. Place ¾ cup of the chicken-vegetable filling near one narrow end of layered filo dough.

4. Fold in longer sides of filo dough about 1½ inches and roll up along length, forming a log about 5 inches long and 2 inches in diameter. Place log, seam side down, on a buttered baking sheet. Repeat with remaining dough and filling to make 6 logs. Brush tops with melted butter.

5. Bake until golden brown and flaky (25 minutes). To serve, slice each log in half on the diagonal.

Serves 6.

MEDITERRANEAN GREEN SALAD

Small, black Niçoise olives have a distinctive briny flavor that infuses this salad with a touch of Provence.

> 8 cups assorted greens, torn into bite-sized pieces
> Dijon Vinaigrette (see page 21)
> 3 hard-cooked eggs, quartered
> 24 Niçoise olives
> 1 can (6 oz) artichoke hearts, drained

In a large salad bowl, toss greens with Dijon Vinaigrette; divide greens among 6 salad plates. Garnish with hard-cooked eggs, olives, and artichoke hearts.

Serves 6.

FASHION A MARRIAGE OF FOOD AND HERBS

Over the centuries certain combinations of herbs and foods have become traditional because they work so well together. The following are complementary pairings. Refer to them for ideas or for substitutions if you run out of a needed herb during cooking. Also try new combinations, making notes on your favorites.

The most flavorful and economical way to cook with herbs is to grow them yourself, but this isn't always practical. Store purchased dried herbs in a dry cupboard away from heat and light. Rotate inventory of dried herbs every three months since herbs lose potency during storage.

Herbs intensify in flavor when they are dried. If substituting fresh herbs for dried herbs, use three times the suggested amount. The exception is rosemary, which retains its natural strength when dried. Fresh herbs are often added to dishes at the last minute so they keep their intensity of flavor. Dried herbs, which need heat and moisture to regain their intensity, can be added earlier in the cooking. To release oils, crush dried herbs before adding to food.

Meat, Fish, and Eggs

Beef Basil, bay, marjoram, oregano, parsley

Chicken Basil, bay, chervil, chives, dill, marjoram, mint, oregano, parsley, rosemary, sage, tarragon, thyme

Eggs Basil, bay, chervil, chives, dill, marjoram, mint, oregano, parsley, tarragon, thyme

Fish Basil, bay, chervil, chives, dill, marjoram, mint, oregano, parsley, tarragon, thyme

Lamb Basil, bay, marjoram, mint, oregano, parsley, rosemary, sage, thyme

Pork Basil, bay, chives, marjoram, oregano, parsley, rosemary, sage, thyme

Veal Basil, bay, chervil, chives, dill, marjoram, oregano, parsley, sage, tarragon, thyme

Fruits and Vegetables

Corn Basil, chervil, chives, cilantro, dill, mint, parsley, rosemary, sage, tarragon, thyme

Cruciferous vegetables (broccoli, Brussels sprouts, cauliflower, cabbage) Chives, cilantro, dill, marjoram, mint, oregano, parsley, sage

Fruits Basil, bay, chervil, chives, dill, marjoram, mint, oregano, parsley, rosemary, sage, tarragon, thyme

Gourds (chayote, cucumber, summer and winter squash) Chervil, chives, cilantro, dill, marjoram, mint, oregano, parsley, tarragon, thyme

Leafy green vegetables (chard, kale, spinach) Chives, dill, marjoram, oregano, parsley, thyme

Legumes (green beans, jicama, shell beans) Basil, bay, chervil, chives, cilantro, dill, marjoram, mint, oregano, parsley, rosemary, sage, tarragon, thyme

Lettuces Basil, chervil, chives, cilantro, dill, marjoram, mint, oregano, parsley, rosemary, tarragon, thyme

Mushrooms Basil, bay, chervil, chives, dill, marjoram, oregano, parsley, tarragon, thyme

Onion family (garlic, leek, onion, shallot) Basil, bay, chervil, chives, cilantro, dill, marjoram, oregano, parsley, rosemary, sage, tarragon, thyme

Root and bulb vegetables (beet, carrot, celery, fennel) Chervil, chives, dill, mint, parsley, rosemary, sage, tarragon, thyme

Tomato family (eggplant, pepper, potato, tomato) Basil, bay, chervil, chives, cilantro, dill, marjoram, mint, oregano, parsley, rosemary, tarragon, thyme

STOCKING UP ON STOCKS

Homemade stocks add a special dimension to cooking. A supply of the following basic stocks, stored in serving-sized portions in the freezer, will simplify meal preparation, as well as improve flavor. Beef and veal bones are available from butcher shops and at many supermarkets. Chicken wings or necks are found in almost every supermarket; poultry bones and carcasses left over from other preparations can be frozen for later use in stock. Fish bones for stock can be obtained at seafood markets.

Canned broth is often excessively salty and will never have the same taste as homemade stock; however, it is convenient. Dilute canned broth with an equal part water to make it more palatable. Canned chicken stock can be improved by simmering 5 cups stock with 4 green onions (cut in pieces), 1 clove garlic, 1 carrot (cut in pieces), 1 sprig parsley, and 1 bay leaf for 20 minutes. Strain before using.

BEEF STOCK

The bones and vegetables in this recipe are first roasted to give the stock a brown color and rich taste. For the best flavor, use knuckle bones with some meat attached. If possible, include a mixture of beef soup bones and veal knuckle bones; the combination will make a more flavorful stock, with the veal bones also serving as a natural thickener. Or, if desired, use only veal bones (see Brown Veal Stock, at right). Meat scraps, completely trimmed of fat, can be added to the stock during the last hour of cooking time.

4	pounds beef soup bones, chopped in a few pieces by butcher
2	medium onions, unpeeled, root end cut off, and quartered
2	medium carrots, scrubbed but not peeled, and quartered
2	stalks celery, cut in 2-inch pieces
2	bay leaves
10	stems parsley, leaves removed
4	cloves garlic, unpeeled
½	teaspoon black peppercorns
½	teaspoon dried thyme
16	cups (approximately) cold water

1. Preheat oven to 450° F. Place bones in a roasting pan; roast, turning occasionally with a slotted metal spatula, until they begin to brown (about 30 minutes). Add onions, carrots, and celery; roast until browned (about 30 minutes).

2. Drain off fat. With a slotted spatula transfer bones and vegetables to a stockpot, kettle, or other large pot. To ingredients in stockpot add bay leaves, parsley stems, garlic, peppercorns, thyme, and enough of the cold water to cover.

3. Bring just to a boil. Add a little more of the cold water to reduce to below boiling; stir once. Bring back just to a boil and reduce heat to very low so that liquid bubbles very gently. Skim off foam that collects on surface. Partially cover and cook, skimming foam and fat occasionally, for 4 to 6 hours. During first 2 hours of cooking, add hot water as needed to keep ingredients covered.

4. Strain stock through a colander lined with several thicknesses of dampened cheesecloth, discarding solids. If stock is not to be used immediately, cool to lukewarm. Refrigerate until fat rises to surface and congeals (about 8 hours). If stock will be used within 3 to 5 days, leave fat; skim fat when ready to use. If stock is to be frozen, skim fat.

Makes about 8 cups.

Brown Veal Stock Substitute veal bones, preferably knuckle bones, for the beef bones.

CHICKEN STOCK

Chicken and turkey are most common in stock, but other fowl, such as duck or pheasant, are also used. The process for making poultry stock is the same regardless of which bird is the main ingredient. The most flavorful result is produced from an older bird such as a stewing hen. Use whatever parts are available—carcass, cooked scraps, wing tips, giblets (excluding livers), skin, or any leftovers. For more flavor, roast bones, carcass, necks, and back in a 450° F oven until brown (15 to 30 minutes); watch carefully, turn occasionally, and drain off all fat.

>   3 pounds chicken wings, chicken backs, or a mixture of wings, backs, necks, and giblets (excluding livers)
> 16 cups (approximately) cold water
>   2 medium onions, peeled and quartered
>   2 medium carrots, peeled and quartered
>   2 bay leaves
> 10 stems parsley, leaves removed
>   ½ teaspoon black peppercorns
>   ½ teaspoon dried thyme

1. Put chicken in a stockpot, kettle, or other large pot. Add enough of the cold water to cover. Bring just to a boil. Add a little more of the cold water to reduce to below boiling; stir once. Bring back just to a boil and reduce heat to very low so that liquid bubbles very gently. Skim off foam that collects on surface.

2. Add onions, carrots, bay leaves, parsley stems, peppercorns, and thyme. Adjust heat to keep surface just breaking with bubbles, but not boiling. Partially cover and cook for 2 to 3 hours, skimming foam and fat occasionally.

3. Strain stock through a colander lined with several thicknesses of dampened cheesecloth, and discard solids. If stock is not to be used immediately, cool to lukewarm. Refrigerate until fat rises to surface and congeals (about 8 hours). If stock will be used within 3 to 5 days, leave fat; skim fat when ready to use or if freezing stock.

Makes about 10 cups.

Rich Chicken Stock   For a more strongly flavored stock, add beef, pork, or veal bones and trimmings. Increase the simmering time by 1 hour or more to extract additional flavor and body. Or, follow the recipe for Chicken Stock, but begin with a previous batch of stock in place of the water. The resulting "double stock" will make an excellent soup. Adding cut-up chicken regularly is a good way to keep a batch of stock fresh, and it gets richer with each extraction. Rich stock can always be diluted with water when a basic or thin stock is needed.

FISH STOCK

The best bones for fish stock come from mild fish, such as sea bass or halibut. Do not use bones from strong-flavored fish, such as tuna or mackerel.

>   2 pounds fish bones, tails, and heads
>   1 tablespoon unsalted butter
>   1 medium onion, sliced
>   ½ cup dry white wine
> 7½ cups cold water
>   1 stalk celery, cut in 2-inch pieces
>   1 bay leaf
>   8 stems parsley, leaves removed
>   ½ teaspoon dried thyme

1. Put fish bones in bowl in sink. Let cold water run over bones for 5 minutes.

2. In a stockpot, kettle, or large saucepan over low heat, melt butter. Add onion and cook, stirring often, until soft but not brown (about 10 minutes).

3. Add fish bones, wine, the water, celery, bay leaf, parsley, and thyme. Mix well. Bring just to a boil and skim thoroughly to remove foam. Reduce heat to low and simmer, uncovered, skimming occasionally, for 20 minutes.

4. Drain contents of pot by pouring through a fine wire-mesh strainer into a bowl without pressing down on the mass; discard solids. (Pressing down on solids will cloud liquid, making it unsuitable for an aspic or a clear sauce.)

5. If not using stock immediately, cool to room temperature. Pour into 1- to 2-cup containers. Refrigerate, covered, up to 2 days or freeze up to 3 months.

Makes about 6 cups.

GINGER BEEF

Cut and measure all the ingredients for a stir-fry before turning on the stove. Then all the cooking can be done in less than 5 minutes. Store flank steak in the freezer, or freeze 30 minutes, for easier slicing. For variety, substitute 1½ pounds prawns for the steak. Serve with steamed rice.

>   1 pound flank steak
>   3 tablespoons soy sauce
>   3 tablespoons sherry or white wine
>   4 tablespoons peanut oil
>   2 cloves garlic, minced
>   3 tablespoons minced fresh ginger
>   1 small onion, thinly sliced
>   1 red bell pepper, thinly sliced
>   1 yellow bell pepper, thinly sliced
>   4 green onions, cut diagonally into 1-inch lengths
>   1 teaspoon cornstarch
>   2 tablespoons water
>   4 cups steamed rice, for accompaniment

1. Slice flank steak, across the grain, into strips about 3 inches long and ⅛ inch thick. Place in a 1-quart nonaluminum bowl, toss with soy sauce and sherry, and marinate 30 minutes to 8 hours.

2. In a wok or 14-inch skillet over high heat, heat 2 tablespoons oil. Add garlic, 1½ tablespoons of the ginger, and onion slices, and stir constantly until tender but not browned (2 to 3 minutes). Add bell peppers and cook for 2 to 3 minutes. Remove.

3. Add remaining oil to wok and stir in remaining ginger and beef. Toss while cooking over high heat until meat is medium-rare (2 to 3 minutes). Return onion and peppers to beef. Add green onions and toss to combine all ingredients thoroughly.

4. In a small bowl stir together cornstarch and the water and toss with beef mixture. Boil briefly, stirring, until thickened (about 30 seconds). Serve immediately with steamed rice.

Serves 6.

CHIHUAHUA CHILAQUILES

Chilaquiles (pronounced chee-la-*kee*-less) beautifully utilize leftover roast beef, pork, turkey, or chicken. It's also worth a trip to the market to purchase fresh meat for this dish. Buy approximately 4 pounds beef chuck roast and simmer, covered with homemade Beef Stock (see page 56) or water, until tender and falling apart (about 4 hours).

    2 onions, diced
    4 cloves garlic, sliced
    2 tablespoons vegetable oil
    6 dried New Mexico chiles, diced
    1 or 2 jalapeño chiles, sliced
    7 cups Beef Stock (see page 56)
    6 to 8 cups leftover shredded
       beef chuck roast
    1 package (10 oz) frozen corn
       kernels
    1 can (15 oz) plum tomatoes,
       drained and diced
    1 tablespoon toasted cumin seed
    1 tablespoon salt
    ¼ teaspoon freshly ground
       black pepper
    ½ teaspoon hot-pepper flakes
    6 corn tortillas, cut into
       thin strips
    1 cup sour cream, for garnish
    ¼ cup sliced green onions,
       for garnish
    6 sprigs cilantro, for garnish
       Marinated Onions (see page
       46), for garnish (optional)

1. In a 4-quart saucepan over medium heat, sauté onion and garlic in oil until softened and translucent (4 to 5 minutes). Add chiles, stock, beef, corn, tomatoes, cumin, salt, black pepper, and hot-pepper flakes. Reduce heat to low and simmer, uncovered, for 45 minutes.

2. While chilaquiles simmer, heat oven to 350° F. Toast tortilla strips on a baking sheet in the oven until dried out and lightly browned (12 to 15 minutes); reserve.

3. Serve chilaquiles in a shallow soup bowl, topped with toasted tortilla strips, sour cream, green onions, and cilantro sprigs. Serve Marinated Onions (if used), on the side.

Serves 6.

ACCOMPANIMENTS

Pantry side dishes emphasize easily stored root vegetables such as potatoes, carrots, and onions, and other staples such as frozen spinach and dried grains. Many ingredients are interchangeable in these recipes: Substitute baking potatoes for sweet potatoes in Sweet Potato Pancakes (at right), or add blanched broccoli, sautéed red bell pepper, or cooked cauliflower to Crustless Spinach and Zucchini Quiche (see opposite page).

FONTINA POLENTA

Polenta can be prepared at the last minute or hours ahead. Top it with Fresh Tomato Sauce (see page 47) and sprinkle with basil. It is also delicious with ratatouille (see Ratatouille Mille-Feuilles, page 115).

    2½ cups Chicken Stock
        (see page 56)
    1   cup polenta (coarse cornmeal)
    1   tablespoon butter
    1¼ teaspoons salt
    2   tablespoons whipping cream
        (optional)
    ½   cup grated fontina cheese

1. In a 3-quart saucepan over medium-high heat, bring stock to a boil. Reduce to medium heat. Add polenta by the tablespoon, stirring constantly to prevent lumps from forming. Continue stirring as mixture cooks (about 20 minutes). Polenta will pull away from sides of pan.

2. Stir in butter, salt, and cream (if used). Top with grated fontina and serve immediately.

Serves 6.

Baked Fontina Polenta   Prepare Fontina Polenta as directed, reserving grated fontina. Pour polenta into a buttered 8- by 8-inch baking pan. Cover with plastic wrap if not serving immediately. At serving time, preheat oven to 375° F. Sprinkle polenta with grated fontina and bake until cheese melts (15 to 20 minutes).

Creamy Gorgonzola Polenta
Omit fontina cheese. Stir 4 ounces crumbled Gorgonzola cheese into warm polenta with butter and salt.

ROASTED ONIONS WITH BALSAMIC VINEGAR

Red, white, or yellow onions can be marinated and roasted in this fashion, making a tasty dish to accompany roast chicken, lamb, or beef. The onions can also be made ahead and served at room temperature as part of an antipasto platter. Balsamic vinegar is a pungent, almost sweet, aged Italian vinegar.

    3 cloves garlic, minced
    4 tablespoons balsamic vinegar
    4 tablespoons olive oil
    ½ teaspoon salt
    ¼ teaspoon freshly ground
       pepper
    3 red onions, peeled and halved

1. In a 9- by 12-inch baking pan, mix garlic, 2 tablespoons of the vinegar, oil, salt, and pepper to make a marinade. Add onions and coat with marinade. Let stand 1 hour.

2. Preheat oven to 350° F. Bake onions until easily pierced in center with a knife (about 1¼ hours). Remove to a serving dish and drizzle with remaining vinegar.

Serves 6.

SWEET POTATO PANCAKES

Although wonderful when baked, vitamin-rich sweet potatoes are also tasty when sautéed with garlic and tarragon. For variety shred apples and add to the sweet potatoes. The mixture can be prepared in advance and held in the refrigerator for several hours before cooking.

    2 medium sweet potatoes (about
       1 lb), peeled and shredded
    1 small onion, minced
    3 cloves garlic, minced
    2 teaspoons dried tarragon
    1 teaspoon salt
    ¼ teaspoon freshly ground
       pepper
    2 tablespoons dried bread
       crumbs
    2 eggs, lightly beaten
    1 tablespoon butter
    2 tablespoons vegetable oil

1. Place shredded sweet potatoes in a 2-quart bowl. Stir in onion, garlic, tarragon, salt, pepper, bread crumbs, and eggs.

2. In a 14-inch skillet over medium heat, melt butter with oil. For each pancake place 2 heaping tablespoons sweet potato mixture in pan and flatten to a pancake about 4 inches in diameter. Cook until each side is browned and appears dry (10 minutes on the first side, 8 minutes on second side). Serve immediately.

Serves 6.

FENNEL-ROASTED POTATOES

The potatoes do not need to be peeled, simply scrubbed clean. Toss potatoes in the same roasting pan with roast poultry or pork loin, and vary their flavor by substituting rosemary, lavender, basil, or jalapeño chiles for the fennel. Baste with the pan juices from time to time for a crispy, flavorful side dish. As a separately prepared dish, serve with Chris's Mushroom-Stuffed Chicken (see page 50) or Sautéed Duck Breast in Gooseberry Sauce (see page 51).

> 2 *pounds small red boiling potatoes*
> ¼ *cup olive oil*
> 2 *teaspoons whole fennel seed*
> 1 *teaspoon salt*
> ½ *teaspoon freshly ground pepper*
> 6 *whole cloves garlic, peeled*

1. Preheat oven to 350° F. Wash and dry potatoes; place in a 9- by 12-inch baking dish. Drizzle with olive oil. Roll potatoes in oil to coat thoroughly. Crush fennel seed slightly by placing on work surface and pressing with a heavy pan or meat pounder. Sprinkle potatoes with fennel seed, salt, and pepper; add garlic to pan.

2. Roast until potatoes are easily pierced with a knife (45 to 60 minutes, depending on the size of potatoes). Serve immediately.

Serves 6 to 8.

ORANGE-ACCENTED CARROTS

Oranges and carrots are a classic and colorful combination. Orange juice, sherry, brandy, or vodka will taste equally delicious in lieu of orange-flavored liqueur.

> 4 *large carrots, peeled and sliced*
> 2 *tablespoons butter*
> 2 *tablespoons orange-flavored liqueur*
> 2 *tablespoons orange juice or water*
> 1 *tablespoon grated orange rind*
> 1 *teaspoon salt*
> ¼ *teaspoon ground white pepper*

1. In a medium, heavy-bottomed saucepan, combine carrots, butter, liqueur, orange juice, orange rind, salt, and pepper.

2. Cover saucepan tightly and cook over medium-low heat until carrots are tender when pierced with a knife (about 16 minutes). Serve carrots immediately with sauce.

Serves 6.

CRUSTLESS SPINACH AND ZUCCHINI QUICHE

If desired, substitute leftover cooked broccoli, cauliflower, or raw carrots for the zucchini. Whether served hot or cold, the quiche is delicious.

> 3 *tablespoons butter*
> 1 *onion, diced*
> 2 *cloves garlic, minced*
> 2 *medium zucchini, shredded*
> 1 *pound fresh spinach, chopped, or 1 package (10 oz) frozen chopped spinach, thawed*
> 1 *tin (2 oz) anchovies*
> 2 *tablespoons flour*
> 1 *cup milk*
> 1 *cup (4 oz) grated Swiss cheese*
> 4 *eggs*
> ⅛ *teaspoon ground nutmeg*
> ¼ *teaspoon freshly ground pepper*
> 3 *tablespoons minced parsley*

1. Using 1 tablespoon of the butter, grease a 10-inch quiche pan. Preheat oven to 400° F.

2. In a 12-inch skillet over medium heat, melt remaining butter. Sauté onion until softened and translucent (5 minutes). Add garlic and cook 3 minutes more. Stir in zucchini, spinach, and anchovies, mashing anchovies while mixing. Cook, stirring occasionally, until moisture is absorbed (5 to 8 minutes).

3. Add flour and stir until well coated. Stir in milk, cheese, eggs, nutmeg, pepper, and parsley. Pour into prepared pan and bake until top is lightly browned and a knife inserted 2 inches from edge comes out dry (about 35 minutes). Let rest 5 minutes before serving. Cut into 8 wedges and serve warm.

Serves 8.

SOUBISE CASSEROLE

This classic mixture of onions and rice is a versatile side dish that will hold over low heat (200° F) for about 1 hour before serving. It can also be prepared ahead: Follow directions but in step 2 reduce cooking time to 45 minutes; to reheat add 1 cup Chicken Stock and bake in a 350° F oven until hot (about 30 minutes).

> 2 *tablespoons unsalted butter*
> 3 *onions, coarsely diced*
> 1 *cup long-grain white rice*
> 2½ *cups Chicken Stock (see page 56)*
> ½ *teaspoon salt*
> ¼ *teaspoon ground white pepper*
> ½ *tablespoon sweet paprika*
> ¼ *cup freshly grated Parmesan cheese*

1. Preheat oven to 350° F. In a 3-quart ovenproof casserole over medium heat, melt butter. Sauté onions until translucent (about 5 minutes); do not brown. Remove from heat.

2. Stir rice into onions and cook 5 minutes. Add Chicken Stock, salt, pepper, and paprika. Bake 1 hour. Remove, stir in Parmesan, and serve immediately.

Serves 6 to 8.

DESSERTS

Ice cream, purchased cookies, and fresh fruit are only part of the dessert pantry. Home-baked goods can be frozen after a Saturday baking spree, and many ingredients can be purchased and earmarked for the inevitable last-minute dessert. Remember that frozen berries will frequently work as well as fresh, almost always with less effort. A ready supply of flour, sugar, and butter is all that is necessary to turn chocolate, nuts, or fruit into a simple dessert tart. Eggs are useful for meringues, soufflés, or the simplest dessert omelet.

LEMON MOUSSE

When the refrigerator pantry is well stocked with homemade Lemon Curd (see page 47), a dessert such as luscious Lemon Mousse is always quick and easy to make. Here, it is spooned over fresh (or, in a pinch, frozen) blueberries for a tasty final course. The dessert can be served right away or can wait several hours in the refrigerator.

> *1 pound fresh or partially thawed frozen blueberries*
> *Juice of 1 lemon*
> *2 tablespoons granulated sugar*
> *1 cup whipping cream, whipped*
> *2 tablespoons confectioners' sugar*
> *Lemon Curd (see page 47)*

1. Place blueberries in a 1-quart serving dish. Drizzle with lemon juice and sprinkle with granulated sugar. Stir together gently; set aside.

2. In a 2-quart bowl fold together whipped cream and confectioners' sugar. Fold in Lemon Curd. Gently scoop mixture over blueberries. Serve immediately or hold in refrigerator for up to 4 hours.

Serves 6 to 8.

DUTCH BABIE

This simple oven pancake, topped with sautéed Grand Marnier Bananas, is a treat for dessert or a special brunch. If a seasonal fruit is preferred, peaches, pears, apples, strawberries, or boysenberries can replace the bananas.

> *4 eggs*
> *¾ cup milk*
> *¾ cup flour*
> *Pinch salt*
> *4 tablespoons butter*
> *¼ cup confectioners' sugar*
> *1 lemon, cut in 6 wedges*

Grand Marnier Bananas

> *3 bananas*
> *2 tablespoons butter*
> *2 tablespoons brown sugar*
> *1 tablespoon Grand Marnier*
> *Juice of 1 orange*

1. Preheat oven to 425° F. In a medium bowl or a blender, whisk together eggs and milk. Sift in flour and salt and whisk until smooth.

2. In a 12-inch ovenproof skillet over medium heat, melt butter and tilt pan to coat with butter. Pour batter in hot skillet over melted butter. Immediately place into preheated oven and bake until puffy and golden brown (about 25 minutes).

3. Sift confectioners' sugar over top of pancake. Accompany each serving with a lemon wedge to drizzle juice over top. Serve Grand Marnier Bananas on the side.

Serves 6.

Grand Marnier Bananas While pancake is baking, slice bananas into ½-inch pieces. In an 8-inch skillet over medium heat, melt butter; stir in bananas to coat with butter. Sprinkle with brown sugar, Grand Marnier, and orange juice. Cook, stirring, to allow sugar to melt and bananas to heat thoroughly. Reserve over low heat until pancake is done. Serve with pancake as an accompaniment.

GINGER CRÈME BRÛLÉE TART

Crème brûlée is French for *burnt cream*. Actually, the dish is carefully caramelized rather than burned. If desired, the same mixture can be poured into ramekins rather than a tart shell for a simpler presentation. Both crust and filling can be prepared two days ahead, and the filling can be caramelized and refrigerated a day before serving—truly the perfect party dessert.

> *2 cups whipping cream*
> *1 piece (1 in. long) vanilla bean*
> *1 piece fresh ginger, peeled and minced (about 1½ tablespoons)*
> *4 egg yolks*
> *4 tablespoons granulated sugar*
> *1 8-inch baked tart shell (½ recipe Butter Pastry, see page 12)*
> *½ cup plus 2 tablespoons brown sugar*

1. In a 2-quart saucepan over medium heat, bring cream, vanilla bean, and ginger to a boil.

2. In a 3-quart bowl beat egg yolks with granulated sugar until thick and pale yellow. Strain cream over eggs, scraping saucepan thoroughly; return egg-cream mixture to saucepan. Stir, over medium heat, with a wooden spoon until mixture coats spoon (about 3 minutes; 180° F on an instant-read thermometer). Pour into prepared tart shell, cover surface with plastic wrap, and chill 4 hours or overnight.

3. Sift brown sugar over cream filling to cover completely. Set tart in a larger pan and surround tart with crushed ice. Broil about 3 inches from heat just until top is caramelized (2 to 3 minutes). Chill for up to 24 hours and serve.

Serves 6 to 8.

BANANA SPLIT PAVLOVA

This elegant recipe combines two national favorites—meringue-based Pavlova from Australia and the soda fountain delight from the United States, the banana split. Meringues, which are baked until dry, are best made on a cool day with little humidity; they can be stored in an airtight container for about one week. Meringues will be easier to remove from baking sheets if sheets are lined with parchment paper; cleanup will go faster as well.

1 cup toasted pecans
1 cup sugar
4 egg whites
⅛ teaspoon cream of tartar
¼ teaspoon salt
1 teaspoon vanilla extract
3 cups whipping cream
3 tablespoons sugar
1 recipe Chocolate Fudge Sauce (see page 37)
3 bananas
1 pint vanilla, chocolate, or strawberry ice cream
Fresh strawberries or maraschino cherries, for garnish

1. Preheat oven to 300° F. Line a baking sheet with parchment paper or coat with butter and flour. Draw 6 small ovals (with a pencil if using parchment or with a wooden pick on floured baking sheet), each approximately 4 inches wide by 6 inches long to resemble a banana split dish; place ovals about 1 inch apart.

2. To grind pecans in food processor or blender, place ½ cup of the sugar in work bowl or blender with pecans; process until finely ground. If using purchased ground pecans, toss with ½ cup of the sugar.

3. In a large mixing bowl or bowl of a heavy-duty electric mixer, beat egg whites with cream of tartar and salt to form soft peaks. Beat in remaining sugar. Fold in vanilla and pecan-sugar mixture.

4. Using a spoon or pastry bag, spread meringue mixture within each outline to form an oval. Push meringue to form edges that resemble sides of a dish.

5. Bake meringues until dry and lightly browned (about 1 hour). Cool completely. Remove from parchment and place on individual plates.

6. Beat whipping cream to soft peaks. Whisk in the 2 tablespoons sugar. Warm Chocolate Fudge Sauce over low heat. Up to 1 hour before serving, but no less than 15 minutes ahead, spread whipped cream evenly over interior of the 6 meringue "dishes." Slice bananas in half lengthwise and place a banana half over the whipped cream on each meringue. Place 2 small scoops ice cream on each banana, drizzle with Chocolate Fudge Sauce, add a swirl of whipped cream, and garnish with fresh strawberries.

Serves 6.

Include fanciful Banana Split Pavlova, a meringue-based ice cream sundae, in a self-serve soda fountain party.

61

With one stop at the market, for fresh food and cut flowers, and a knowledge of how to put a meal together quickly, you can prepare for a party in minutes, not hours.

On Short Notice

Entertaining against the clock can be stressful. Time will be on your side if you can draw on a collection of fast-to-assemble recipes such as those offered in this chapter. A market stop is part of the game plan: Fresh ingredients are a key to quick cooking since they need little attention to develop their naturally good flavor. Simple cooking methods such as grilling, broiling, stir-frying, and sautéing also speed preparation. To that end, this chapter offers tips on how to sauté (see pages 70 and 71), plus a trove of easy appetizers (see page 66) to get the party going. A menu for an elegant and speedy veal dinner (see page 73) will enable you to host a party on even your most hectic days.

MAKING MARVELOUS MEALS

The ties that keep people together are often woven over a friendly meal. Dinner with dear friends and new acquaintances is a relaxing way to end a hectic day. Perhaps you'd like to invite co-workers for a simple supper after a late night at the office, comfortably accommodate drop-in dinner guests, or breeze through a long-planned invitation that is now jammed between the school rummage sale and an overdue report. Knowing how to organize and prepare a meal simply and quickly, when time is at a premium, is the key.

PARE DOWN MENUS

Cooking foods that are fast and simple to prepare will help you entertain successfully. Plan a manageable menu. This is not the time to serve a new recipe or a seven-course dinner. Choose recipes that can be completed, including preparation time, in minutes, not hours. Don't be afraid to offer foods that you have served before. Instead, present them as your specialty. Guests will be pleased to be invited.

Prepare only as much food as you need. Portion control avoids wasting perishable food, and cuts down on extra preparation and cooking time. Think in number of servings, restaurant style, rather than in number of pounds required. To appease hearty appetites, plan to have a little bit more of some of the courses. Although several courses should satisfy most guests, remember that guests do not want to be uncomfortably full.

Incorporate a market stop into the schedule, so you can buy the freshest and simplest foods. Don't attempt a month's worth of shopping at this time. Be organized at the market. Always have a list, and get to know the prepared foods that are available. Some markets even carry washed salad greens and grilled chickens.

FOCUS ON QUICK-COOKING TECHNIQUES

This chapter emphasizes fresh ingredients, simply sautéed, grilled, baked, panfried, stir-fried, steamed, or boiled. Although fast, these techniques depend on planning for success, perhaps more so than do-ahead or pantry cooking. Timing and preparation are essential: Make sure ingredients are washed, diced, and premeasured, and equipment is at hand. Store equipment such as wooden spoons, spatulas, tongs, and cookware conveniently near the work area.

BE PREPARED

A confident attitude, a mastery of basic cooking skills, and a carefully stocked pantry allow parties to succeed impressively. Being organized is important. Keep silver polished, fresh candles ready in the cupboard, and a selection of linens ironed, so that you can concentrate on preparing food and visiting with guests.

Draw up a clear, step-by-step preparation plan, then follow it. Estimate how long it will take to assemble and cook each dish, and break down each recipe into tasks. Determine the amount of time available for preparation, then organize the work to match your schedule (see Working From Lists, page 7).

Practice will sharpen your ability to accurately estimate preparation time and to know which tasks can logically be grouped together. For example, plan to do some chopping while you watch the skillet. Use a timer to track the progress of oven-cooked foods so you can concentrate on another dish. Pair dishes that can be cooked concurrently and that finish at the same time, such as a risotto and a sauté. Also, keep in mind that every course doesn't have to be ready when the meal begins: You may want to select a slow-cooking dessert that bakes while you sit down for the first course. As this pattern becomes second nature, you may not need a written plan, but with a list you will minimize the possibility that something will be overlooked.

APPETIZERS AND FIRST COURSES

Speedy appetizers and first courses fit the bill for something that starts the meal on the right note, but isn't too filling. Each could be extended with a sandwich or series of small courses to become the focus of the meal. Appetizers should be easy and, of course, appetizing, and this selection is just that: straightforward, quick to prepare, and attractive.

AVOCADO AND SALSA SOUP

The dark-skinned Hass avocado has the firmest flesh of all avocado varieties, a rich flavor, and a creamy texture. It is a winter variety and, when available, should be the one you choose. A sprinkling of South-of-the-Border Salsa (see page 47) makes a colorful garnish, as does a simple swirl of sour cream. This soup is also delicious on a hot summer day served chilled, with hearty salad.

4 *large dark-skinned avocados*
1 *cup whipping cream*
½ *teaspoon ground white pepper*
½ *teaspoon cayenne pepper*
4 *cups Chicken Stock (see page 56) or purchased chicken broth*
  Juice of 1 lemon
  Salt, to taste
¾ *to 1 cup South-of-the-Border Salsa (see page 47)*

1. Halve avocados lengthwise. Remove pit and skin; discard. Purée avocado, cream, white pepper, and cayenne in a food processor; remove purée to a 2-quart saucepan. Or, place avocados in a 2-quart saucepan and mash with a potato masher, then add cream, white pepper, and cayenne. Add lemon juice to taste. Season with salt if needed.

2. Over low heat, whisk in stock; warm while stirring constantly. Serve soup warm in shallow bowls. Garnish each bowl with 2 tablespoons salsa.

Makes 8 cups; 8 servings as a first course, 6 servings as a main course.

CORN AND CRAB CHOWDER

For a substantial, main-dish soup, stir leftover cubed, cooked potatoes into the chowder with the bell pepper and corn. If you prefer to eliminate the bacon, substitute 3 tablespoons butter for the sautéing.

½ pound bacon, diced
2 onions, diced
2 cloves garlic, minced
4 tablespoons flour
4½ cups milk
    Kernels from 5 ears corn,
    or 2½ cups corn kernels
1 large green bell pepper, diced
1 teaspoon salt
½ teaspoon ground white pepper
½ teaspoon cayenne pepper
1 teaspoon dried thyme leaves
1 pound crabmeat
    Juice of 1 lemon
3 tablespoons minced parsley,
    for garnish

1. In a 4-quart saucepan over medium heat, fry bacon until most of the fat is rendered and bacon is crisp. Remove bacon with a slotted spoon to a paper-towel–lined plate and reserve.

2. Stir onions into bacon fat and sauté until translucent (3 to 4 minutes). Add garlic and cook 2 minutes more. Whisk in flour, coating onion and garlic; cook, whisking, about 2 minutes. Whisk in milk and cook until mixture has thickened slightly (2 to 3 minutes).

3. Stir in corn kernels, bell pepper, salt, white pepper, cayenne, and thyme. Bring mixture to a boil, reduce heat, and simmer for 6 to 8 minutes.

4. Stir in crabmeat, season with lemon juice, and warm over low heat 3 to 5 minutes. Serve immediately, sprinkled with parsley.

Makes about 10 cups; 8 servings as a first course, 6 as a main course.

Rich and creamy Corn and Crab Chowder is an outstanding choice for luncheon or late evening supper. The soup can be prepared ahead and chilled or frozen.

Special Feature

EFFORTLESS APPETIZERS

Each cook needs a few hors d'oeuvres that will be a snap to prepare. However, other than a wedge of cheese and a box of crackers, there are very few work-free appetizers. Simplicity and good planning will help lessen the burden of coming up with that perfect little something before dinner.

Bacon-Wrapped Dried Fruit Wrap dried pears, apples, or apricots in a 3-inch length of bacon, spear with a toothpick, and broil until bacon is crisp (2 to 3 minutes).

Baked Brie Place a 1-pound wedge of Brie on an ovenproof serving platter with a 1-inch-deep rim. Bake in a preheated 350° F oven until softened and slightly runny (20 minutes). Serve with crackers.

Crostini of Salami and Parmesan Cheese Cut a baguette into ¼-inch-thick slices. Top with a slice of salami and grated Parmesan cheese. Bake in a preheated 350° F oven until warmed (2 to 3 minutes).

Cucumber Rounds With Sour Cream and Chutney Slice English cucumbers crosswise about ¼ inch thick. Top each slice with 1 teaspoon sour cream and ½ teaspoon purchased chutney.

Endive Spears With Guacamole, Bay Shrimp, and Salsa Trim root end from a head of Belgian endive; separate endive into spears. Place ½ teaspoon prepared guacamole near cut end, 2 or 3 bay shrimp next to guacamole, and ¼ teaspoon tomato salsa next to shrimp.

Endive Spears With Gorgonzola and Toasted Walnuts Wash and pat dry 24 endive spears. Place ½ teaspoon Gorgonzola cheese on each spear and garnish with 1 large toasted walnut half.

Grilled Sausage With Spicy Mustard Grill or broil mild Italian sausage; cut into pieces and serve on skewers, accompanied with favorite spicy mustard.

Herring in Cherry Tomatoes Remove stems from 1 basket of cherry tomatoes. Slice top off stem end and hollow out interior by gently squeezing out seeds. Dice prepared herring in sour cream sauce and spoon into tomatoes.

Jane's Pesto–Crème Fraîche Stir together 1 cup crème fraîche and 1 cup Pesto Sauce (see page 47; or use prepared sauce). Serve as a dip for skewered tortellini and crudités.

Parmesan Pita Triangles Cut 8-inch pita circles in 6 wedges; split each wedge, brush with garlic oil (see Pepper Bruschetta introduction, page 26), sprinkle with 1 teaspoon grated Parmesan cheese, and bake in a 375° F oven until crispy and lightly browned (about 5 minutes).

Prosciutto-Wrapped Bread Sticks Wrap a paper-thin piece of prosciutto diagonally along the length of a good-quality bread stick. Leave a small amount of bread stick showing for a handle.

Skewered Chicken Breast With Italian Salsa Verde Cut boned chicken breast halves into 8 to 10 cubes (about ½ inch) and thread on a bamboo skewer. Broil 3 inches from heat for 2 minutes; turn and cook for 1 minute more. Serve with Italian Salsa Verde (see page 21), for dipping.

Smoked Salmon Mousse In a blender or food processor, purée 4 ounces smoked salmon, 4 ounces softened cream cheese, and juice of ½ lemon. Place in a small serving dish and serve with baguette slices or crackers.

Steamed Potatoes With Aioli Steam 2 pounds (about 16) tiny red-skinned potatoes until tender when pierced with a knife (30 to 35 minutes). Cool slightly. Slice and arrange around a bowl of garlicky Aioli (see page 20).

Steamed Potatoes With Sour Cream and Caviar Steam 2 pounds red-skinned potatoes as directed above. Using a melon ball cutter, scoop a small ball of flesh from the top of each potato. Fill with 1 teaspoon sour cream and dot with tiny caviar.

QUICK HUNAN PANCAKES WITH SPICY CARROT SALAD

Although Quick Hunan Pancakes are delicious served plain as an accompaniment, when topped with Spicy Carrot Salad they are transformed into a special first course. Serve alongside Kumi's Mushroom Soup (see page 45) or Thai Noodle Salad (see page 50) for a simple light meal. Coarse salt, such as sea salt or kosher salt, will stand out in the pancakes and not be completely absorbed like finely ground table salt.

    12 flour tortillas
     6 teaspoons Asian sesame oil
    ¾ teaspoon coarse salt
     6 green onions, minced
     6 teaspoons vegetable oil,
       for frying
       Coarse salt, for topping

Spicy Carrot Salad

     2 cloves garlic, minced
    ¼ teaspoon hot-pepper flakes
     3 tablespoons red wine vinegar
     2 tablespoons sugar
     2 tablespoons water
     1 tablespoon tomato paste
     2 carrots, peeled and shredded

1. Brush 6 flour tortillas with ½ teaspoon sesame oil each; sprinkle each with ⅛ teaspoon coarse salt and 1 minced green onion. Top each prepared tortilla with a plain tortilla.

2. In a 14-inch skillet over medium heat, sauté tortilla pancake in vegetable oil until light and golden brown (about 2 minutes) on first side; turn and brown on second side (about 1 minute). Sprinkle top with coarse salt before serving.

3. To serve as an appetizer, cut each tortilla into 6 pieces and serve while warm, either plain or topped with Spicy Carrot Salad.

Serves 6 to 8 as a first course.

Spicy Carrot Salad Place garlic, hot-pepper flakes, vinegar, sugar, the water, and tomato paste in a small saucepan. Mix thoroughly and bring mixture to a boil. Place carrots in a 1-quart mixing bowl. Pour hot sauce over carrots. Let marinate 20 minutes before serving. Spicy Carrot Salad will keep in the refrigerator for several days.

Makes about 2 cups.

SMOKED SALMON–CREAM PASTA

Smoked salmon and caviar symbolize elegant dining. In combination with pasta, they also create a quick first course that looks a lot more complicated than it actually is.

     5 tablespoons butter
     3 shallots, minced
     3 cloves garlic, minced
    1½ cups whipping cream
     2 tablespoons vodka
    ¼ teaspoon ground white
       pepper
    4½ ounces smoked salmon, diced
    1½ pounds fresh fettuccine or
       1 pound (approximately)
       dried fettuccine
     2 ounces salmon caviar,
       for garnish
     3 tablespoons minced chives,
       for garnish

1. In a 12-inch skillet over medium heat, melt butter and sauté shallots and garlic 2 minutes. Pour in cream and stir while bringing to a boil. Lower heat and simmer until cream has reduced slightly (about 10 minutes). Stir in vodka, white pepper, and smoked salmon. Heat thoroughly. Remove from heat and reserve.

2. In a 4½-quart saucepan bring 4 quarts water to a boil. Cook pasta until slightly chewy or al dente (about 30 seconds); drain pasta in a colander and place in skillet with sauce. Toss pasta to coat completely with sauce.

3. Serve on warmed plates, sprinkled with salmon caviar and chives.

Serves 6.

WARM CHICKEN LIVER FRISÉE SALAD

The pale green inner leaves of baby curly endive (*frisée*), are strong flavored and slightly bitter—a good counterpart to the pungency of the chicken livers. Dicing the chicken livers lets them cook more quickly and evenly.

     6 ounces baby curly endive
     2 ounces radicchio
       Dijon Vinaigrette
       (see page 21)
    ¾ pound chicken livers
     2 cloves garlic, sliced
     4 tablespoons olive oil
    ½ teaspoon salt
    ¼ teaspoon freshly ground
       pepper
       Juice of 2 oranges

1. Wash curly endive and radicchio and pat dry; tear into small pieces. Place greens in a 3-quart bowl and toss with Dijon Vinaigrette. Distribute greens among 6 chilled salad plates.

2. Cut chicken livers in ½-inch dice. In an 8-inch skillet over medium-high heat, sauté chicken livers and garlic in oil, stirring constantly, until crisp and browned on outside and slightly pink on inside (about 6 minutes). Season with salt, pepper, and orange juice. Stir to coat.

3. Evenly distribute chicken livers on salad greens. Serve immediately.

Serves 6.

ANTIPASTO PLATTER

Italian antipasto, named because it was traditionally served before pasta, can consist of any combination of favorite foods. It can be expanded for large parties or last-minute, unexpected guests by increasing the components. In this case, the course is extended by including pasta in the form of a salad. If not used immediately, the pasta salad should be reseasoned just before serving.

Four or five of the following:
½ *pound salami, sliced thinly*
½ *pound mortadella, sliced thinly*
¼ *pound Provolone cheese*
12 *ounces Niçoise olives*
1 *jar (8 oz) peperoncini*
1 *jar (6 oz) artichoke hearts, drained*
1 *red bell pepper, cut in strips*
1 *green bell pepper, cut in strips*
Marinated Onions (see page 46)

Pasta Salad

1½ *cups dried pasta shells*
2 *tomatoes, diced*
½ *pound mozzarella cheese, cubed*
1 *red onion, minced*
2 *cloves garlic, minced*
1 *bunch basil, chopped*
3½ *tablespoons red wine vinegar*
2 *tablespoons vegetable oil*
1 *teaspoon salt*
1 *teaspoon freshly ground pepper*

To arrange the platter, distribute antipasti around Pasta Salad.

Serves 8.

Pasta Salad   Bring 3 quarts water to a boil. Add pasta, stirring occasionally to prevent sticking. Cook until al dente (about 12 minutes, depending on size of pasta). In a 3-quart bowl stir together tomatoes, mozzarella, red onion, garlic, basil, vinegar, oil, salt, and pepper. Drain pasta, cool briefly (about 5 minutes), and toss with dressing while still warm. Serve as centerpiece of antipasto platter.

Makes 10 cups.

MAIN COURSES

Speed and ease are the hallmark of these main dishes. For convenience, purchase boned meats, rib and loin chops, tender prime kabobs, ground meat, fish fillets, and loin steaks in individual portions. This simplifies preparation, maintains exact serving size, and reduces cleanup time.

PICANTE PRAWNS

Spicy cumin-scented prawns pair well with Arroz Verde. In some markets preshelled prawns are available to save preparation time.

1½ *teaspoons cornstarch*
1 *tablespoon water*
3 *tablespoons vegetable oil*
1 *pound prawns (about 24), shelled*
3 *shallots, minced*
2 *cloves garlic, minced*
1 *teaspoon cumin seed*
½ *teaspoon hot-pepper flakes*
¼ *cup white wine or water*
¼ *cup tomato paste*
3 *green onions, minced*
Juice of 1 lime
Avocado Salsa (see page 47), for accompaniment
Arroz Verde (see page 76), for accompaniment

1. In a small bowl stir together cornstarch and the water; set aside.

2. In a 14-inch skillet over high heat, swirl vegetable oil and sauté prawns, shallots, garlic, cumin, and hot-pepper flakes until prawns start to turn pink and become coated with cooking mixture (2 minutes).

3. Add white wine and tomato paste, stirring well to combine. Bring mixture to a boil; stir cornstarch-water mixture into prawns. Stir in green onions and lime juice. Mix thoroughly and cook 1 minute more.

4. Place in a serving dish; accompany with Avocado Salsa and Arroz Verde. Serve immediately.

Serves 8.

SCALLOPS EN PAPILLOTE

Not only is this recipe delicious and quick to prepare, but the technique of steaming in foil packages is equally successful with cubes of other firm-fleshed fish such as salmon, sea bass, halibut, and turbot. Mint, fennel seed, or thyme would be a fine substitute when basil is out of season. The packages can be prepared ahead and stored in the refrigerator for up to 24 hours. Bake about 7 minutes longer when baking refrigerated fish.

8 *shallots, minced*
3 *large tomatoes, diced*
1 *large bulb fennel, sliced thinly*
4 *tablespoons olive oil*
1 *teaspoon salt*
½ *teaspoon freshly ground pepper*
1 *cup plus 4 tablespoons unsalted butter*
2 *pounds scallops*
8 *tablespoons minced fresh basil*
Grated rind of 1 lemon

1. Preheat oven to 400° F. In a 12-inch skillet over medium heat, sauté shallots, tomatoes, and fennel in oil until most of the liquid has evaporated (about 2 minutes). Add salt and pepper and continue cooking until liquid is absorbed (about 3 minutes); set aside to cool.

2. Cut 8 squares of aluminum foil, about 10 inches by 10 inches each; smear each with 2 tablespoons butter. Place an equal amount of tomato-fennel mixture in center of each foil square. Place ¼ pound (about ¾ cup) scallops on tomato-fennel mixture. Cut any very large scallops so they will cook evenly. Place 1 tablespoon basil on each mound of scallops, top with 1½ teaspoons butter, and ½ teaspoon lemon rind. Seal foil package securely. Refrigerate if not baking immediately.

3. Place packages on a baking sheet and bake until package puffs (12 to 14 minutes, depending on size of scallops). To serve, place a package on a dinner plate and open at the table so the aroma can be enjoyed.

Serves 8.

Prepare Antipasto Platter with a combination of your favorite foods. The homemade Pasta Salad makes this a substantial first course.

... ON SAUTÉ ESSENTIALS

The French word *sauter* means *to jump*. This simple cooking method uses a shallow-sided, lightly greased skillet or straight-sided sauté pan. Food is tossed in the pan, or made to jump, but the technique has also come to mean food cooked lightly and quickly whether tossed or not. Unlike panfrying, sautéing uses little fat and no liquid; the slick coat of fat and relatively high cooking temperature combine to keep food from sticking to the pan. Bits of food that remain on the bottom of the pan are often used to flavor a simple pan sauce or deglazing sauce, made by adding stock, liqueur, cream, or water to the pan after cooking.

☐ Match size of pan to amount of food it will contain: If pan is too small, food will be crowded and will steam rather than brown; if pan is too large, surface of pan not covered with food will burn.

☐ Sauté with a combination of butter and oil—butter for its flavor and oil for its ability to cook at high temperatures without burning. Olive oil also adds a definitive flavor to sautéed food.

☐ Fry food quickly, over fairly high heat, to seal in flavor. Liquid is not used for a sauté, although it may be added later for the sauce.

☐ High-quality, tender cuts of uniform size and thickness are preferred for sautéing since they cook evenly. All food to be sautéed should be patted dry.

BAKED SEA BASS PROVENÇALE

Reminiscent of the south of France, home of delicious olives, fragrant olive oil, ripe tomatoes, and pungent capers, this dish features a sauce that can be served with grilled sausages, sautéed turkey cutlets, or broiled veal steaks in addition to fish. The rule of fish cookery, whether poaching, grilling, or sautéing, is to cook 10 minutes per inch of thickness (measured at the thickest part). The fish will appear opaque when done and will flake when gently pressed with a metal spatula.

3 pounds (about 8 small) sea bass fillets
½ cup flour
2 tablespoons olive oil
1 tablespoon butter
¼ cup minced parsley, for garnish

Provençal Sauce

2 tablespoons olive oil
1 small onion, diced
2 cloves garlic, minced
6 plum tomatoes, diced
1 teaspoon herbes de Provence or ½ teaspoon each oregano and basil
1 teaspoon salt
½ teaspoon freshly ground pepper
1½ tablespoons capers
20 black olives, pitted and halved

1. Lightly coat sea bass fillets with flour. In a 14-inch skillet over medium heat, sauté fillets in olive oil and butter until light golden brown (about 8 minutes). Turn and sauté second side until lightly browned (about 5 minutes). When properly cooked fish will be golden brown on exterior and opaque on inside.

2. Spoon about ⅓ cup Provençal Sauce on each sea bass fillet and sprinkle with parsley.

Serves 8.

Provençal Sauce In a heavy-bottomed, 10-inch sauté pan over medium heat, swirl pan with oil and sauté onion until translucent (4 minutes); add garlic and sauté until softened and translucent (2 to 3 minutes). Add tomatoes, *herbes de Provence,* salt, pepper, capers, and black olives. Reduce heat and simmer for 10 minutes; keep warm over low heat while fish cooks.

Makes about 3 cups.

TURKEY PICCATA

Turkey cutlets (turkey breast sliced about ¼ inch thick) are substituted for the more traditional and expensive veal in this classic recipe. If you wish to use veal scallops, which are much thinner, reduce the cooking time by half. Serve with Saffron Risotto (see page 30) or Grandma's Herbed Spaetzle (see page 76).

6 tablespoons flour
½ teaspoon salt
¼ teaspoon ground white pepper
4 boneless turkey cutlets (about 1½ lb total), sliced ¼ inch thick
2 tablespoons butter
2 tablespoons olive oil
Juice of 1 lemon
Salt and ground white pepper, to taste
3 tablespoons minced parsley
2 tablespoons capers, drained

1. Sift together flour, salt, and pepper. Dredge turkey cutlets in flour mixture.

2. In a 12-inch sauté pan over medium heat, swirl butter and oil. Sauté cutlets in butter-oil mixture until lightly browned (4 minutes). Turn and cook second side until lightly browned (about 3 minutes). Thicker pieces of turkey cutlet will need to cook a bit longer.

3. Remove cutlets to a serving plate and cover loosely with aluminum foil. Add lemon juice to pan to deglaze, stirring to loosen any flavorful browned bits in pan. Season with salt and pepper. Stir in parsley and capers and pour sauce over cutlets.

Serves 6.

GRILLED VEAL CHOPS WITH CHIVE CREAM

Small veal rib chops each consist of just a few tender bites. Serve 2 or 3 rib chops to each guest for an ample portion. The sauce adds an elegant finale, although the veal chops are also delicious served plain, simply grilled or broiled.

      2 tablespoons freshly squeezed
         lemon juice
      2 tablespoons vegetable oil
      1 teaspoon salt
      ½ teaspoon ground white pepper
      3 shallots, minced
     2½ pounds small veal rib
         chops (about 12)

Chive Cream

     1½ cups whipping cream
     1½ tablespoons freshly squeezed
         lemon juice
      ¼ teaspoon salt
      ⅛ teaspoon ground white pepper
      4 tablespoons minced fresh
         chives

1. In a shallow pan stir together lemon juice, oil, salt, pepper, and shallots. Place veal chops in pan, coat with marinade on both sides, and let rest for 15 to 30 minutes.

2. Prepare grill or preheat broiler. Place veal chops on grill or under broiler, about 4 inches from heat, and cook until browned on one side (about 4 minutes). Turn and cook second side until lightly browned and slightly firm (but not rigid) when pressed with a metal spatula (about 3 minutes). Serve veal chops immediately, drizzled with Chive Cream.

Serves 4 to 6.

Chive Cream   In a 1-quart saucepan over medium heat, place cream and lemon juice. Simmer until reduced by about one third; keep warm over low heat. Just before serving, season with salt and pepper, then stir chives into warm cream sauce.

Makes 1 cup.

Step-by-Step

HOW TO SAUTÉ AND DEGLAZE

The following sequence shows how to sauté Turkey Piccata (opposite page) and make a simple deglazing sauce from the pan juices and the browned, crusty bits that form on the bottom of the pan.

1. *Place a large, heavy skillet or sauté pan over medium-high heat. Coat with butter and oil. Place floured turkey cutlets in butter-oil mixture. Leave some space between pieces of food (¼ to ½ inch) so that food will brown and not steam.*

2. *Cook cutlets in butter-oil mixture until lightly browned on first side. With a spatula, turn cutlet and cook second side until lightly browned. Thicker pieces of turkey cutlet will require a longer cooking time. Remove cutlets to a serving plate and cover loosely with aluminum foil to keep warm while the sauce is made.*

3. *To prepare a pan sauce, add lemon juice to natural juices left in pan from sautéing turkey.*

4. *Stir and scrape bottom of pan to loosen any flavorful browned bits of turkey or flour coating stuck to the pan. Cook briefly to blend flavors.*

5. *For a more refined sauce, strain through a fine-mesh wire sieve. Season with salt and pepper to taste. Stir in parsley and capers. Pour sauce over turkey cutlets and serve immediately.*

A fast and fancy party dinner is possible with a carefully chosen menu such as this one. Recipes begin on opposite page.

A QUICK AND ELEGANT DINNER

*Avocado and Poached Salmon
With Lemon Vinaigrette*

Veal Paillards With Sage

*Stir-fried Broccoli, Red Onion,
And Red Pepper*

Saffron Risotto (see page 30)

Almond Amor Polenta

Chardonnay

*This glorious and
glamorous dinner can be
accomplished between five
p.m. and eight p.m. even on
the most pressured day
because the techniques are
well-practiced and
uncomplicated. Stop at the
market on the way home,
and use your well-stocked
pantry. Turn on some
relaxing music, chill the
wine, and relax—this lovely
meal will be a snap to
prepare. This menu serves 6.*

Preparation Plan

Start the oven for the cake when you walk in the door. Make the cake and put it in the oven. Slice the vegetables for sautéing and reserve. Poach the salmon and prepare the vinaigrette. Pound and season the veal, and arrange the other ingredients nearby. Pull Raspberry Purée (see page 37) from the freezer. Start risotto while you set the table.

AVOCADO AND POACHED SALMON WITH LEMON VINAIGRETTE

For a more casual dinner, you might want to use a spicier sauce such as Jalapeño Rémoulade (see page 20).

　1　lemon, sliced
　3　shallots, sliced
　6　salmon steaks (about
　　　2 lb total)
　6　lettuce leaves
　1　avocado, peeled and sliced
　　　Lemon Vinaigrette
　　　(see page 21)

1. Fill a 12-inch skillet with about 1½ inches of water. Bring to boil over medium heat. Reduce heat to low; add lemon slices and shallots. Place salmon steaks in simmering water and poach, uncovered, 4 minutes. Turn off heat and leave salmon in pan 15 minutes.

2. Place lettuce leaves on six individual chilled salad plates. Top with a salmon steak and garnish with slices of avocado. Drizzle with Lemon Vinaigrette.

Serves 6.

VEAL PAILLARDS WITH SAGE

A paillard is a thinly sliced cut of meat. With veal, it is usually from the leg. You may find that your market calls them scallops.

　6　veal scallops (1½ lb total)
　1　teaspoon salt
　½　teaspoon freshly ground
　　　pepper
　3　tablespoons butter
　2　tablespoons olive oil
　2　tablespoons fresh sage or
　　　2 teaspoons dried sage

　¼　pound Bel Paese or fontina
　　　cheese, sliced
　6　slices prosciutto or ham
　¼　cup Brown Veal Stock
　　　(see page 56) or Chicken
　　　Stock (see page 56), optional

1. Pound veal slightly to even any thick portions. Season veal with salt and pepper. In a 14-inch skillet over medium heat, heat butter and oil; cook veal on one side until barely browned (about 3 minutes).

2. Turn veal and sprinkle with sage. Place one sixth of the cheese on each piece of veal. Cover with prosciutto. Cook on second side until lightly browned (2 minutes); remove veal and keep warm. Add stock to pan to deglaze, stirring to loosen browned bits on bottom. Spoon this sauce over veal. Serve immediately.

Serves 6.

STIR-FRIED BROCCOLI, RED ONION, AND RED PEPPER

Blanching the broccoli will shorten the time it needs to stir-fry: Boil the broccoli florets for about 3 minutes. Remove to ice water to stop the cooking. Cooking time in step 1 is for unblanched broccoli.

　3　tablespoons olive oil
　1　tablespoon butter
　1　head broccoli, cut into florets
　½　red onion, thinly sliced
　1　red bell pepper, sliced
　2　tablespoons fresh basil or
　　　2 teaspoons dried basil
　1　tablespoon fresh oregano or
　　　1 teaspoon dried oregano

1. In a 12-inch sauté pan over medium-high heat, add oil and butter. Add broccoli; toss to coat with oil and butter. Cook until bright green and heated through (5 to 8 minutes).

2. Add onion slices; cook, tossing with broccoli, until onion is translucent (about 5 minutes). Add red pepper and continue cooking until pepper is soft but still holds its shape (2 minutes). Toss basil and oregano with broccoli, onion, and red pepper, and serve immediately.

Serves 6.

ALMOND AMOR POLENTA

This version of a simple Italian cornmeal pound cake has almonds and is an excellent foil for poached fruit or Chocolate Fudge Sauce (see page 37). A traditional pan for *amor polenta* is a deerback cake pan, which resembles a half cylinder with ridges across the curved side. A ring mold can be substituted. If desired, use strawberries instead of raspberries to prepare the fruit purée.

> *Butter and flour, to prepare pan*
> ¾ cup unsalted butter, at room temperature
> 2 cups confectioners' sugar
> 3 eggs
> 1 teaspoon vanilla extract
> ½ teaspoon almond extract
> ½ cup cornmeal
> ½ cup toasted almonds, finely ground
> ¾ cup flour
> 2 teaspoons baking powder
> 1 teaspoon salt
> *Confectioners' sugar, for dusting*
> *Raspberry Purée (see page 37)*

1. Preheat oven to 375° F. Butter and flour two deerback cake pans (about 3 cups each) or one 5-cup tube pan.

2. In a 3-quart bowl cream butter and sugar until light and fluffy. Add eggs, one at a time, beating well after each addition. Mix in vanilla and almond extracts. Stir in cornmeal and ground almonds. In a separate bowl, sift together flour, baking powder, and salt. Fold into creamed mixture.

3. Bake the two small molds or one large mold until a skewer inserted into center of cake comes out clean (30 minutes for small molds, 50 minutes for large mold). Cool in pan on wire rack 10 minutes; unmold onto rack and finish cooling.

4. Dust cooled cake with confectioners' sugar. To serve, spoon Raspberry Purée on individual dessert plates; set a slice of cake on each plate.

Serves 8 to 10.

MEDITERRANEAN LAMB MEATBALLS WITH MINT-CHILE SAUCE

Prepare packaged quick couscous or steamed rice to serve with these meatballs. Drizzle both the skewered lamb and the accompanying couscous or rice with Mint-Chile Sauce. For variety the lamb mixture can be sautéed in a skillet rather than broiled on skewers.

> 2 pounds ground lamb
> 1 onion, minced
> 2 cloves garlic, minced
> 6 tablespoons minced parsley
> ½ jalapeño chile, minced
> ¼ cup dried bread crumbs
> 2 eggs
> 1 teaspoon salt
> ½ teaspoon freshly ground black pepper
> ½ cup cornmeal
> *Oil, for coating*
> *Couscous or steamed rice, for accompaniment*

Mint-Chile Sauce

> 1 cup plain yogurt
> 1 cup fresh mint or ¼ cup dried mint
> ½ cup minced cilantro
> ½ jalapeño chile, minced
> 1 teaspoon salt
> ¼ teaspoon freshly ground pepper

1. Soak bamboo skewers in water 15 minutes. In a 3-quart bowl thoroughly mix together ground lamb, onion, garlic, parsley, minced chile, bread crumbs, eggs, salt, and pepper.

2. Preheat broiler. Wrap ⅓ cup lamb mixture around each of sixteen 8-inch bamboo skewers to form a meatball about 3 inches long by 1½ inches in diameter. Place cornmeal on a plate and roll skewered meatball in cornmeal to coat completely.

3. Brush broiler pan with a thin film of oil. Place meatball skewers on broiler pan and broil 3 inches from heat until lightly browned on one side (about 3 minutes). Turn and broil second side until lightly browned (about 2 minutes).

4. Place couscous on individual dinner plates, top with 2 Mediterranean Lamb Meatballs on skewers, and drizzle with Mint-Chile Sauce.

Serves 8.

Mint-Chile Sauce In a small bowl stir together all ingredients. Let sit 30 minutes for flavors to meld.

Makes about 2 cups.

SMOKED PORK CHOP SAUTÉ

Serve Multigrain Pilaf (see page 30) and Carrot Purée (see page 34) with Smoked Pork Chop Sauté. Because a large amount of salt is used to cure meats such as ham, smoked pork, smoked salmon, and bacon, very little additional salt is needed when cooking with these meats.

> 4 tablespoons olive oil
> 4 tablespoons butter
> 8 smoked pork chops
> *Juice and grated rind of 2 oranges*
> 4 shallots, minced
> 1½ cups Pineapple Salsa (see page 89), for accompaniment

1. In a large skillet over medium-high heat, swirl oil and 2 tablespoons butter. Sauté smoked pork chops until lightly browned (5 minutes); turn chops over and cook other side until lightly browned (about 3 minutes). Remove pork chops to serving dish and loosely cover with foil. Keep warm while finishing sauce.

2. Drain all but 2 tablespoons fat from skillet; add grated orange rind and shallots. Cook 1 minute; whisk in orange juice. Swirl in remaining butter and pour sauce over pork chops. Serve with Pineapple Salsa.

Serves 8.

ACCOMPANIMENTS

Whether as simple as a slice of fresh fruit on a sandwich plate or as elaborate-looking as Olive and Asparagus Sauté (at right), side dishes are an indispensable complement to any main course. Colorful steamed vegetables, easily prepared ahead of time and reheated, are delicious served plain or with a simple sauce. Compound butters, seasoned with herbs, spices, and citrus peels, contribute variety to grilled fish and poultry, as well as to vegetables. Many of the ingredients for the side dishes can be sliced and diced in the morning, covered with plastic wrap, and chilled until cooking time.

STEAMED VEGETABLES

The simplest of all side dishes consists of steamed vegetables dressed up with lemon juice or a pat of flavored butter. Herb butters, a convenient finishing touch, are appealing because they can be wrapped in aluminum foil and frozen. Recipes for herb butter begin at right.

> One of the following vegetables: asparagus, broccoli, Brussels sprouts, carrots, cauliflower, green beans, or sugar snap peas
> Salt, freshly ground pepper, and lemon juice, or herb butter of choice (at right)

1. Place a steamer, wire basket, or rack in a pan with 1 to 2 inches of simmering water, add vegetables, and cover tightly. *For asparagus:* Snap asparagus stalks where they naturally break; steam 4 to 6 minutes. *For broccoli:* Trim florets to about 2 inches in diameter; steam 3 to 4 minutes. *For Brussels sprouts:* Trim stem ends and cut an *X* in bottom of each; steam 5 minutes. *For carrots:* Peel and cut in ½-inch-thick slices; steam 4 to 6 minutes. *For cauliflower:* Trim florets to about 2 inches in diameter; steam 3 to 4 minutes. *For green beans:* Trim stem ends; steam 7 minutes. *For sugar snap peas:* Trim stem ends; steam 1 to 2 minutes.

2. Season with salt, pepper, and lemon juice, or drizzle with herb butter of choice.

GREEN ONION–DILL BUTTER

Delicately flecked with green, this butter is beautiful on grilled fish, particularly salmon and halibut.

> ½ cup unsalted butter, softened
> 4 tablespoons fresh dill, minced
> 2 green onions, minced
> Juice of 1 lime
> ¼ teaspoon cayenne pepper
> ½ teaspoon salt

In small bowl stir together all ingredients.

Makes ½ cup.

ROSEMARY-GARLIC BUTTER

The strong flavor of this combination complements lamb and veal. It's also delicious spread on toast.

> ½ cup unsalted butter, softened
> 2 cloves garlic, minced
> 2 tablespoons fresh rosemary, minced
> 1 tablespoon freshly squeezed lemon juice
> ½ teaspoon salt
> ¼ teaspoon freshly ground white pepper

In a small bowl stir together all ingredients.

Makes ½ cup.

TARRAGON-SHALLOT BUTTER

This butter pairs well with poultry— both chicken and turkey—as well as seafood.

> ½ cup unsalted butter, softened
> 2 shallots, minced
> 3 tablespoons fresh tarragon, minced
> 1 tablespoon white wine vinegar
> ½ teaspoon salt
> ⅛ teaspoon ground white pepper

In a small bowl stir together all ingredients.

Makes ½ cup.

OLIVE AND ASPARAGUS SAUTÉ

This simple sauté uses pungent Greek olives. The dish is equally good with carrots, eggplant, or zucchini.

> 1 pound thin asparagus
> 2 cloves garlic, minced
> 20 Kalamata olives, pitted and halved
> 2 tablespoons olive oil
> ½ teaspoon salt
> ¼ teaspoon freshly ground pepper
> ½ cup water

1. Trim tough stems from asparagus. In a 12-inch skillet over medium heat, sauté garlic and olives in oil about 5 minutes.

2. Add asparagus, salt, pepper, and the water. Cover and cook over medium heat until asparagus is tender (3 to 5 minutes).

Serves 6.

WARM CABBAGE SALAD

Pancetta is Italian bacon. Substitute commercial bacon if pancetta is unavailable.

> ¼ pound pancetta, diced
> 2 pounds red cabbage, shredded
> 4 shallots, chopped
> 1 teaspoon salt
> ½ teaspoon freshly ground pepper
> 2 tablespoons red wine vinegar
> 1 cup chopped toasted pecans
> ½ pound Roquefort cheese, crumbled

1. In a deep, 14-inch sauté pan over medium-high heat, cook pancetta until fat is rendered (about 4 minutes); remove to paper-towel–lined plate. To pan add cabbage, shallots, salt, and pepper. Cook until cabbage begins to wilt (3 to 4 minutes).

2. Stir in vinegar, pecans, Roquefort cheese, and reserved pancetta. Cook 1 to 2 minutes, tossing to combine thoroughly. Serve immediately.

Serves 8.

SPINACH IN SESAME DRESSING

Tahini is found in Middle Eastern markets or health-food stores; if unavailable substitute peanut butter. This is a quick-moving preparation. Be sure to have all ingredients measured, ready to toss with the spinach after it has sautéed.

    5 tablespoons vegetable oil
    3 bunches spinach, washed
      and dried
    ¼ cup tahini
    1½ teaspoons Asian sesame oil
    1 teaspoon salt
    ½ teaspoon freshly ground
      pepper
    ½ cup toasted sesame seed,
      for garnish

1. In a deep sauté pan or Dutch oven over medium-high heat, add vegetable oil and stir in one third of the spinach; sauté until spinach begins to wilt (about 2 minutes). Add one third more spinach and cook by tossing with oil and hot spinach already in pan (about 2 minutes more). As second batch of spinach begins to wilt, add remaining spinach and sauté until wilted (2 to 3 minutes).

2. As soon as last addition of spinach has wilted and any moisture in the pan has evaporated, quickly stir in tahini, sesame oil, salt, and pepper. Toss to combine. Remove from pan to a serving dish and sprinkle with toasted sesame seed.

Serves 6.

ARROZ VERDE

Tone down the heat in this rice dish by omitting the diced green chiles.

    1 onion, diced
    2 cloves garlic, minced
    2 tablespoons vegetable oil
    ½ cup minced parsley
    2 cups long-grain white rice
    4½ cups Chicken Stock
      (see page 56)
    2 teaspoons salt
    8 green onions, minced
    ½ cup minced cilantro
    1 small can (3½ oz) diced
      green chiles

1. In a 2-quart saucepan over medium heat, sauté onion and garlic in oil until softened and translucent (3 to 4 minutes). Stir in parsley, rice, Chicken Stock, and salt.

2. Cover and simmer over low heat until all liquid is absorbed (18 to 20 minutes). Remove from heat and stir in green onions, cilantro, and diced green chiles. Serve warm.

Serves 8.

GRANDMA'S HERBED SPAETZLE

Spaetzle are the traditional dumplings of Germany. Most Spaetzle makers are small boxes that sit over a series of small holes. When the box is moved on its track over the holes, the batter drops out in short ribbons. Spaetzle can be prepared ahead and reheated in a buttered, ovenproof dish in a 350° F oven for 10 minutes.

    ½ cup minced parsley
    1½ cups flour
    4 eggs
    ½ cup milk or water
    1 teaspoon salt
    ½ teaspoon ground nutmeg
    3 tablespoons butter, for
      garnish
    ¼ teaspoon freshly ground
      pepper

1. In a 2-quart bowl stir together parsley, flour, eggs, milk, salt, and nutmeg to form a batter. Let sit 30 minutes.

2. In a 4½-quart saucepan, bring 4 quarts water to a rapid boil. *To use a Spaetzle maker:* Pour batter into Spaetzle maker and, over boiling water, move box over holes. Batter will drop in short ribbons. *To shape by hand:* Drop batter by teaspoonful into boiling water. Or, spread batter on a cutting board and place board at edge of pot of boiling water. With a knife slice batter into ribbons and push into boiling water.

3. Spaetzle are done when they float to surface of water. Remove with a slotted spoon, drain thoroughly, and serve tossed with butter and sprinkled with freshly ground pepper.

Serves 6 to 8.

DESSERTS

Quick desserts range from sliced pears and a wedge of blue cheese to Tart Red-Cherry Clafoutis (see opposite page). Ice cream, whipped cream, confectioners' sugar, Quick Caramel Sauce (see page 37), Chocolate Fudge Sauce (see page 37), Raspberry Purée (see page 37), and purchased *amaretti* cookies can complement simple desserts such as Caramel Citrus Slices (see below), and Strawberry Sorbet (see opposite page).

CARAMEL CITRUS SLICES

Oranges, tangerines, and grapefruit, sliced and wearing a glaze of caramel, make a refreshing dessert for a substantial dinner. The hot caramel mixture must be handled with extreme care, especially when pouring over the fruit. The easiest way to clean the pan is by filling with water and bringing the water to a boil, which will dissolve the sugar.

    2 oranges, peeled
    2 tangerines, peeled
    2 pink grapefruit, peeled
    1 cup sugar
    ¼ cup water
    2 tablespoons dark rum

1. Remove membrane from fruit, and separate into sections; place sections in a shallow, 10-inch-diameter dish.

2. In a deep, heavy-bottomed saucepan over low heat, place sugar and the water. Swirl pan to dissolve sugar. Simmer over low heat, without stirring, until sugar turns a deep, golden brown (12 to 18 minutes).

3. Hold pan by handle, carefully pour in rum, and swirl gently until rum and caramelized sugar are mixed. Mixture will start to bubble and rise up because of the extreme difference in temperatures. As soon as bubbling stops, drizzle caramel syrup over citrus sections. Serve fruit at room temperature.

Serves 6 to 8.

STRAWBERRY SORBET

A food processor is mandatory for this incredibly quick dessert for six. Extend the sorbet to serve eight by topping with fresh fruit. The leftover sugar syrup will keep indefinitely in the refrigerator.

    1 pound whole frozen
        strawberries
    4 cups mixed, fresh fruit
        (blueberries, strawberries,
        raspberries, peaches), for
        accompaniment (optional)

Sugar Syrup

    1 cup sugar
    ¼ cup water

Purée frozen berries in food processor 1 minute. Add ¼ cup Sugar Syrup and process until smooth (about 2 minutes). Serve immediately, topped with mixed fresh fruit, if desired.

Makes about 2 cups, 6 to 8 servings.

Sugar Syrup   In a clean 1-quart saucepan over medium-low heat, place sugar and the water. Stir once to mix. Cover for 8 minutes. Remove from heat. Pour into a clean storage jar and cool completely.

Makes 1 cup.

TART RED-CHERRY CLAFOUTIS

Claufoutis is a French pudding made with fresh, canned, or frozen fruit. Blueberries, blackberries, peaches, and raspberries can be used instead of cherries. Vanilla ice cream is a dramatic accent for this simple dessert.

    3 tablespoons butter
    1 pound tart red cherries, pitted
        if fresh, drained if canned
    1 cup sugar
    ½ cup flour
    6 eggs, separated
    1⅓ cups milk
    ⅛ teaspoon salt
    1 teaspoon vanilla extract
    ⅛ teaspoon cream of tartar
        Confectioners' sugar, for
        garnish
        Vanilla ice cream, for
        accompaniment (optional)

1. Using 1 tablespoon of the butter, grease a shallow, 10-inch-diameter baking or gratin dish. Preheat oven to 350° F.

2. Toss cherries with ¼ cup sugar and place in buttered baking dish. Dot cherries with remaining butter.

3. In a 3-quart bowl, whisk remaining sugar, flour, egg yolks, milk, salt, and vanilla.

4. Beat egg whites with cream of tartar to form soft peaks. Fold into flour mixture and pour over cherries in prepared dish. Bake until light golden brown (about 35 minutes). Dust with confectioners' sugar, and serve warm with vanilla ice cream (if desired).

Serves 6.

Make-Ahead Tip   The batter can be made through step 3 early in the day and left out at cool room temperature until needed. Forty minutes before serving, proceed with step 4.

This French fruit-strewn pudding tastes best eaten while it is still warm. Bake the clafoutis in a pretty dish and serve at the table with ice cream.

When you have the luxury of time, an occasion can assume a more formal tone, both in table decor and in menu.

Do-Ahead Entertaining

The ideal entertaining situation is one that you can prepare for at a leisurely pace. This chapter offers you party recipes that can be assembled partly or completely in advance—recipes that will be treasured by even the most experienced host. These dishes are often stews and other slow-cooking foods that improve with sitting. Individually packaged servings of either main course or accompaniment will streamline planning, so you'll learn how to wrap food in filo pastry (see page 88) and cooking parchment (see page 89). Cookies to make ahead and freeze are another feature (see page 96). The menu (see page 91) is wonderfully creative; it covers a weekend of entertaining. Learn to have houseguests and survive.

COOKING IN STAGES

Cooking for friends is pure pleasure if you can join them in the dining room without nervously checking your watch and intermittently rushing to the kitchen. The recipes in this chapter will give you peace of mind because much of the preparation can be accomplished ahead of time, yet the dishes still taste fresh and flavorful when served. If your schedule won't permit last-minute cooking or you are an insecure chef, these recipes are perfect—not only can they be done hours or days before the first guest arrives, but they will benefit from the wait. They are ideal for those occasions where you have the luxury of at least several days to plan and prepare a meal.

Hearty stews, main-dish soups, and substantial main-course salads epitomize the do-ahead dinner. Made with economical, less tender cuts of meat, long-simmered dishes welcome guests with their aroma and rich visual appeal. Most of these dishes should be prepared days before serving to allow flavors to meld and intensify. Some dishes, such as the Moroccan Chicken Pie (see page 85), will store beautifully in the freezer and can be baked while still frozen. Carefully wrapped stews and chilis can be frozen, then defrosted and reheated as they are needed. These are excellent dishes to double and triple for stand-up suppers. Such party foods as Winter Lamb Ragout (see page 87), Breakfast Bread Pudding (see page 95), or Chafing Dish Chili (see page 87) can be served from an ovenproof casserole or chafing dish.

Preparing food in advance takes careful thought, the right recipes and ingredients, and a master plan that will allow the most elaborate dinner to succeed without a hitch. The greatest asset to any dinner party is the calm host whose well-planned menu is under control.

DIVIDE AND CONQUER

With all entertaining, planning is the key. Divide the menu into smaller, more manageable components: tomato sauce, chicken stock, or dessert can be made a week ahead and stored in the freezer. Some fresh foods, prepared several days in advance, won't wilt in the refrigerator. Raw vegetables and greens for dipping or salads can be cut, layered with paper towels in plastic bags, and stored in the refrigerator for 24 hours. Include in the meal some foods that are served directly from the refrigerator or freezer or that will taste wonderful at room temperature. Also, many foods can be assembled the day before a meal, and roasted, grilled, or baked at the last minute.

Use available increments of time, over several days, to prepare and chill components of a dinner. Wherever possible, store the food in the dish in which it will be served. At the last minute, top with attractive fresh garnishes such as tomato slices, parsley sprigs, or confectioners' sugar to freshen the appearance.

Your entertaining and creative genius can surface when you don't have to hurry. You will also have time to correct an error or improve a dish. You will feel secure knowing that any problems that occur can be solved long before guests arrive.

MAKE THE MENU YOURS

Plan the menu carefully. Write out the menu to help visualize and vary the colors of the food selections and the cooking techniques. Think about which foods will cook in the oven, which will be prepared on the stovetop, and how many items need to be chilled. Decide which serving dishes to use. Preparing ahead also means storing food safely at the proper temperature.

Don't feel pressured to create an overly ambitious menu. The main purpose of the invitation is to get together with friends, not impress them. Work with your favorite types of food and serving styles. Plan the menu around your capabilities, budget, and friends' preferences. Create a balance of main dishes and side dishes. Serve stews with French bread, rice pilaf casseroles, or buttered noodles—accompaniments that will absorb rich, tasty sauces. Rather than a traditional green salad, make the salad course a simple romaine leaf topped with a slice of triple cream cheese, or serve a basket of crudités and a dipping sauce.

MATCH SERVICE TO FOOD

Chafing dishes, either with a candle or an alcohol burner, make appropriate serving containers for sauced foods. Antique or heirloom terrines and platters add character to the table; oven-to-table ware is especially useful for these occasions. Cover tables with brightly colored cloths, terra-cotta plates, and papier-mâché animals from Mexico—guests will enjoy a playful approach to a dinner party. Serve chili from a chafing dish surrounded by colorful, edible condiments. Let a fresh fruit centerpiece stand in for dessert, accompanied by lots of homemade cookies. If serving buffet-style, wrap flatware in oversized cloth napkins so that it can be picked up easily.

APPETIZERS AND FIRST COURSES

The cook can tailor do-ahead cooking to a personal agenda, whether that means preparing the food several days before, one day before, or early on the day of the party. Delicious appetizers and first courses are a cinch to prepare in advance. The following salads and soups taste even better after they have marinated and their flavors have melded. They can be doubled or tripled easily to serve large buffet dinners or accommodate extra guests. They also can easily transform simple dinners into a multicourse menu.

MINTY GAZPACHO

This version of a refreshing summer favorite is loaded with fresh mint and tangy tomatoes. To turn this soup into a main course, serve it with grilled tiger prawns—colorful freshwater shellfish with distinctive dark stripes across their tails. (But if these prawns are unavailable, any prawns can be substituted.) Lay the grilled prawns on the chilled soup as a garnish.

  3 large, ripe tomatoes, diced (3½ cups)
  1 English cucumber, diced
  1 large green bell pepper, diced
  3 stalks celery, diced
  1 large red onion, diced
  1 bunch green onions, diced
  3 cloves garlic, minced
1¼ cups minced parsley
  3 cups minced fresh mint
  ½ cup white wine vinegar
  ½ cup extravirgin olive oil
  5 cups tomato juice
  1 teaspoon salt
  ½ teaspoon freshly ground pepper

1. In a 4-quart serving bowl, stir together all ingredients.

2. Let mixture marinate in refrigerator for 1 to 24 hours. Serve chilled, but not ice-cold.

Makes 12 cups, 8 servings.

With vine-ripened tomatoes, hearty bell peppers, and crisp, cool cucumbers, Minty Gazpacho features the best of summer produce. Make the soup the day before so that the flavors will meld, then serve with grilled prawns and a crunchy garlic bread to fashion a marvelous meal.

If you love tuna salads, try this Italian version, made hearty with the addition of beans, moistened with a vinaigrette, and flecked with fresh herbs and minced onion.

Remove bacon with a slotted spoon to a paper-towel–lined plate. Reserve bacon fat in pan.

2. Sauté shallots in bacon fat 2 to 3 minutes. Add spinach, potatoes, stock, salt, and pepper. Simmer over low heat until potatoes are tender when pierced with a knife (about 25 minutes).

3. Add baby oysters to soup; simmer until heated through (about 3 minutes). Stir in cream (if used). Serve immediately.

Makes 7 cups, 6 servings.

Make-Ahead Tip To prepare ahead, make recipe through step 2. Just before serving, continue with step 3 and refrigerate up to 2 days.

SPINACH AND OYSTER SOUP

This delicious soup is reason enough to keep spinach in the freezer and oysters on the pantry shelf. One bunch of fresh spinach can substitute for the frozen, if desired. For a fresh-from-the-beach flavor, one pound of freshly shucked oysters can replace the canned shellfish. If omitting bacon, sauté shallots in 2 tablespoons vegetable oil.

- 4 *strips bacon*
- 6 *shallots, minced*
- 2 *packages (10 oz each) frozen spinach, thawed*
- 2 *small potatoes, peeled and diced*
- 4 *cups Fish Stock (see page 57) or Chicken Stock (see page 56) Salt and freshly ground pepper, to taste*
- 2 *cans (8 oz each) baby oysters*
- ¼ *cup whipping cream (optional)*

1. Cut bacon into ½-inch strips. In a 3-quart saucepan over medium heat, fry bacon until fat is rendered and bacon is crisp (4 to 5 minutes).

TUSCAN WHITE BEAN AND TUNA SALAD

The cook will laud this hearty salad as the ideal menu item—a combination of pantry food and do-ahead dish. Guests will enjoy its Italian flavor. Serve as a first-course salad to complement grilled chicken or a lamb dish, or offer hearty portions with crusty bread as a main course.

- 2 *cans (15 oz each) cooked white cannellini beans, drained*
- 1 *large red onion, minced*
- 1 *clove garlic, minced*
- 2 *cans (6 oz each) imported tuna, packed in olive oil*
- 1 *tablespoon olive oil*
- 3 *tablespoons red wine vinegar*
- 4 *tablespoons minced parsley*
- 4 *tablespoons dried sage*
- 1 *teaspoon salt*
- ½ *teaspoon freshly ground pepper*
- 4 *tablespoons minced chives, for garnish*

In a 2-quart bowl gently stir together beans, onion, garlic, tuna, olive oil, vinegar, parsley, sage, salt, and pepper. Marinate 4 to 48 hours to let flavors meld. Serve at room temperature garnished with chives.

Serves 6 to 8.

RED PEPPER TERRINE

Both the terrine and the Rémoulade Sauce will hold for up to one week in the refrigerator, ready for a planned occasion or for an impromptu meal. The terrine can become a substantial lunch when garnished with grilled oysters, scallops, or crayfish. Note that the terrine must be refrigerated 24 hours to set.

2 large eggplants (about
      1 lb each)
    Salt, for sprinkling
4 red bell peppers
5 tablespoons olive oil
2 teaspoons salt
1 cup fresh basil leaves
    Parsley sprigs, for garnish
18 to 24 black olives, for garnish
2 cups Rémoulade Sauce
    (see page 20)

1. Wash and dry eggplant; do not peel. Cut a ½-inch-thick lengthwise slice from 2 sides of each eggplant; these will be the first layer of terrine. Cut remainder of both eggplants into ¼-inch-thick slices. Place slices (including 2 thicker slices) on a paper-towel–lined tray or baking sheet, sprinkle with salt, and let rest for 30 minutes. Toward end of 30-minute period, preheat oven to 450° F.

2. While eggplant slices are resting, roast red peppers over an open flame or under a broiler to remove skin more easily. Turn peppers several times to char evenly. Place roasted peppers in a paper bag and close tightly; let rest 20 minutes. Remove from bag and, under running water, slip off skin. Pat peppers dry. Halve lengthwise and remove seeds.

3. Rinse salt from eggplant slices and pat dry. Lightly brush a baking sheet with 1 tablespoon olive oil. Brush both sides of eggplant slices with 3 tablespoons olive oil, and place on prepared baking sheet. Bake 10 minutes, turn slices over, and bake 10 minutes more. Remove and cool.

4. Lightly brush a 4½- by 8½-inch loaf pan with remaining olive oil. Place ½-inch eggplant slices, skin side down, on bottom of loaf pan. Cover with 2 pieces of red bell pepper; sprinkle with ½ teaspoon salt, then top with 6 to 8 basil leaves. Alternately layer remaining eggplant, bell pepper, salt, and basil leaves three more times. Place a weight on the terrine and refrigerate 24 hours to set.

5. To unmold, invert terrine on a serving platter. Lift off baking dish. To serve, cut terrine into ¾-inch-thick slices, serving 1 slice as a first course or 2 for a light luncheon. Garnish with Rémoulade Sauce, sprigs of parsley, and black olives.

Serves 12 as a side dish or first course, 6 as a main course.

Layers of roasted red bell peppers and sliced eggplant form a colorful and unusual vegetable loaf. A dollop of Rémoulade Sauce (see page 20) and a garnish of black olives add the finishing touches.

*Wrapped in filo pastry, savory
and sophisticated Moroccan
Chicken Pie is easy to prepare
and freezes beautifully.*

MAIN COURSES

A main course often takes the most preparation time, but is worth it because it is the heart of a menu. The following dishes permit you to prepare, in advance and at leisure, special foods for special parties. Some recipes lend themselves to individual servings—Flaky Beef Fillet en Croûte (see page 88) is best put on plates in the kitchen—and others, such as Chafing Dish Chili (see page 87) or Winter Lamb Ragout (see page 87), are best served as buffet fare. However, don't hesitate to place the beef on a buffet table or serve the ragout on a dinner plate if either presentation will work better for you.

MOROCCAN CHICKEN PIE

This unusual chicken pie will tantalize guests with its exotic flavor. Don't omit the unusual confectioners' sugar and cinnamon topping; it adds the critical sparkle. Frozen filo dough will thaw in one hour at room temperature or six hours to overnight in the refrigerator.

  3 pounds chicken breasts
  1 onion, quartered
  2 tablespoons butter
  ¼ pound whole almonds,
      chopped roughly
  1 medium onion, diced
  2 cloves garlic, minced
  1 cup minced cilantro
  ½ cup minced parsley
  2 tablespoons ground
      cinnamon
  2 teaspoons turmeric
  1 teaspoon salt
  1 tablespoon finely grated
      fresh ginger
  ¾ teaspoon freshly ground
      pepper
  ½ teaspoon hot-pepper flakes
  1 cup dried currants
  ½ cup Chicken Stock
      (see page 56)
  4 eggs
  8 tablespoons butter, melted
  9 sheets filo dough, thawed
      according to package
      directions
  2 tablespoons confectioners'
      sugar, for topping

1. In a 3-quart saucepan place chicken breasts and quartered onion and cover with water; bring to a boil, reduce heat, and simmer until breast meat is firm to the touch and juices run clear when meat is pierced (25 to 30 minutes; about 165° F on an instant-read thermometer); cool. Discard quartered onion. Shred chicken into long thin strips.

2. In a 14-inch skillet over medium heat, add the 2 tablespoons butter. Stir in almonds, diced onion, and garlic, and cook until onion is translucent (4 to 5 minutes). Add cilantro, parsley, 1 tablespoon cinnamon, turmeric, salt, ginger, pepper, hot-pepper flakes, currants, stock, and shredded chicken. Stir to combine thoroughly. Beat eggs together in a small bowl and stir into chicken mixture. Cook until mixture thickens slightly (about 3 minutes). Remove from heat and reserve.

3. Preheat oven to 350° F. Brush 1 tablespoon melted butter on bottom of a 9-inch springform pan. Place 1 sheet filo dough in pan; brush with melted butter. Place a second sheet in pan at right angles to first sheet and brush with butter. Place a third sheet in pan, arranged so that one of the short sides is in center of pan bottom and other side drapes over pan edge; brush with butter. Arrange 5 more sheets of dough in the same manner as the third sheet, overlapping them slightly, and brushing each with butter. Place filling in pan. Gather draped ends of filo sheets and gently twist to close; brush top of pie with butter. Brush remaining sheet of dough with butter; fold in half lengthwise, butter, and fold in half lengthwise again. Roll loosely into a cylinder; pinch bottom and fan top slightly to form a rose. Set filo flower on twisted pastry sheets. Reserve in refrigerator until 55 minutes before serving time.

4. Bake until lightly browned on top (about 55 minutes). Remove from oven. Dust with confectioners' sugar and sprinkle with remaining cinnamon.

Serves 8.

SKEWERED PRAWNS AND GRAPE LEAVES

Tender young grape leaves are an essential part of this recipe. However, if they are unavailable, you could substitute large spinach leaves. The grape leaves can be stuffed two to three days ahead. The prawns should be shelled and skewered early on the day of the dinner party. Accompany with Rabat Rice Pilaf (see page 30). Grape leaves are available packed in jars at Greek delicatessens and in the foreign food section of most supermarkets. Try to cull the smaller grape leaves from the jar; they are younger and therefore more tender.

  32 medium prawns
  ¼ cup olive oil
  1 teaspoon dried basil
  1 teaspoon dried oregano
  1 log (11 oz) goat cheese,
      cut in 16 slices
  16 young, tender grape leaves
      Spicy Tomato Sauce
      (see page 47)
      Lemon wedges, for garnish

1. Shell prawns. Whisk together olive oil, basil, and oregano in a small bowl; reserve.

2. Place 1 slice goat cheese in the center of each grape leaf. Fold grape leaf to enclose cheese. Skewer 1 prawn with a bamboo pick, securing it in 2 places, then skewer stuffed grape leaf, and a second prawn. Repeat with remaining prawns and grape leaves to make 16 skewers. Brush with olive oil marinade. Chill in refrigerator until serving time.

3. Just before serving, preheat broiler. In a 2-quart saucepan over medium heat, warm Spicy Tomato Sauce. Place skewered prawns and grape leaves on broiling pan and broil about 4 inches from heat source until prawns turn bright pink on one side (about 3 minutes); turn skewers and cook second side 3 minutes more.

4. For each serving, place a pool of warm tomato sauce (about ½ cup) on a serving plate and lay 2 skewers on sauce; squeeze lemon juice over prawns and grape leaves.

Serves 8.

As the weather cools, welcome the change of season with this substantial Winter Lamb Ragout, a basket of warm whole-grain rolls, and a fire in the hearth.

CHICKEN BREAST ITALIENNE

This do-ahead dish—pretty pinwheels of chicken, prosciutto, and cheese—is perfect buffet food. Serve warm with risotto, or cold with pasta salad.

   8 *chicken breast halves, boned and skinned*
   1 *teaspoon salt*
  ½ *teaspoon freshly ground pepper*
  ½ *cup Pesto Sauce (see page 47)*
   8 *slices prosciutto*
  ½ *pound provolone cheese, cut into 8 pieces*
   2 *eggs, beaten*
1¼ *cups toasted bread crumbs*
  ½ *cup butter, melted*

1. Place chicken breasts flat on work surface. Pound lightly to flatten to a uniform ¼ inch. Season with salt and pepper.

2. Spread each chicken breast with 1 tablespoon Pesto Sauce. Place a strip of prosciutto on each pesto-covered breast. Place 1 piece provolone at narrow end of chicken breast.

3. Preheat oven to 350° F. Roll up each breast to form a cylinder, enclosing the cheese. Roll cylinder in egg, then bread crumbs. Chill 30 to 60 minutes.

4. One hour before serving time, place cold chicken breasts on an ungreased baking sheet. Pour melted butter over rolls and bake for 1 hour. Remove from baking sheet and slice each roll diagonally into 3 pieces to show spiral of prosciutto, cheese, and chicken.

Serves 8.

CHAFING DISH CHILI

A bountiful chafing dish of spicy chili, accompanied by a variety of colorful condiments, creates a festive buffet supper. If you prefer, substitute beef, veal, duck, or pork for the less traditional lamb suggested in this recipe. This is sized for a large party; for fewer guests, cut the recipe in half or freeze some for future entertaining. For the best flavor, let the chili sit in the refrigerator at least 8 hours and up to 48 hours before serving.

- 6 tablespoons vegetable oil
- 6 pounds boneless lamb shoulder, cut in 1½-inch cubes
- 8 onions, sliced
- 10 cloves garlic, sliced
- 2 green bell peppers, sliced
- 2 cans (28 oz each) plum tomatoes, drained and diced
- 4 tablespoons toasted cumin seed
- 4 tablespoons dried oregano
- 2 tablespoons salt
- 2 tablespoons hot-pepper flakes
- 2 teaspoons cayenne pepper
- 2 teaspoons ground cinnamon
- 12 cups water
- 12 green onions, diced
- 1 can (6 oz) pickled jalapeño chiles, sliced
- 2 cups sour cream
- 3 cups (12 oz) grated Cheddar cheese
  Borracho Beans (see page 89)
  Corn tortilla chips
  South-of-the-Border Salsa (see page 47)

1. In an 8-quart Dutch oven over medium heat, place 3 tablespoons oil. Add one fourth of the lamb cubes, and stir while browning on all sides (4 to 5 minutes). Remove lamb with a slotted spoon to a serving dish and reserve. Add 2 more tablespoons oil and another fourth of the lamb cubes, browning all sides and stirring to prevent sticking. Repeat, without adding more oil, until all the lamb is browned.

2. Return reserved lamb cubes to pan and add remaining oil. Stir in onions and garlic and cook until translucent (4 to 5 minutes). Stir in bell peppers, tomatoes, cumin seed, oregano, salt, hot-pepper flakes, cayenne, cinnamon, and the water.

3. Bring to a boil, reduce heat to simmer, and cook slowly until lamb is tender (about 2 hours); cool. Place in refrigerator for 8 to 48 hours before serving for maximum flavor.

4. At serving time, reheat chili in an 8-quart Dutch oven over low heat; transfer to a chafing dish and hold over low heat to serve buffet style. Surround with terra-cotta bowls filled with green onions, pickled jalapeños, sour cream, Cheddar cheese, Borracho Beans, corn tortilla chips, and South-of-the-Border Salsa.

Serves 16 to 20.

WINTER LAMB RAGOUT

In the spring, add small green beans, asparagus, new peas, tiny potatoes, or green onions for a bright variation.

- 6 tablespoons olive oil
- 3 pounds lamb stew meat, cut in 2-inch cubes
- 4 medium yellow onions, diced
- 2 cloves garlic, sliced
- 2 tablespoons tomato paste
- 4 tablespoons minced parsley
- 2 teaspoons salt
- 1 teaspoon freshly ground pepper
- 1½ teaspoons dried thyme
- 2 bay leaves
- 1 pound small turnips, peeled and quartered
- 1 pound carrots, peeled
- 12 ounces pearl onions, peeled

1. In an 8-quart Dutch oven over medium heat, add 2 tablespoons olive oil and toss half the lamb cubes in oil; brown lamb on all sides (5 to 7 minutes). Remove to a work bowl or platter and reserve.

2. Add 2 more tablespoons oil and remaining lamb cubes, browning while stirring constantly (5 to 7 minutes). Push meat to one side and add remaining oil, yellow onions, and garlic. Return reserved lamb cubes to pan and cook until onions are translucent (4 to 5 minutes).

3. Add tomato paste, parsley, salt, pepper, thyme, bay leaves, turnips, and water to cover. Reduce heat to simmer, cover, and cook 1 hour. Cut carrots into 2-inch lengths.

4. After 1 hour add carrots and pearl onions to ragout. Cook 1 hour and 10 minutes. Serve hot.

Serves 8.

TERIYAKI PORK TENDERLOIN

Marinate Teriyaki Pork Tenderloin in its roasting pan for up to 48 hours. Then simply roast in the oven, slice, and serve. This same marinade also enhances prawns, chicken, scallops, or beef. Serve with sautéed Swiss chard and Potatoes, Shallots, and Garlic en Papillote (see page 89).

- 1 tablespoon grated fresh ginger
- 2 cloves garlic, minced
- 2 green onions, chopped
- ¼ cup soy sauce
- 2 tablespoons honey
- 1 tablespoon rice-wine vinegar or apple cider vinegar
- ½ tablespoon Asian sesame oil
- 1 tablespoon vegetable oil
- 1 teaspoon cornstarch
- 1 tablespoon water
- 2 pork tenderloins (1 lb each)
- 2 tablespoons toasted sesame seed

1. Stir together ginger, garlic, green onions, soy sauce, honey, rice-wine vinegar, oils, cornstarch, and the water. Whisk until smooth.

2. Trim any fat from pork tenderloins and place in a shallow roasting pan. Pour marinade over pork and marinate 1 hour to 2 days. From time to time turn pork tenderloins to be sure they marinate evenly.

3. About 1 hour before serving, preheat oven to 350° F. Drain off marinade and sprinkle pork with toasted sesame seed. Cook until medium (40 to 45 minutes; about 140° F on an instant-read thermometer).

4. To serve, slice pork thinly across grain of meat.

Serves 8.

FILO PACKAGES

Filo dough, a gift from several Mediterranean cuisines, has found its way into all styles of food preparation. Its flaky lightness is used to create individual, handheld appetizers for the cocktail hour or to wrap an unconventional chicken pie (see Moroccan Chicken Pie, page 85). Flaky Beef Fillet en Croûte (at right) is a simplified variation of an old favorite, beef Wellington. Fruit strudels are often made with filo rather than time-consuming handmade strudel dough (see Apple and Walnut Strudel, page 119). Filo transforms a simple dish into a special one, and most filo recipes can be prepared well in advance of a party. Purchase filo dough in the freezer section of the supermarket or in a market specializing in Mediterranean cuisines.

☐ Defrost frozen filo sheets, still wrapped tightly, but taken out of the box, for about one hour at room temperature, about six hours in the refrigerator, or according to package directions. Seal extra dough carefully before re-freezing.

☐ Before assembling a filo-based dish, have the filling ready and chilled, butter for brushing already melted, and dough thawed.

☐ To avoid soggy filo packages, cool all food before wrapping.

☐ Filo sheets dry out easily and will crumble. As you work, keep unused sheets of dough stacked under a damp towel on the counter until you need them.

☐ Although sheets are fragile, once they are brushed with melted butter, layered, and baked, any tears will be disguised.

FLAKY BEEF FILLET EN CROÛTE

Filo replaces puff pastry in this quick variation on an old favorite. Note that frozen filo dough will thaw in one hour at room temperature or six hours to overnight in the refrigerator.

  6 pieces beef fillet (about
    3 lb total, each 2 in. thick)
  3 cloves garlic, minced
  4 shallots, minced
  ¾ cup butter, melted
  ½ pound mushrooms,
    finely diced
  ½ teaspoon salt
  ¼ teaspoon freshly ground
    pepper
  ¼ teaspoon nutmeg
  18 sheets (about ¾ lb) filo
    dough, thawed according
    to package directions

1. Trim excess fat from beef fillet. In a 12-inch sauté pan over medium heat, place ¼ cup butter. Sauté beef fillets until browned (2 to 3 minutes); turn and cook second side until browned (2 to 3 minutes). Remove and reserve.

2. In an 8-inch skillet over medium heat, cook garlic and shallots in butter until softened (3 to 4 minutes). Add mushrooms; cook until lightly browned and no moisture remains in pan (12 to 15 minutes). Season with salt, pepper, and nutmeg; reserve.

3. Place 1 sheet filo dough on work surface. Brush with melted butter. Cover with another sheet of filo. Brush with melted butter, place another sheet of filo on top, and brush with more butter. Place 1 fillet on filo and top with 2 tablespoons mushroom mixture. Working quickly so that dough does not dry out, gather dough into a pouch enclosing beef fillet; seal with a 2-inch-high ruffle on top. Twist slightly to fasten. Brush pouch and ruffle with melted butter. Place on a baking sheet. Repeat with remaining beef and mushroom mixture.

4. Thirty minutes before serving, preheat oven to 425° F. Bake filo pouches 12 minutes for rare or 15 minutes for medium-rare. Serve immediately.

Serves 6.

ACCOMPANIMENTS

Long-simmered beans, combination pastas, and vegetables *en papillote* are highlighted in this chapter. Cooking the beans and sturdy vegetables in olive oil rather than butter gives you the option of turning leftovers into salads. These are great dishes to double and freeze; store in attractive oven-to-table ware.

BACON, BROCCOLI, AND GREEN BEAN PASTA

Vegetable pastas are simple to prepare using this technique. Bring pasta water to a boil, drop prepared vegetables into the boiling water to cook partially, remove with a slotted spoon, and reserve. Turn off heat under hot water and reserve if not continuing immediately. About 20 minutes before serving, bring water back to a boil and add pasta. While pasta is cooking, toss vegetables in a separate skillet with pasta sauce or melted butter and cheese. The combination of sauce and warm pasta will reheat vegetables.

  ½ pound small Blue Lake green
    beans, trimmed
  1 head broccoli, cut in florets
  1 pound dried pasta
    (such as fusilli)
  ¼ pound bacon, diced
  2 shallots, minced
  2 tomatoes, diced
  1 cup whipping cream
    Salt and freshly ground
    pepper, to taste
  ½ cup (2½ oz) grated
    Asiago cheese

1. In a 4½-quart saucepan over high heat, bring 4 quarts water to a boil. Add beans and cook until one of the smaller beans is tender when pierced with a knife (4 to 7 minutes, depending on size of beans). If not using beans immediately, chill in ice water to stop cooking and set bright color. Drain and pat dry. Continue by adding broccoli to boiling water and cooking until bright green and tender when pierced with a knife (2 to 3 minutes, depending on size). Cool as directed for green beans.

2. At serving time, bring water back to a boil and add dried pasta. Boil until al dente (about 10 minutes, depending on shape).

3. In a 12-inch sauté pan or skillet over medium-high heat, fry bacon until crisp (3 to 4 minutes); remove to a paper-towel–lined plate and reserve.

4. Reduce heat to medium and stir shallots and tomatoes into bacon fat. Cook for about 1 minute. Stir in cream, beans, and broccoli, mixing thoroughly. Toss with hot, cooked pasta, coating with sauce. Serve immediately tossed with salt, freshly ground pepper, and Asiago cheese.

Serves 8.

BORRACHO BEANS

Drunken (*borracho*) beans accompany myriad entrées from south of the border. They can be garnished with South-of-the-Border Salsa (see page 47), sour cream, or Avocado Salsa (see page 47), and paired with Quesadillas (see page 43) for a simple lunch. To prepare beans, soak 2½ cups dried beans 8 to 10 hours, drain liquid, add fresh water to cover, and simmer 2 hours until tender. Borracho Beans can be made as much as one week ahead and kept in the refrigerator until needed.

½ pound bacon, diced
2 onions, diced
2 cloves garlic, diced
6 cups cooked black beans
2 teaspoons salt
1 teaspoon pepper
1 teaspoon toasted cumin seed
1 can (12 oz) beer

1. In a 6-quart bean pot or deep stockpot over medium heat, cook bacon until some of the fat is rendered (4 minutes). Stir in onions and garlic and sauté until onion is translucent (4 to 5 minutes).

2. Add beans, salt, pepper, cumin seed, and beer. Simmer 25 minutes. Serve warm or refrigerate up to 1 week; reheat to serve.

Serves 8 to 10.

PINEAPPLE SALSA

Fresh fruit salsas satisfy the taste for salad and fruit in one dish. Peaches, nectarines, or plums can also be used. Serve as a condiment with pork, chicken, or duck.

½ pineapple, diced in ¼-inch pieces
2 medium tomatoes, diced
1 small cucumber, seeded and diced
2 shallots, minced
½ jalapeño chile, minced
¼ cup minced cilantro
2 tablespoons freshly squeezed lime juice
1 tablespoon white wine vinegar
1 tablespoon vegetable oil
½ teaspoon salt

In a 2-quart bowl stir together all ingredients. Cover and refrigerate at least 1 hour.

Makes 4 cups.

POTATOES, SHALLOTS, AND GARLIC EN PAPILLOTE

These seasoned potato packages can be readied early in the day and baked at dinnertime.

16 small (about 2 lb total) red potatoes
16 shallots, peeled
16 cloves garlic, peeled
12 tablespoons Rosemary-Garlic Butter (see page 75)
8 tablespoons water
2 teaspoons salt
1 teaspoon freshly ground pepper

1. Preheat oven to 350° F. Slice potatoes ¼ inch thick. On each of eight 8-inch squares of aluminum foil, place 2 sliced potatoes, 2 shallots, and 2 cloves garlic. Dot each with 1½ tablespoons Rosemary-Garlic Butter, and add 1 tablespoon of the water, ¼ teaspoon salt, and ⅛ teaspoon pepper. Seal packets tightly.

2. Place packets on a baking sheet; bake 40 minutes. Remove from oven, open packets, and slide potatoes, shallots, and garlic onto plates.

Serves 8.

Special Feature

PARCHMENT PACKAGES

For centuries the French have steamed food *en papillote*—in heart-shaped paper packages. With this moist cooking method—really a type of steaming—the food creates its own sauce from natural juices as it cooks. This technique is often used for foods that dry out when cooked conventionally—lean fish, vegetables, scallops, or chicken breast. Herb butters, fresh herbs, and sautéed vegetables all contribute flavor to the steamed dish. Parchment paper is available at better cookware stores and well-stocked supermarkets. Although parchment paper is more elegant, aluminum foil will serve the same purpose and could be used if the packages are opened in the kitchen rather than by each guest at the table.

☐ Be sure that parchment paper or aluminum foil is cut large enough to securely hold the food to be steamed; usually a recipe will specify the size. To form the classic heart shape, first fold paper in half. Beginning and ending at fold, cut paper in teardrop shape.

☐ Food packages may be assembled early in the day, refrigerated, and brought to room temperature before baking.

☐ To maintain a tight seal for steaming, securely crimp packages before placing in oven. Seal edges by folding ¼ inch of edge all the way around, then fold another ¼ inch over the first fold; repeat a third time.

☐ If possible, let guests open packages at the table. They will be delighted with the wonderful aroma that is released as the paper is torn.

With careful planning, and this delicious series of meals, the well-organized cook can easily host a houseful of guests for the weekend.

A WEEKEND OF ENTERTAINING

FRIDAY DINNER

Tandoori Chicken (see page 92)

Rabat Rice Pilaf (see page 30)

Greek Orzo Salad (see page 92)

Crusty French Bread

Tiramisu (see page 92)

Beer or Gewürztraminer

SATURDAY BREAKFAST

Joe's Special Filo Rolls (see page 93)

Sweet Potato and Cinnamon Muffins (see page 94)

Poached Fruit With Walnuts (see page 94)

Coffee or Tea

SATURDAY LUNCH

Mango Chutney Chicken Salad (see page 94)

Pumate and Basil Biscuits (see Mom's Buttermilk Biscuits, page 94)

Cookies of Choice and Fresh Fruit

Chenin Blanc

SATURDAY DINNER

Fajitas (see page 95)

Arroz Verde (see page 76)

Black Bean Salsa Salad (see page 95)

Peaches en Papillote (see page 95)

Beer or Zinfandel

SUNDAY BRUNCH

Breakfast Bread Pudding (see page 95)

Fresh Fruit

Tossed Green Salad

Orange Juice Spritzers

The menus serve 8.

Get Ready, Get Set, Relax

Having weekend guests offers the opportunity for back-to-back entertaining. Houseguests are a treat, as long as everything is ready before they arrive so that you can enjoy their visit too.

Preparation Plan

Write up an extensive shopping list one week before and purchase all staples. Make a separate list for the perishables to be bought the day that guests arrive. Bake the sponge roll for the Tiramisu (see page 92) early in the week; roll and wrap airtight before freezing. The morning of the day that guests arrive, defrost sponge roll at room temperature and fill. Chill until dinner.

Tandoori Chicken (see page 92) can marinate for two days in the refrigerator. Extra Tandoori Chicken can be incorporated into Saturday's Mango Chutney Chicken Salad (see page 94). On Friday cook orzo, make vinaigrette, and dice cucumbers and tomatoes for Greek Orzo Salad (see page 92); reserve and toss together one hour before serving.

Joe's Special Filo Rolls (see page 93) can be frozen up to one month before visitors arrive. Transfer directly from freezer to oven (allow about 10 minutes of extra baking time). Muffin batter can be prepared several days in advance and chilled. Bake on Saturday morning.

The dressing for the Mango Chutney Chicken Salad (see page 94) will store in the refrigerator for one week. Toss with leftover Tandoori Chicken or freshly poached chicken early on Saturday while breakfast is cooking and let marinate while you are out sightseeing.

For the final breakfast on Sunday morning, pull the Breakfast Bread Pudding (see page 95) directly from the freezer and bake. Slice fruit, left from breakfast or lunch on Saturday, add a simple green salad (if it's brunch-time) and top fresh orange juice with a spritz of sparkling wine. Wash a selection of whole fruit and let it shine as an edible centerpiece.

TANDOORI CHICKEN

A tandoor is an Indian clay oven, but even without such an oven the style and flavor of this cuisine can be reproduced at home on a barbecue or in a hot oven. Tandoori Chicken is great at room temperature for salads and sandwiches, so plan to make extra for leftovers. Note that the chicken must marinate at least two hours, or overnight.

    8 chicken breast halves
    2 teaspoons cumin seed
    1 teaspoon whole coriander,
       crushed
    ⅛ gram (¼ teaspoon) saffron
       threads
    2 tablespoons boiling water
    1 teaspoon turmeric
    2 shallots, minced
    3 cloves garlic, minced
    1 teaspoon minced fresh ginger
    ¼ cup minced cilantro
    1 jalapeño chile, minced
    1 tablespoon paprika
    ¼ teaspoon cayenne pepper
    1 teaspoon salt
    1 cup plain yogurt
    3 tablespoons freshly squeezed
       lemon juice
    6 tablespoons unsalted
       butter, melted
       Rabat Rice Pilaf
       (see page 30),
       for accompaniment

1. Score chicken breast halves on the diagonal, cutting slashes 3 inches long, almost to the bone in 3 or 4 places.

2. In a dry skillet over medium heat, toast cumin seed and coriander until barely browned (4 to 5 minutes). In a 1-quart bowl stir together saffron and the boiling water.

3. Into the saffron liquid stir cumin seed, coriander, turmeric, shallots, garlic, ginger, cilantro, chile, paprika, cayenne, salt, yogurt, lemon juice, and 3 tablespoons melted butter. Mix thoroughly. Rub this marinade into chicken; let marinate in refrigerator for 2 hours, or overnight.

4. Preheat oven to 500° F. Place chicken pieces on a broiler rack in a shallow pan and roast, skin side down, for 10 minutes. Turn skin side up, baste with remaining melted butter, and brown second side (20 to 25 minutes, depending on size of breasts). Serve with Rabat Rice Pilaf.

Serves 8.

GREEK ORZO SALAD

Orzo, sometimes called *riso,* is a pasta that, when cooked, resembles rice. It is an excellent complement to grilled lamb. Note that the pasta marinates at least two hours, or as long as overnight.

    1 cup orzo
    6 tablespoons olive oil
    5 tablespoons red wine vinegar
    1 small red onion, minced
   1½ teaspoons salt
    ½ teaspoon freshly ground
       pepper
    1 teaspoon dried oregano
    ¼ cup minced parsley
    2 large tomatoes, diced
    1 English cucumber, diced
   12 to 18 Greek olives, halved
       and pitted
    6 ounces feta cheese

1. In a 3-quart saucepan bring 2 quarts water to a vigorous boil. Add orzo and cook until slightly al dente (8 to 10 minutes). Drain, place in a 2-quart serving dish, and toss with 1 tablespoon olive oil.

2. Whisk together remaining olive oil, vinegar, onion, salt, pepper, oregano, and parsley. Pour over orzo and let marinate for 2 to 24 hours.

3. At serving time, toss tomatoes, cucumber, olives, and feta with marinated orzo. Season again if necessary. Serve immediately.

Serves 8.

TIRAMISU

Tiramisu, which means *pick me up* in Italian, is a luscious cake roll with a rich, sweet cheese filling. It is a dessert that is easy to make and delicious to eat. *Mascarpone* is a rich Italian cream cheese. If mascarpone is unavailable, you can substitute natural cream cheese.

   1½ cups whipping cream
   1¼ cups confectioners' sugar
    1 pound mascarpone cheese
    ½ teaspoon vanilla extract
    5 tablespoons dark rum
    1 plain sponge roll (see
       Milk Sponge Roll With Jam,
       page 36)
    3 tablespoons unsweetened
       cocoa powder
       Grated semisweet chocolate,
       for garnish

1. In a 3-quart bowl whip cream and 1 cup confectioners' sugar to soft peaks. Fold in mascarpone, vanilla, and 2 tablespoons rum; reserve.

2. Set sponge roll on a flat baking sheet; sprinkle with remaining rum. Dust with unsweetened cocoa, spread with reserved filling, and roll up jelly-roll fashion.

3. Carefully transfer filled Tiramisu from flat baking sheet to a long, narrow serving tray, so that seam side is on bottom. Sprinkle top with remaining confectioners' sugar and grated chocolate.

Serves 8 to 10.

JOE'S SPECIAL FILO ROLLS

The easiest way to clean sand from spinach leaves is to place the spinach in a large bowl or in the sink and cover with cool water. Gently press leaves in the water; the sand will drop to the bottom of the bowl. Lift spinach out of the water. Drain water and repeat until there is no more sand in the bottom of the bowl. Pat spinach dry before using. Note that the filo dough must thaw six to eight hours, overnight, in the refrigerator, or one hour at room temperature.

      1 cup butter, melted
  1¼ pounds Italian sausage meat
      1 medium onion, diced
      2 cloves garlic, minced
      2 bunches spinach (about
            1 lb each)
      1 teaspoon dried basil
      ½ teaspoon ground nutmeg
      6 eggs
    16 sheets frozen filo dough,
            thawed according to
            package directions

1. Preheat oven to 350° F. Brush 2 baking sheets lightly with some of the melted butter. In a 12-inch skillet over medium heat, crumble sausage into small pieces and brown (6 to 8 minutes). Stir in onion and garlic and cook until onion is translucent (3 to 4 minutes). Add spinach, basil, and nutmeg. Stir constantly until spinach is wilted.

2. Beat eggs together in a small bowl and add to sausage mixture; remove from heat and let cool. Place 1 sheet of filo dough on the work surface and brush with melted butter. Cover with a second sheet and brush with butter. Place a scant ½ cup sausage mixture in an approximately 4-inch-long strip along short end of filo dough. Fold in sides of filo about 1½ inches and roll up to enclose filling.

3. Place roll seam side down on one of the prepared baking sheets and repeat with remaining filo dough and filling. Brush rolls with remaining butter. Bake until golden brown (35 to 40 minutes).

Serves 8.

Joe's Special Filo Rolls, Sweet Potato and Cinnamon Muffins, and Poached Fruit With Walnuts—Saturday breakfast—can all be readied days or weeks before guests arrive. Substitute purchased muffins and a huge bowl of strawberries for home-made rolls and poached fruit if time or the season alters your menu.

SWEET POTATO AND CINNAMON MUFFINS

Scrub 1 medium-large sweet potato, cut into 2-inch-long pieces, place in a small saucepan, and cover with water. Cook about 25 minutes before pureeing in a food processor. Remove purée and cream the butter and sugar.

Butter and flour, for preparing pan
½ cup *butter, softened*
1½ cups *firmly packed brown sugar*
1 cup *sweet potato purée*
1 *egg*
1¾ cups *flour*
½ teaspoon *each salt, ground nutmeg, and ground ginger*
1 teaspoon *baking soda*
2 teaspoons *ground cinnamon*
⅛ teaspoon *ground cloves*
⅓ cup *water*

1. Preheat oven to 375° F. Butter and flour muffin pan or line with muffin papers. Cream the ½ cup butter and sugar until light and fluffy; stir in sweet potato purée and egg.

2. Sift together flour, salt, nutmeg, ginger, baking soda, cinnamon, and cloves. Stir half the dry ingredients into creamed mixture; stir in water, then remaining dry ingredients.

3. Using an ice cream scoop, fill muffin cups two thirds full of batter; bake until dry on top and a skewer inserted in center comes out clean (18 to 20 minutes). Serve warm.

Makes 1 dozen muffins.

POACHED FRUIT WITH WALNUTS

Turn simple fresh fruit into a compote fit for breakfast or for dessert. Serve plain for breakfast or warm with vanilla ice cream for dessert.

4 *apples, peeled and cored*
4 *pears, peeled and cored*
12 *dried apricots*
2 cups *white wine or apple juice*
½ cup *sugar*
1 *vanilla bean, cut in half lengthwise*
½ cup *toasted walnut halves*

1. In a 3-quart saucepan, place apples, pears, and dried apricots; add white wine, sugar, and vanilla bean. Bring to a boil, reduce heat, and simmer until apples and pears are tender but still firm (15 to 20 minutes).

2. Stir in walnuts, place in a serving dish, and cool completely. Chill until serving time.

Serves 8.

MANGO CHUTNEY CHICKEN SALAD

Use leftover Tandoori Chicken (see page 92) in this salad for a special treat or simmer boneless chicken breasts, covered with water, until tender (25 to 35 minutes). Note that the chicken must marinate from 2 to 24 hours.

1 cup *Homemade Mayonnaise (see page 20)*
1 cup *sour cream*
½ cup *mango chutney*
¼ cup *minced cilantro*
¼ cup *minced green onion*
1 teaspoon *salt*
6 cups *diced Tandoori Chicken or diced, cooked boneless chicken breast*
1 cup *toasted pecans*

1. In a 3-quart bowl combine mayonnaise, sour cream, chutney, cilantro, green onion, and salt.

2. Toss with chicken and let marinate for 2 to 24 hours. Sprinkle with pecans before serving.

Serves 8.

MOM'S BUTTERMILK BISCUITS

Biscuits are quick and easy to prepare and can frequently be flavored with ingredients on hand. Enhance by stirring in fresh herbs, Parmesan cheese, or sun-dried tomatoes (see variations at end of recipe). Stir 2 tablespoons lemon juice into ¾ cup milk to make a buttermilk substitute.

2 cups *flour, plus flour for dusting*
2 tablespoons *sugar (optional)*
4 teaspoons *baking powder*
½ teaspoon *salt*
½ cup *butter, chilled*
¾ cup *buttermilk*
2 tablespoons *butter, melted*

1. Preheat oven to 425° F. In a 3-quart bowl sift together flour, sugar (if used), baking powder, and salt. Dice chilled butter into ½-inch cubes and, using 2 knives or a pastry blender, cut butter cubes into flour mixture until mixture resembles coarse crumbs.

2. Make a depression in center of flour-butter mixture and gently stir in buttermilk, taking care not to overmix dough. Mix only until dry ingredients are moistened.

3. Lightly dust a work surface with flour. Place dough on work surface and pat into a 1½-inch-thick rectangle. Cut biscuits with a round cutter or into squares with a knife. Place on an ungreased baking sheet. Brush with melted butter and bake until golden brown on top (15 minutes).

Makes 1 dozen biscuits.

Cheddar Biscuits   In step 1 add ½ cup grated Cheddar cheese and ½ teaspoon cayenne pepper to flour-baking powder mixture. Proceed with recipe as directed.

Pumate and Basil Biscuits   In step 1 add 12 julienned basil leaves and 3 tablespoons diced sun-dried tomatoes (*pumate*) to flour-baking powder mixture. Proceed with recipe as directed.

FAJITAS

Marinate skirt steak or strips of sirloin for up to 48 hours. Grill or sauté steak pieces and wrap in warm flour tortillas for a southwestern dinner.

    3 pounds sirloin steak or skirt
       steak, cut in strips ¼ inch
       thick by 3 inches long
    1 small onion, minced
    3 cloves garlic, minced
    2 jalapeño chiles, cut in strips
    1 bunch cilantro, minced
    5 tablespoons vegetable oil
       Juice of 3 limes
   16 flour tortillas, warmed,
       for accompaniment
       Avocado Salsa (see page 47),
       for garnish
    1 cup sour cream, for garnish
       Arroz Verde (see page 76),
       for accompaniment

1. Place strips of steak in a mixing bowl. Toss with onion, garlic, jalapeños, cilantro, 3 tablespoons oil, and lime juice. Marinate for 2 to 48 hours.

2. At serving time, wrap tortillas in aluminum foil and warm in oven. In a 12-inch skillet over medium-high heat, place remaining oil. Drain off marinade and sauté steak strips, stirring constantly, until browned but still rare (4 to 6 minutes).

3. Serve immediately with warm tortillas, Avocado Salsa, sour cream, and Arroz Verde.

Serves 8.

BLACK BEAN SALSA SALAD

Combine all the ingredients for this salad the day before the party but don't fuss with the flavor. Beans, and other starches such as pasta, need to be reseasoned with salt, pepper, and perhaps a touch of vinegar just before serving.

    2 cups corn kernels
       (from 3 ears corn)
    2 cans (15 oz each) cooked
       black beans
    1 red bell pepper, diced
    1 red onion, minced

    2 jalapeño chiles, minced
    1 clove garlic, minced
    1 bunch cilantro, minced
       Juice of 1 lime
    1 teaspoon salt
    ½ teaspoon freshly ground
       pepper
    5 tablespoons vegetable oil
    5 tablespoons red wine vinegar

In a 3-quart bowl combine all ingredients. Chill for 1 to 24 hours. Taste for seasoning before serving.

Serves 8.

PEACHES EN PAPILLOTE

Desserts wrapped in parchment paper or aluminum foil can be assembled hours ahead and popped into a preheated oven while the main course is being enjoyed.

    ½ cup sour cream or
       plain yogurt
    1 teaspoon vanilla extract
    3 tablespoons confectioners'
       sugar
    6 peaches, peeled and sliced
       in eighths
    ¼ cup firmly packed
       brown sugar
    4 tablespoons orange-flavored
       liqueur or orange juice
       Grated rind and juice
       of 1 lemon

1. Preheat oven to 400° F. Cut eight 12-inch squares of aluminum foil.

2. In a small bowl stir together sour cream, vanilla, and confectioners' sugar. Reserve.

3. Place 6 peach slices on each foil square. Sprinkle each with ½ tablespoon brown sugar, ½ tablespoon liqueur, 1 teaspoon lemon juice, and about ⅛ teaspoon lemon rind. Place 1 tablespoon sour cream mixture on peaches. Tightly seal foil and place on a baking sheet.

4. Bake until packages puff slightly (8 to 10 minutes). Warm ovenproof dessert plates during last 2 minutes of baking. Open peach packages, remove foil, and slip fruit onto warm serving plates. Serve immediately.

Serves 8.

BREAKFAST BREAD PUDDING

A savory do-ahead version of an old-fashioned dessert favorite, this pudding works well for brunch or for a wintery evening supper. Vary the taste with diced red bell pepper, spinach, and leftover ham or roast turkey tossed with pieces of broccoli. The longer the pudding rests before baking, the creamier the interior will be, since the bread will absorb more liquid. Note that the bread slices should dry overnight, if possible, before using.

    8 slices rye or French bread
    ¼ pound butter, melted
    1 cup sauerkraut
    1 teaspoon caraway seed
    2 cups diced corned beef
   1½ cups (6 oz) grated
       Swiss cheese
    2 cups milk
    5 eggs
    1 teaspoon salt
    ½ teaspoon freshly ground
       pepper
    2 tomatoes, sliced

1. Let bread dry out at room temperature 8 hours or place in one layer on a baking sheet and bake 10 minutes in a preheated 350° F oven.

2. Brush dried bread with melted butter and place in a 9- by 12-inch baking dish. Spread sauerkraut over bread, and sprinkle with caraway seed, corned beef, and cheese.

3. Whisk milk, eggs, salt, and pepper together. Pour over contents of baking dish. Cover with aluminum foil and let rest at room temperature for 1 hour or in the refrigerator for up to 24 hours.

4. Preheat oven to 350° F. Bake pudding 30 minutes, then remove foil and arrange sliced tomatoes in one layer on top of pudding; continue to bake until golden brown and slightly puffy (about 20 minutes more if started at room temperature, 30 minutes if started cold). Serve warm.

Serves 8.

QUICK COOKIES

Cookies are a wonderful dessert. They can make an attractive centerpiece, glamorize a plate of fruit, or garnish a bowl of ice cream. Taking only minutes to stir together and baking in 10 to 15 minutes, cookies are one of the easiest and quickest desserts to prepare. Whether baked and waiting in the freezer or sitting, ready to bake, in the refrigerator, cookies are also the perfect do-ahead dessert. Offering a selection of personal favorites can become your trademark. Even a selection of small cookies can look like a substantial dessert.

Refrigerator cookies such as Pecan Icebox Cookies (see opposite page) and Susan's Triple-Chocolate Cookies (at right) are best served the same day they are baked. If necessary, the dough can be prepared up to one week in advance and stored in the refrigerator, wrapped in foil, ready to slice and bake. These doughs also freeze well if you are planning a large party or anticipating several houseguests. Cream Cheese Cookies (at right) can be dressed up with confectioners' sugar, garnished with raspberry jam or chocolate sprinkles, or filled with peanut butter and dipped in chocolate.

RUTHEE'S IRISH LACE COOKIES

Inexpensive rolled oats take the place of chopped pecans in this crisp, elegant cookie. If making these cookies ahead, store airtight after baking. Recrisp by warming on a baking sheet in a 350° F oven 5 minutes. Cool completely before serving.

- *½ cup unsalted butter, plus butter for greasing*
- *4 tablespoons flour, plus flour for dusting*
- *1 cup firmly packed brown sugar*
- *1 tablespoon vanilla extract*
- *2 tablespoons milk*
- *1 cup old-fashioned rolled oats*

1. Preheat oven to 350° F. Grease and flour 2 baking sheets.

2. Cream butter and sugar. Add vanilla; stir in flour, milk, and rolled oats. Drop batter by the tablespoon onto prepared baking sheets; allow room for cookies to spread to about 3 inches in diameter. Each baking sheet will hold about 6 cookies.

3. Bake until cookies flatten and look dry (10 minutes). Let cookies cool for 4 to 5 minutes on baking sheets. Lift from baking sheet with a metal spatula and cool completely.

Makes 2 dozen cookies.

CREAM CHEESE COOKIES

These make wonderful refrigerator cookies—simply roll the dough into a cylinder, wrap tightly to seal, and chill. The dough can be frozen for up to three months, an asset for the busy cook. Decorate with chocolate sprinkles, a dot of cherry jam, or a whole toasted pecan. Thinner cookies (which bake in less time) can be cut and filled with a layer of cool Chocolate Fudge Sauce (see page 37) or raspberry jam. Dust the tops with confectioners' sugar. The dough can also be pressed into miniature tart tins and filled with Lemon Curd (see page 47). For yet another variation, cut rounds, bake, then dip one half of each cookie in melted chocolate.

- *½ cup unsalted butter, at room temperature*
- *3 ounces cream cheese, at room temperature*
- *2 cups granulated sugar*
- *2 eggs*
- *1 teaspoon vanilla extract*
  Grated rind of 1 lemon
- *4 cups flour*
- *1 teaspoon baking powder*
- *½ teaspoon salt*
- *½ cup raspberry jam*
  Confectioners' sugar, for dusting

1. Cream butter, cream cheese, and granulated sugar until light and fluffy. Add eggs, one at a time, beating well after each addition. Stir in vanilla and lemon rind.

2. Sift together flour, baking powder, and salt. Stir into butter–cream cheese mixture.

3. Roll dough into a log about 18 inches long. Place on a 20-inch-long sheet of aluminum foil, roll up, and seal ends. Chill 2 hours or freeze for up to 3 months.

4. To bake, preheat oven to 350° F. Slice dough into ⅜-inch-thick rounds and place on parchment-lined baking sheets. Spoon ½ teaspoon jam in center of each cookie. Bake until firm on top and golden brown on underside (8 to 10 minutes). Remove from baking sheet to a cooling rack. Dust with confectioners' sugar before serving.

Makes about 4 dozen cookies.

SUSAN'S TRIPLE-CHOCOLATE COOKIES

Chocoholics never feel cheated when these triple-rich cookies are the only dessert served. Use a stainless steel mixing bowl and make this a one-bowl recipe.

- *4 ounces unsweetened chocolate, chopped roughly*
- *12 ounces semisweet chocolate, chopped roughly*
- *4 tablespoons unsalted butter*
- *½ cup all-purpose flour*
- *½ teaspoon baking powder*
- *½ teaspoon baking soda*
- *⅛ teaspoon salt*
- *4 eggs*
- *2 cups sugar*
- *1 tablespoon dark rum*
- *1 teaspoon vanilla extract*
- *2 cups chocolate chips*
- *2 cups chopped walnuts*

1. Fill a shallow pan with 1½ inches water; bring to a boil over medium heat. Place chocolates and butter in a 2-quart metal mixing bowl. Place bowl in the shallow pan of boiling water and turn off heat. Stir to mix chocolates and butter while they melt.

2. Sift together flour, baking powder, baking soda, and salt onto a piece of aluminum foil or parchment paper.

3. Beat eggs, sugar, rum, and vanilla into melted chocolate mixture until mixture thickens. Stir in sifted flour mixture and combine thoroughly. Stir in chocolate chips and walnuts. Let mixture sit until easy to shape (5 to 10 minutes); it will be sticky.

4. Place dough on a sheet of aluminum foil about 18 inches long and roll into a log 2 inches in diameter. (For a more elegant cookie, roll 2 cylinders each about 1 inch in diameter.) Wrap carefully and chill overnight.

5. Preheat oven to 350° F. Line baking sheets with aluminum foil. Slice cookie dough with a hot knife. Place slices on foil. Bake until cracks form on top of cookies and surfaces appear dry; interiors of cookies as seen through cracks will be moist (10 to 12 minutes). Let cool 5 minutes on baking sheets before removing to a wire rack to finish cooling.

Makes 2 dozen large cookies or 4 dozen small cookies.

MRS. KELLER'S OATMEAL RAISIN COOKIES

For ease and exactness, professional bakers scoop and measure cookie dough with a spring-operated ice cream scoop. If drop cookies are a favorite, you might want to purchase this type of scoop, available at well-stocked cookware stores and hardware stores.

>   1 cup butter, at room
>   temperature
>   1 cup firmly packed
>   brown sugar
>   1 cup granulated sugar
>   2 eggs
>   1 teaspoon vanilla extract
>   1½ cups flour
>   1 teaspoon salt
>   1 teaspoon baking soda
>   3 cups quick oatmeal
>   1 cup raisins

1. Preheat oven to 350° F. Line 2 baking sheets with parchment paper or butter and flour sheets.

2. In a 3-quart bowl cream butter, brown sugar, and granulated sugar until light and fluffy. Thoroughly mix in eggs and vanilla. Sift together flour, salt, and baking soda. Stir into batter with oatmeal. Mix in raisins.

3. Using ice cream scoop or a spoon, form dough into 2-inch mounds; set about 3 inches apart on prepared baking sheets. Bake until lightly browned (15 to 17 minutes). Cool on wire racks.

Makes fourteen 4-inch cookies.

PECAN ICEBOX COOKIES

Icebox cookies allow you to serve cookies fresh from the oven almost anytime.

>   1 cup unsalted butter
>   2 cups firmly packed light
>   brown sugar
>   2 eggs
>   1 teaspoon vanilla extract
>   3 cups flour
>   1 tablespoon baking powder
>   1 teaspoon salt
>   ½ cup chopped pecans

1. If baking cookies immediately after making dough, preheat oven to 375° F. Line 2 baking sheets with parchment, or butter and flour.

2. Cream together butter and sugar; add eggs, one at a time, beating thoroughly after each addition. Stir in vanilla.

3. Sift together flour, baking powder, and salt. Stir into creamed mixture. Stir in pecans.

4. Place half the dough on a 12- by 15-inch sheet of aluminum foil. Shape dough into a log and wrap well in aluminum foil. Repeat with remaining dough. Chill 2 hours or place rolls in airtight freezer bags and freeze.

5. Unwrap chilled dough and slice into ½-inch-thick rounds. (Frozen dough may be too hard to slice; let dough soften slightly, then slice into rounds.) Place on prepared baking sheets. Bake until dry on top and lightly browned on underside (10 to 12 minutes). Remove from baking sheets to cool on wire racks.

Makes 7 dozen cookies.

DESSERTS

Preparing dessert ahead has been a traditional practice in most homes. Pumpkin pies for Thanksgiving, tall layer cakes for birthdays, cheesecakes for elaborate dinners, and frothy fruit mousses all can be made days or weeks before a party. Cake layers can be baked and frozen weeks in advance and assembled early in the day they will be served. Airy cream puffs can wait in the freezer, filled or empty, ready for guests. Cheesecake also freezes well, and the Blackberry Summer Pudding (see below) can wait in the refrigerator.

BLACKBERRY SUMMER PUDDING

Traditional deep, white English pudding basins are available at well-stocked cookware stores, but an 8-cup mold or mixing bowl makes a good substitute.

> 3 pounds blackberries
> 1 cup granulated sugar
> 12 slices (each ½ in. thick) Vanilla-Nutmeg Pound Cake (see page 35)
> 2 cups whipping cream
> 2 tablespoons confectioners' sugar
> 1 teaspoon vanilla extract

1. Wash berries and discard any stems. Toss with granulated sugar in a 2-quart mixing bowl; set aside 15 to 30 minutes.

2. Line an 8-cup mold or English pudding basin with plastic wrap. Line sides and bottom of mold with overlapping cake slices. Fill with half of the blackberry mixture. Place 3 cake slices over blackberries and cover with remaining blackberries, then with remaining cake slices. Place plastic wrap over top layer. Cover pudding with a plate slightly smaller in diameter than mold, and place a heavy weight on plate. Refrigerate 12 to 24 hours. Cake will be completely saturated with fruit syrup and will turn a royal purple.

3. At serving time, lift off weight and plate, remove plastic wrap, and loosen edges with a knife. Invert a serving dish over pudding basin and invert both together to unmold. There

may be some excess blackberry liquid in basin, so unmold over a sink or work surface.

4. Beat whipping cream to soft peaks and whisk in confectioners' sugar and vanilla. Serve a dollop of whipped cream on top of each slice of pudding.

Serves 8 to 10.

CHOCOLATE AND RASPBERRY SWIRL CHEESECAKE

Tightly wrapped and stored in the freezer, this cheesecake will keep for two months, ready for surprise guests or future parties.

> 6 ounces semisweet chocolate
> 2 pounds cream cheese, softened
> 1 cup sugar
> 5 eggs
> 3 tablespoons flour
> 1 teaspoon vanilla extract
> 4 tablespoons raspberry liqueur
> 1 pint fresh raspberries or 1 pound unsweetened frozen raspberries (do not thaw)
> ¼ cup currant jelly

Crust

> 1¼ cups flour
> 3 tablespoons sugar
> ¼ teaspoon salt
> 6 tablespoons unsalted butter
> 1 to 2 tablespoons water

1. Prepare Crust; set aside. Leave oven at 350° F while preparing filling.

2. Break chocolate into pieces and place in a small bowl. Place bowl in a shallow pan of water and simmer until chocolate melts. With an electric mixer or food processor, beat cream cheese until smooth; gradually add sugar. Beat in eggs, one at a time. Add flour, vanilla, and 2 tablespoons raspberry liqueur.

3. Place two thirds of the cream cheese filling into crust. Stir melted chocolate and 1 cup raspberries into remaining filling. Divide chocolate-raspberry filling into sixths and drop each by the spoonful into the plain filling. Swirl with a dinner knife to marble batter. Bake until top is set

and center wiggles slightly if cake is gently shaken (1 hour and 10 minutes). Let cool in pan 1 hour.

4. Chill 4 to 12 hours (cake will keep in refrigerator for 10 days). Two to four hours before serving, heat currant jelly with remaining raspberry liqueur. Gently toss remaining raspberries with currant jelly glaze and arrange on top of cheesecake.

Serves 10 to 12.

Crust In a 3-quart bowl stir together flour, sugar, and salt. Cut butter into small cubes and rub into flour with 2 knives, a pastry blender, or your fingertips until it resembles coarse crumbs. Add enough of the water to form a dough and chill 30 minutes. Preheat oven to 350° F. Roll out to fit a 9-inch springform pan. Bake 12 minutes; remove and cool.

BOSTON CREAM TRIFLE

A trifle, as the name suggests, is quite simple to put together. Have the sponge cake roll ready in the freezer, then layer the cake, rum-flavored pastry cream, and fudge sauce.

> 1 Milk Sponge Roll (see page 36)
> 2 cups milk
> ½ cup sugar
> 4 egg yolks
> 2 tablespoons cornstarch
> 2 tablespoons flour
> ½ teaspoon vanilla extract
> 3 tablespoons unsalted butter
> 2 tablespoons dark rum Chocolate Fudge Sauce (see page 37)

1. Choose a 1½-quart serving bowl about 8 inches in diameter. Cut two 8-inch circles from cake roll. Place one in bottom of serving bowl. Reserve second circle and trimmings.

2. To make pastry cream, in a 2-quart saucepan bring milk just barely to a boil (bubbles will appear around edges of pan). While milk is heating, in a 2-quart bowl whisk together sugar, egg yolks, cornstarch, and flour. Pour hot milk over egg-yolk mixture, whisking constantly to prevent lumps and to blend well. Return egg-milk mixture to saucepan.

3. Over medium heat stir egg-milk mixture until thickened (about 4 minutes). Mixture will pull away from sides of pan as it thickens. Strain into a clean mixing bowl. Stir in vanilla extract, butter, and dark rum. Place plastic wrap on surface of mixture and chill until it reaches room temperature.

4. Pour half of the pastry cream into cake-lined serving bowl. Cover pastry cream with cake trimmings. Fill serving bowl with remaining pastry cream. Top with second cake circle.

5. Warm Chocolate Fudge Sauce and pour over cake circle. Chill 2 to 24 hours before serving.

Serves 8 to 10.

ICE CREAM ÉCLAIRS

Cream puffs can be made ahead, when you have some free time, and frozen for future use. After cooling completely, fill cream puffs with coffee ice cream and wrap, being careful to seal tightly, then freeze. Fifteen to twenty minutes before serving, remove from freezer and drizzle with warm fudge sauce.

     1 cup water
     ¾ teaspoon salt
     1 teaspoon sugar
     6 tablespoons butter, diced
     1 cup flour
     4 eggs
     1 quart coffee ice cream,
        for filling
        Chocolate Fudge Sauce
        (see page 37), for
        topping

1. Preheat oven to 400° F. Line 2 baking sheets with parchment paper or coat with butter and flour. In a 1½-quart saucepan over medium heat, bring the water, salt, sugar, and butter to a boil. Remove from heat and stir in flour. Return pan to heat and stir until mixture pulls away from sides of pan (1 minute).

2. Place mixture in a 2-quart bowl, food processor, or bowl of heavy-duty mixer. Cover and let cool 20 minutes.

3. Add eggs, one at a time, beating thoroughly after each is added. Mixture will appear shiny and be thick when mixed. Using a teaspoon or a pastry bag, form strips of dough, about 4 inches long by 1 inch wide, on baking sheets, placing them 1½ inches apart to allow room for expansion.

4. Bake until doubled in size and light golden brown (25 to 30 minutes). Cool completely on wire racks.

5. When cream puffs are cool, halve horizontally with a serrated knife. Place 2 rounded tablespoons of coffee ice cream on each bottom half. Cover with top half. Place on dessert plates. Warm Chocolate Fudge Sauce in a small saucepan over low heat and drizzle over éclairs.

Makes 12 to 15 éclairs.

After one taste, this spectacular swirled cheesecake will become everyone's favorite splurge dessert. At serving time, glaze the raspberries with currant jelly and raspberry liqueur for a jeweled finish.

With planning and a solid
repertoire of familiar recipes,
entertaining on a large scale is no
more complicated than preparing
an intimate dinner for two.

Cooking for a Crowd

This chapter will demonstrate that it's as easy to cook for many guests as it is for just a few. The key is consolidation of time and energy, plus a good understanding of one's cooking and serving style and the limitations of home and equipment. The menus are innovative: The first (see page 107) encourages back-to-back entertaining with a formal, sit-down dinner for 8 on Friday evening and an open house for 30 on Sunday afternoon. The trick is to use the same foods, modifying them to suit the occasion. The second menu (see page 121) features a Thanksgiving meal that can be prepared in a day if you suddenly learn that this year it's at your house.

MASTERING THE MASSES

Big celebrations are a practical way of entertaining. The behind-the-scenes preparation—cleaning house, arranging flowers, polishing silver, choosing dishes and serving pieces—is almost the same regardless of the size of the guest list. Your time and energy are expended for a single event, but for scores of guests.

The pleasure of having the company of many friends is one major benefit of large-scale entertaining. Consolidation of time and energy when planning and cooking is another. You can purchase food in advance, order wine (and have it delivered because you are buying in volume), and perhaps even have a friend or family member assist with the cooking. Suddenly handling 20 or even 40 guests becomes as easy as dinner for 8. You can entertain without exhaustion, and with a flourish.

SETTING THE STAGE

Unless you have space to set up tables (outdoors on a lawn, in a clean garage spruced up with decorations, or in a room that is easily cleared of furniture), sit-down dinners for more than the usual eight or ten guests are impossible. A cocktail buffet or stand-up supper makes the most sense.

Casual parties can feature a soup-based menu, which is particularly festive if the soup is served from copper or other decorative pots directly from the stove. Informal get-togethers can also take the form of a make-your-own-salad bar. Crusty bread and a delicious dessert are the only extras you need. For easy service, wrap silverware in napkins and place at the end of a buffet line (guests will have less to hold as they fill their plates). If you have room for two or three tables, each seating eight, set them with glasses, silver, and napkins, but still let guests help themselves to the food buffet style. Set out dessert in another room, so that you don't have to clean up until after the party is over. Adjoining rooms are ideal for placing multiple tables.

CHOOSING A THEME

After you've resolved the logistics (size of guest list and placement of tables), you can think about a theme. A theme or special occasion can give focus to a dinner party, simplify planning, and make the evening go more smoothly. Certain foods may lend themselves to the season, your culinary skills, or a special guest.

Major holiday gatherings and special occasions, such as Thanksgiving and Christmas dinner, a baby shower, a New Year's cocktail party, or an annual Super Bowl party, are events that you can plan well in advance. You can also establish a dining format for entertaining that best matches your home and cooking skills. Alter menus to suit the time of year and choose traditional or favorite foods. Recipes that are good for 8 guests may work beautifully for 12 to 25, but the way you serve the dish might differ, depending upon the size of the crowd.

BACK-TO-BACK ENTERTAINING

Planning several parties within days of one another is often advantageous; cooking, cleaning, and decorating for many guests on a single weekend is a great time-saver. You can alleviate some of the fatigue by skipping a day between parties. Consider an elegant cocktail party on Saturday night, then leave all day Sunday to set the stage for a formal dinner on Monday night. Or, plan a sit-down dinner for Friday evening and an open house for Sunday afternoon (see page 107). With one shopping list and several well-planned preparation and cooking sessions, you will still have the benefits of entertaining a large number of people, but with a guest list that is divided over two occasions. Planning and preparation are still critical to a party of any size; for back-to-back parties, it's even more important to lay the groundwork exceedingly well.

APPETIZERS AND FIRST COURSES

The simplest part of the menu to increase, whether for large parties or unexpected additions to a guest list, is the appetizer or first course. Many appetizers readily lend themselves to doubling or tripling as well as to careful freezing. For example, marinating extra Buffalo Chicken Wings (see page 110) takes little additional time, and cooking time is identical as long as the oven is not overcrowded (leave space for air to circulate around the baking dish). Consider Basil-Cheese Feuilletée (see page 104), which freezes well and can be baked directly from the freezer.

GRUYÈRE AND SQUASH SOUP SERVED IN A SQUASH SHELL

To form the soup tureen, cut the top from a pumpkin, and remove and discard the seeds. Right before serving time preheat the oven to 350° F and warm the pumpkin for 20 minutes before filling with the soup. Place on a serving platter lined with squash leaves from your garden, if available, or lemon leaves, fern fronds, or oversized ivy. Serve from the table.

3 acorn or Danish squash, cut in large cubes
½ cup butter
4 leeks, cleaned and diced
5 ounces Gruyère cheese, grated
½ teaspoon ground nutmeg
1 teaspoon salt
½ teaspoon dried thyme
¼ teaspoon cayenne pepper
5 cups Chicken Stock (see page 56)
½ cup whipping cream

1. In a 5-quart saucepan place squash cubes and cover with water. Bring to a boil, reduce heat, and simmer until a knife easily pierces squash (30 minutes). Remove skin and purée in food processor or blender.

2. In a 4-quart saucepan or Dutch oven over medium heat, add butter and sauté leeks until softened and translucent (20 minutes).

3. Add squash purée, Gruyère, nutmeg, salt, thyme, cayenne, Chicken Stock, and whipping cream. Stir together and simmer for 15 to 20 minutes to mingle flavors. Pour into prepared pumpkin or serve from a soup tureen.

Makes 11 cups, 10 servings as a first course, 6 as a main course.

CREAMY SHRIMP SOUP

Although this smooth and creamy soup is very elegant—well suited to a formal dinner—it can be topped with South-of-the-Border Salsa when more casual fare is in order.

   1 pound shrimp
   8 tablespoons butter
   1 red bell pepper, diced
   5 shallots, diced
   8 tablespoons flour
   4 cups Fish Stock (see page 57) or water
   1 teaspoon salt
  ⅛ teaspoon ground nutmeg
   4 drops hot-pepper sauce
  ¼ cup minced chives
  ½ cup whipping cream
     South-of-the-Border Salsa (optional; see page 47), for garnish

1. Shell shrimp and reserve the meat. In a 3-quart saucepan over low heat melt 6 tablespoons butter; stir in shrimp shells and cook over low heat until shells turn pink and butter takes on shrimp flavor (10 to 12 minutes). With a slotted spoon remove shells and discard; reserve butter in pan.

2. Add remaining butter to pan. Sauté bell pepper and shallots, stirring, until translucent (about 5 minutes). Whisk flour into shallot-pepper mixture and cook 3 to 4 minutes. Add Fish Stock and whisk until thickened (6 to 7 minutes). Add salt, nutmeg, hot-pepper sauce, chives, and cream.

3. Bring to a boil, add shrimp, and reduce heat. Cook until shrimp turn bright pink (1 to 2 minutes). Serve immediately, plain or garnished with South-of-the-Border Salsa.

Makes 7 cups; 8 servings as an appetizer, 6 as a main course.

Special Note

THE QUANTITY QUANDARY

To plan menus for large groups successfully, keep in mind the amount of time available, your skills, and your equipment.

☐ Incorporate into the menu a do-ahead dish such as a soup or stew that can rest in the refrigerator for 1 or 2 days, and a dish that can be chopped in advance and then sautéed or steamed at the last minute. This will spread out preparation and keep storage facilities from being overcrowded.

☐ Shop for do-ahead recipes at one time, prepare them, and then store in the refrigerator or freezer until serving time.

☐ Read each recipe through before attempting it in order to make sure that techniques and timing are clear, and to confirm that you have all ingredients on hand.

☐ The first time you prepare a recipe, weigh ingredients and keep a record for future use. Weight is always a more accurate measure than volume.

☐ Before increasing the yield of a recipe, be familiar with how the dish looks when done. Cooking time does not always increase proportionately, so when doubling recipes, judge doneness by eye rather than by strict timing.

☐ Break recipes into components and prepare the components—such as sauces, fillings, cake bases, vinaigrettes, pastry, and marinades—separately. Then combine the components to finish each dish.

☐ Wash, slice, dice, and measure ingredients beforehand when possible. Store washed salad greens (wrapped in towels), premeasured dry ingredients, and soft (but not liquid) cooked foods in plastic food-storage bags.

☐ Be aware of equipment requirements. You may need oversized mixing bowls, large stockpots, special heavy-duty cookware, and large baking pans. If the food is crowded, the results may suffer.

☐ For health reasons, be careful to chill food properly. If the refrigerator will not quickly chill large quantities at one time consider placing food over ice until cold and then refrigerating.

RICE SALAD IN PROSCIUTTO-LINED MOLD

This beautiful buffet salad, which is easily made the day before serving, extends the use of expensive prosciutto. For family meals, omit the prosciutto layer and enjoy the refreshing rice.

4 cups water
1 teaspoon salt
2 cups long-grain white rice
Wine Vinaigrette (see page 21; use white wine)
40 slices prosciutto (each about 7 in. long, about ¾ lb total)
6 green onions, diced
1 green bell pepper, diced
1 red bell pepper, diced

1. In a 2-quart saucepan bring the water and salt to a boil; stir in rice, reduce heat, and cover. Cook until water is absorbed and rice is tender (18 to 20 minutes). Toss with Wine Vinaigrette; cool.

2. Dice 6 slices prosciutto. Toss prosciutto, green onions, and peppers with rice. Reserve.

3. Line a 3-quart, round-bottomed mixing bowl with plastic wrap. Lay a slice of prosciutto along side of bowl, with one end in the center of the bottom and the other at the rim. Continue placing prosciutto around inside of bowl, overlapping slices about ½ inch, to cover interior completely.

4. Carefully fill prosciutto-lined bowl with rice salad. Cover top of salad with plastic wrap and gently press rice to remove any air pockets. Place a weight on salad and chill for 1 to 24 hours.

5. To unmold, remove plastic wrap and invert a serving plate over salad. Invert salad and serving plate together and lift off bowl. Gently remove plastic wrap and discard. Peel back prosciutto partway to reveal some of the rice; let prosciutto slices fall back like the petals of an opening flower.

Makes 10 cups; 8 to 10 servings as an appetizer, 12 to 20 as part of a buffet supper.

BASIL-CHEESE FEUILLETÉE

This dish can be held in the freezer for entertaining on a busy day. Serve it as a first course or cut in thin strips for cocktail fare. The amount of salt needed in the recipe will vary, depending on the taste of the cheeses.

¾ cup (4 oz) grated Parmesan cheese
½ cup (4 oz) grated fontina cheese
½ cup (4 oz) grated Jarlsberg cheese
1 pound ricotta cheese
¾ cup julienned fresh basil
Salt and ground white pepper, to taste
Quick Puff Pastry (see opposite page)
1 egg beaten with 2 tablespoons water, for glaze

1. In a 3-quart bowl stir together cheeses and basil. Season with salt and pepper, if needed.

2. Line a baking sheet with parchment paper. Roll half the Quick Puff Pastry into a rectangle 6 inches wide by 18 inches long. Place pastry rectangle on baking sheet. Mound filling down center of pastry strip, leaving a 2-inch border on all sides. Brush border with 1 tablespoon water.

3. Roll second half Quick Puff Pastry into same size rectangle; set over first sheet, covering filling. Press border gently but firmly to seal. Press border of pastry all the way around with back of knife to create a decorative edge. Brush top of pastry with egg-water glaze, taking care not to let any glaze drip over sides of pastry. Chill 1 to 24 hours or freeze, tightly wrapped.

4. One hour before serving, preheat the oven to 425° F. Bake Basil-Cheese Feuilletée until golden brown (35 minutes). Cool 5 minutes before serving. To serve, slice into thin strips about ¾ inch wide.

Serves 12.

RILLETTES

Always best when made days ahead, this aromatic and simple pork spread is a wonderful party appetizer. Pack for picnic sandwiches or place in attractive crocks for holiday gifts.

3 pounds pork shoulder, cubed
1 pound pork fat
4 cups water
1 stalk celery, chopped
2 carrots, chopped
4 cloves garlic, sliced
1 tablespoon black peppercorns, crushed
1 tablespoon juniper berries, crushed
1 teaspoon dried thyme
1 dried bay leaf
1 teaspoon dried oregano
1 tablespoon salt
½ tablespoon freshly ground pepper

1. In a deep, 4-quart saucepan, place pork shoulder, pork fat, the water, celery, carrots, garlic, peppercorns, juniper berries, thyme, bay leaf, and oregano. Bring to a boil, reduce heat, and simmer for 3 hours.

2. Remove bay leaf and discard. Place one third of mixture in a mixing bowl or bowl of a heavy-duty mixer. Beat to a smooth paste. Add remaining mixture in thirds, beating to a paste after each addition. Season with salt and pepper. Place in a serving terrine and chill for up to 10 days. Serve with crusty French bread and *cornichons* (tiny French pickles).

Serves 25 to 30 as an appetizer.

QUICK PUFF PASTRY

A tender, flaky alternative to the more time-consuming original, this Quick Puff Pastry can be used in any recipe calling for traditional puff pastry. Traditional puff pastry will rise spectacularly from its original thickness. This Quick Puff Pastry will rise almost as high and is made in half the time. It is well-suited to large-scale entertaining because it freezes beautifully if wrapped airtight, and is therefore one less menu component to prepare at the last minute. Defrost in the refrigerator overnight, ready to use in the morning, or for four hours at room temperature. Shaped puff pastry (such as the rectangles used in Ratatouille Mille-Feuilles, page 115) can be baked directly from the freezer. Wrap this pastry around sausage as directed for the Andouille en Croûte (see page 110) or sprinkle with cheese for Parmesan Cheese Twists (at right) to serve with soup or Champagne.

QUICK PUFF PASTRY

In making this recipe, it is important to use cold butter and ice water and to work quickly. Stop mixing this pastry before it homogenizes and holds together. It should look quite rough and messy after the first mixing in step 1. If freezing dough, roll first to about ½ inch thick; it will defrost faster and be easier to roll. Cold ingredients and careful folds are key to making the pastry rise. When brushing the cut shapes with beaten egg before baking, do not allow any egg to drip over the edge—this prevents the pastry from rising as high. For convenience, freeze pastry in pound and half-pound packages.

   3 cups flour, plus flour for dusting
   1½ teaspoons salt
   2¼ cups cold butter, diced
   ⅔ to ¾ cup ice water

1. In a 3-quart bowl stir together flour and salt. Cut in butter, leaving large pieces the size of almonds (don't let butter warm or soften). Dough will appear rough, with the bits of butter showing. Dust work surface lightly with flour and place dough mass on it.

2. Pat dough into a rectangle about 8 by 14 inches, placing a shorter edge parallel to front edge of work surface. Using a metal spatula or a pastry scraper, lift third of dough nearest you up and fold over center third (as if folding a business letter). Lift farthest third of dough and fold over center. Dust work surface and top of dough lightly with flour as needed. Turn dough so that shorter end is parallel to table edge.

3. Roll dough to form an 8- by 14-inch rectangle and repeat folds to resemble a business letter. Turn, roll, and fold dough 2 more times for a total of 4 turns. Chill dough 30 minutes. Dough can now be frozen in a rectangle or rolled into various shapes before freezing.

Makes about 2½ pounds pastry.

PARMESAN CHEESE TWISTS

These twists can be baked ahead, cooled, and frozen. Refresh in a 350° F oven for 5 to 8 minutes.

   1 pound Quick Puff Pastry
   1 egg, beaten
   ½ cup freshly grated Parmesan cheese

1. Roll Quick Puff Pastry ⅜ inch thick; brush with egg and sprinkle with ¼ cup Parmesan. Lightly press in cheese with a rolling pin. Turn over. Cover with remaining Parmesan; press in.

2. Cut pastry sheets into 24 strips, each ¾ inch wide. Twist gently and place on parchment-lined baking sheets. Chill 30 minutes. Preheat oven to 425° F. Bake until golden brown and crisp (about 12 minutes).

Makes 2 dozen twists.

Salt Sticks   Omit Parmesan cheese. Sprinkle puff pastry with 2 tablespoons coarse salt.

A weekend of parties will burnish your reputation for spectacular entertaining. Host a formal sit-down dinner on Friday evening and a festive buffet on Sunday.

BACK-TO-BACK ENTERTAINING

NEW ORLEANS–STYLE FORMAL DINNER FOR 8 (FRIDAY EVENING)

Rillettes (see page 104) and French Bread

Prawns Rémoulade (see page 108)

Chicken and Andouille Jambalaya (see page 108)

Crisp Asparagus and Red Bell Pepper Sauté (see page 108)

Cheddar Biscuits (see page 94)

Onion and Red Pepper Marmalade (see page 109)

All-American Apple and Quince Pie (see page 109)

Beer (Dinner) and Chicory Coffee (Dessert)

MARDI GRAS OPEN HOUSE FOR 30 (SUNDAY AFTERNOON)

Rillettes (see page 104) and French Bread

Skewered Prawns With Rémoulade Sauce (see page 108)

Buffalo Chicken Wings (see page 110)

Andouille en Croûte (see page 110)

Cheddar Cheese, Crackers, And Apple Slices

Asparagus and Red Bell Pepper Strips With Vinaigrette (see page 108)

Beer and Robust Red Wine

One Menu, Two Parties

On Friday night create a formal atmosphere, with candles, elegant linens, and good silver. An open house on Sunday will use the same decor and food but will have a more casual feel because it is not a sit-down meal.

Preparation Plan

Giving two parties back-to-back makes sense. Shopping, cleaning, cooking, and choosing flowers or other table decor can be organized in advance for both days. Entertaining guests only 48 hours apart may sound frantic, but it is a sensible way to entertain if you allow a day between occasions to get organized for the second meal. Menus should feature similar foods and components so that recipes can be doubled or tripled, thereby saving cooking time.

Make one recipe of Rillettes the weekend before the party; store a small amount in a 2-cup mold for Friday night and the rest in a 1½-quart mold for Sunday. Cook Onion and Red Pepper Marmalade the weekend before; it keeps well in the refrigerator. Make Roquefort Dressing for Buffalo Chicken Wings and store in the refrigerator. Prepare All-American Apple and Quince Pie and freeze; bake from the freezer on Friday. Buy enough apples so that 6 are left over for fruit and cheese tray for Sunday. Make 2 recipes Rémoulade Sauce and store in the refrigerator until needed. You can do most of the cooking for both parties on Wednesday and Thursday evenings, or you can prepare the dinner on Friday and still have all day Saturday to work on the larger Sunday supper buffet. Shop for staples the weekend before and purchase perishables on Thursday. Set the table on

Wednesday night. Purchase French bread fresh each day.

On Thursday buy 6 pounds asparagus and 6 large red bell peppers (enough for both parties). Buy 2½ pounds Cheddar cheese; shred 4 ounces for biscuits. Refrigerate remainder for Sunday's fruit and cheese tray. Trim vegetables and store in clean plastic bags in the refrigerator until needed. Measure the dry ingredients for the Cheese Biscuits; mix, cut, and bake them on Friday.

On Friday purchase 10 pounds chicken drummettes (4 pounds for the chicken jambalaya and 6 pounds for the Buffalo Chicken Wings) and the prawns. Marinate the chicken for Buffalo Chicken Wings and reserve in the refrigerator. Chop and dice ingredients for chicken jambalaya. Five pounds prawns will be enough for both parties, although guests will enjoy it if you provide more.

On Saturday finish cleaning up from Friday night and reset the table, this time for a buffet. Arrange beverages near a copper tub or the kitchen sink (cleanup is easy) and fill the tub with ice on Sunday. Marinate chicken wings for Sunday if this hasn't already been done. Wrap *andouille* in Quick Puff Pastry and chill until you bake it on Sunday. Make Basic Vinaigrette as a dip for the asparagus and red bell pepper strips.

On Sunday arrange Rillettes; slice French bread and store in plastic bags until just before you need it. Place asparagus and red pepper strips on a tray, with Basic Vinaigrette in the center. Use whole apples and quinces for table decorations. Prepare a serving tray of shrimp skewers and store in the refrigerator until guests arrive. Cook Andouille en Croûte and Buffalo Chicken Wings and arrange just before serving. Just before the guests arrive, surround Cheddar cheese on a plate with an array of apple slices and crackers.

PRAWNS RÉMOULADE

Serve five prawns per guest on Friday. Boil the 1½ pounds prawns for Friday dinner separately from Sunday's batch, which will be skewered before boiling (see variation). For Sunday, you will need 3½ pounds prawns.

> 1½ pounds medium (26 per lb) prawns, shelled
> 4 cups shredded lettuce
> Rémoulade Sauce (see page 20)
> Cherry tomatoes and black olives, for garnish

1. In a 4½-quart saucepan bring 4 quarts water to a boil. Reduce heat, add prawns, and simmer until they turn bright pink (1 to 2 minutes). Remove from simmering water and plunge into ice water to stop cooking. Remove and pat dry. Reserve.

2. For each serving, place ½ cup shredded lettuce on a salad plate. Divide prawns among salad plates and top with a dollop of Rémoulade Sauce. Garnish with cherry tomatoes and black olives.

Serves 8.

Skewered Prawns With Rémoulade Sauce   For the Sunday party, cook the 3½ pounds prawns: To cook the prawns on skewers, insert a bamboo skewer into each prawn, starting with the tail and holding the prawn so it is straight when skewered; plunge skewered prawns into simmering water, letting skewers rest on edge of pan, until prawns are bright pink (1 to 2 minutes). Remove from simmering water and plunge into ice water to stop cooking. Remove and pat dry. Accompany with a savoy cabbage that has been hollowed and filled with Rémoulade Sauce, to be used for dipping.

Serves about 30.

CHICKEN AND ANDOUILLE JAMBALAYA

Easily expanded entrées like this jambalaya are great for large parties or formal dinners for eight guests. Serve from a large tureen at the table, family style, or on plates from the kitchen. *Andouille,* a smoked Cajun sausage, lends a characteristic spiciness to this dish.

> 4 pounds chicken drummettes or 2 pounds boneless chicken breast
> 5 tablespoons oil
> 1 pound andouille
> 2 onions, chopped
> 2 stalks celery, chopped
> 1 carrot, chopped
> 1 green bell pepper, chopped
> 2 cloves garlic, minced
> 2 tablespoons flour
> 8 plum tomatoes, peeled, seeded, and chopped, or 1 can (28 oz) plum tomatoes, drained and chopped
> 1 teaspoon cayenne pepper
> 1 teaspoon dried thyme
> 1 tablespoon salt
> ½ tablespoon freshly ground black pepper
> 5 cups Chicken Stock (see page 56)
> 2 cups long-grain white rice
> ¼ cup chopped parsley, for garnish

1. Pat chicken drummettes dry. If using chicken breast, slice each into 5 pieces. In a 6-quart Dutch oven over medium-high heat, add 2 tablespoons oil and sauté chicken until light brown (about 10 minutes); remove and reserve.

2. Cut andouille into pieces about 2½ inches long. In same Dutch oven over medium heat, sauté andouille until lightly browned (about 10 minutes). Remove with a slotted spoon and drain on paper towels.

3. In remaining oil over medium heat, sauté onions, celery, carrot, bell pepper, and garlic until golden brown (10 to 12 minutes). Stir in flour and cook until light brown (about 10 minutes). Stir in tomatoes. Season with cayenne, thyme, salt, and pepper.

4. Add Chicken Stock; bring to a boil over medium-high heat and add rice and chicken. Reduce heat to a simmer and cook, covered, until liquid is absorbed and rice is tender (about 20 minutes). Stir in reserved andouille and cook another 15 minutes. Sprinkle with parsley and serve piping hot.

Serves 8.

CRISP ASPARAGUS AND RED BELL PEPPER SAUTÉ

Prepare the asparagus earlier in the day and reheat at serving time. Any leftover vegetables can be tossed with Basic Vinaigrette (see page 21) or served with the Rémoulade Sauce (see page 20) at Sunday's party.

> 2 pounds thin asparagus
> 4 tablespoons olive oil
> 1 small red onion, sliced thinly
> 2 red bell peppers, sliced thinly
> 1 bunch basil, sliced thinly
> Salt and freshly ground pepper, to taste

1. In a 4½-quart saucepan over medium-high heat, bring 4 quarts water to a boil. Trim any dry stem ends from asparagus. Place asparagus in boiling water, reduce heat to medium, and cook until tender when pierced with a knife (about 3 minutes). Plunge into ice water to stop cooking.

2. In a wok or 14-inch skillet over medium heat, add olive oil and sauté onion until slightly wilted (5 minutes). Stir in bell pepper, asparagus, basil, salt, and pepper and cook until hot (4 to 5 minutes), tossing to combine.

Serves 8.

Asparagus and Red Bell Pepper Strips With Vinaigrette   For the Sunday party, prepare 4 pounds asparagus and 4 bell peppers as directed in Crisp Asparagus and Red Bell Pepper Sauté. Cook asparagus as directed. Serve asparagus and bell pepper strips with a bowl of Basic Vinaigrette (see page 21) for dipping.

Serves 20 to 30.

ONION AND RED BELL PEPPER MARMALADE

Long, slow cooking makes this colorful condiment pungent and sweet. Prepare one week before the party, and refrigerate until needed. It can be served hot or cold, with chicken, sausage, hamburgers, or roast pork.

    8 medium-sized yellow onions,
       diced coarsely
    3 large red bell peppers, diced
    3 cloves garlic, sliced
    ½ cup olive oil
    7 tablespoons good-quality
       white wine vinegar
       (Chardonnay, if available)
    4 teaspoons sugar
    1 teaspoon salt
       Freshly ground pepper, to taste

1. In a deep, 14-inch sauté pan over medium heat, sauté onions, peppers, and garlic in olive oil until onions are translucent (8 to 10 minutes).

2. Add water to onion-pepper mixture to cover and bring to a boil over medium-high heat. Reduce heat to low and simmer 2½ hours, stirring frequently.

3. Stir in vinegar, sugar, salt, and pepper and cook 20 minutes more. Store in an airtight container in the refrigerator.

Makes 6 cups.

ALL-AMERICAN APPLE AND QUINCE PIE

Quince, the "golden apple" of Greek mythology, is a tart fruit that is usually cooked, rather than eaten raw. Apples or pears can be substituted, if desired.

       Butter Pastry (see page 12)
    4 *tart baking apples, peeled
       and cored*
    2 *quinces, peeled and cored*
    ½ *cup sugar*
    3 *tablespoons flour*
    2 *teaspoons ground cardamom*
    1 *teaspoon ground cinnamon*
    2 *teaspoons rose water*
    4 *tablespoons unsalted
       butter, cubed*
    2 *tablespoons whipping
       cream, for glaze*

1. Preheat oven to 400° F. Roll two thirds of the Butter Pastry into a circle about 14 inches in diameter. Transfer to a 9-inch pie plate.

2. Slice apples and quinces into 8 pieces each. Place in a 3-quart bowl and toss with sugar, flour, cardamom, cinnamon, and rose water. Pour into prepared pie crust. Dot with cubes of butter.

3. Roll remaining Butter Pastry 1 inch larger than diameter of pie pan (10 inches) and place over fruit mixture. Crimp edges of pastry to seal, and cut small, decorative slashes in top crust. Brush with cream. (Pie can be frozen at this time.)

4. Bake until lightly browned on top (55 to 65 minutes; if baking frozen pie, add 40 minutes to baking time). Serve warm.

Serves 8.

Jambalaya is a favorite Cajun one-pot meal that is perfect buffet fare. Keep the dish warm over a low flame or a chafing dish candle.

BUFFALO CHICKEN WINGS

Chicken drummettes are the second joint of the chicken wing and resemble miniature chicken legs. Marinate the chicken all day and deep-fry at the last minute, or fry the wings up to 2 hours before the party and warm in a 350° F oven for 15 minutes at serving time. Or, bake the chicken wings at 400° F until golden brown (about 45 minutes). Allow 2 or 3 chicken wings per guest. Roquefort dressing and celery sticks are traditional condiments.

½ pound butter, melted
⅓ cup vegetable oil
6 tablespoons hot-pepper sauce
3 cloves garlic, minced
2 tablespoons dried basil
2 teaspoons salt
½ teaspoon freshly ground pepper
6 pounds (about 60) chicken drummettes
3 cups oil, for deep-frying
12 lemon wedges, for garnish
20 celery sticks, for garnish

Roquefort Dressing

6 ounces Roquefort cheese
1 cup sour cream
2 tablespoons mayonnaise
Freshly ground pepper, to taste

1. In a 1-quart saucepan over low heat, melt butter and oil. Stir in hot-pepper sauce, garlic, basil, salt, and pepper. Place drummettes in a roasting pan in one layer and pour marinade over chicken. Toss to coat thoroughly; marinate 2 to 48 hours.

2. Near end of marinating time, heat the 3 cups oil in a 14-inch wok or deep pan to 375° F. Remove chicken wings from marinade; fry until golden brown (about 4 minutes). Turn and brown other side (about 4 minutes). Drain on paper towels; keep warm in a 200° F oven for up to 2 hours. Serve with Roquefort Dressing, lemon wedges, and celery sticks.

Makes about 60 drummettes, 20 to 30 appetizer servings.

Roquefort Dressing Mix Roquefort, sour cream, and mayonnaise together. Season with pepper.

Makes 1¼ cups.

ANDOUILLE EN CROÛTE

A cooked Italian sausage could be substituted for the *andouille*, but the spicy, smoky flavor of the latter is a dramatic contrast to the light, crisp puff pastry.

1 egg, beaten
2 tablespoons water
¼ cup flour
3 pounds andouille
2 recipes Quick Puff Pastry (see page 105)
Creole mustard, for accompaniment

1. Line 2 baking sheets with parchment paper. In a small bowl beat together egg and the water. Place flour in a shallow dish or on work surface. In a 4½-quart saucepan bring 4 quarts of water to a boil, add andouille, and cook 15 minutes. Remove from cooking water and cool for 10 minutes.

2. Roll out each recipe Quick Puff Pastry into a 10½-inch square that is ½ inch thick. Cut each square into 3 strips, each 3½ inches wide by 10½ inches long. Cut andouille into 10½-inch lengths (if andouille pieces are less than 10½ inches long, place several pieces end to end in order to make correct length). Roll andouille in flour, brush with beaten egg mixture, and place down center of each pastry strip. Brush long edge with water. Roll to enclose sausage in pastry and place, seam side down, on baking sheet; chill 1 to 24 hours. Near end of chilling time, preheat oven to 400° F.

3. Brush andouille rolls with remaining beaten egg mixture and bake until golden brown and hot (about 30 minutes); cool 5 minutes. Slice thinly (about ½ inch thick) and serve with Creole mustard.

Serves about 30.

MAIN COURSES

The main dishes here can be doubled or tripled, or frozen easily for later use. Choose Ground Beef Roulade Pizzaiola (see page 114) and serve one roll at a time while the extra keeps warm in the oven ready for late arrivals. The broth for Indonesian Seafood Stew (see page 113) can be prepared well in advance, with the seafood added at the last minute. Delhi Indian Curry (see page 113) can be frozen and reheated.

CHICKEN MOLE BUDINES

Chicken Mole Budines store well in the refrigerator or in the freezer, although if you are planning to let the dish sit, you may want to use fewer chiles because the spiciness increases with time. Dried chiles can be purchased in Latin American markets or can be found in the specialty food section of the supermarket.

½ cup whole almonds, toasted
6 dried New Mexico chiles
4 dried chiles chipotles
4 tablespoons vegetable oil
5 pounds chicken legs and thighs, boned and cubed
2 onions, diced
2 cloves garlic, minced
1½ teaspoons salt
1 tablespoon ground cinnamon
¼ cup raisins
½ teaspoon cumin seed
¼ cup minced cilantro
½ ounce unsweetened chocolate
3 cups Chicken Stock (see page 56)
14 flour tortillas (10-in. diameter)
2 cups warm refried beans
2 cups Avocado Salsa (see page 47)
½ cup grated Monterey jack cheese
16 sprigs cilantro, for garnish
South-of-the-Border Salsa (see page 47), for garnish
2 cups sour cream, for garnish

1. Toast almonds in a 350° F oven for 8 minutes; grind coarsely and reserve.

2. Place chiles in a 1-quart bowl and cover with boiling water. Let soak 30 minutes. Remove and cut in thin strips. Reserve 2 cups soaking liquid.

3. In an 8-quart Dutch oven over medium-high heat, add 2 tablespoons oil and sauté half the chicken pieces until lightly browned (about 8 minutes). Remove and reserve. Repeat with remaining oil and chicken; remove and reserve.

4. Add onions and garlic to Dutch oven and cook until softened (7 to 8 minutes). Stir in chile strips, reserved soaking liquid, salt, cinnamon, raisins, cumin seed, cilantro, chocolate, and Chicken Stock. Bring to a boil, return browned chicken to pan, reduce heat, and simmer for

30 minutes. Add 6 tablespoons ground almonds and stir to thicken.

5. To assemble *budín*: Place a flour tortilla on an ovenproof serving dish. Spread with 1½ cups chicken mixture. Top with another tortilla. Spread with ½ cup refried beans, top with another tortilla, and spread with ½ cup Avocado Salsa; repeat layers, top with a tortilla, and sprinkle with ¼ cup grated cheese. Make another budín with remaining tortillas, chicken filling, beans, salsa, and cheese. Reserve until serving time.

6. Fifteen minutes before serving, preheat oven to 375° F. Place budines in oven and bake until piping hot and cheese has melted (about 20 minutes). To serve, cut each into 8 wedges; dot with cilantro sprigs; and sprinkle with remaining 2 tablespoons ground almonds. Let guests garnish with salsa and a dollop of sour cream.

Makes 2 budines; 16 servings.

The savory chicken filling of this layered tortilla main course is flavored with unsweetened chocolate, typical of a Mexican mole sauce.

Harvest the best of autumn's flavors with a tart-sweet Cranberry and Corn Bread Stuffing, here used to fill extra-thick pork chops.

CRANBERRY-STUFFED PORK CHOPS

When you have a special guest list, fill the center of a crown roast of pork with a double batch of this savory stuffing. Ask the butcher to tie the two loins, about 24 pork chops, together in a circle. If you don't want to wait for a special occasion, stuff double-thick pork chops with the same tasty corn bread mixture. Serve with Carrot Purée (see page 34) and Crisp Asparagus and Red Bell Pepper Sauté (see page 108).

> 6 *thick pork chops (about 1 in. thick)*
> 5 *cups Cranberry and Corn Bread Stuffing (see page 122)*
> 4 *tablespoons oil*

Sage Marinade

> 3 *tablespoons olive oil*
> 2 *cloves garlic, minced*
> 2 *tablespoons dried sage*

1. Preheat oven to 425° F. Rub marinade into pork chops. Make a horizontal pocket in pork chops, cutting through to bone. Place about ¾ cup Cranberry and Corn Bread Stuffing in each pork chop cavity.

2. In a large skillet over medium heat, add 3 tablespoons oil; cook 2 or 3 chops at a time until browned on one side (about 5 minutes). Turn and brown second side (about 3 minutes). Remove and reserve. Add remaining oil and repeat with remaining chops.

3. Place pork chops in a small roasting pan and bake 25 minutes. Serve immediately.

Serves 6.

Sage Marinade   In a small bowl stir together all ingredients.

Makes about ¼ cup.

INDONESIAN SEAFOOD STEW

This lavish and colorful stew can be served with rice, couscous, or crusty French bread. The broth may be prepared ahead of guests' arrival and simply reheated with the seafood at the last minute. Scrub clams, peel prawns, and cube red snapper, and chill until 10 minutes before serving. Fresh lemongrass is found in Thai or Asian specialty food stores; it can be omitted from the recipe if unavailable. Canned coconut milk is often sold in the specialty food section of the supermarket.

> 1 pound medium prawns
> ½ cup butter
> 4 tablespoons vegetable oil
> 4 onions, finely diced
> 2 carrots, peeled and diced
> 2 cloves garlic, minced
> 2 tablespoons grated fresh ginger
> 1 stalk fresh lemongrass, diced (optional)
> 2½ tablespoons kosher salt
> 2 teaspoons freshly ground black pepper
> 1 teaspoon cayenne pepper
> ¼ gram (½ teaspoon) saffron threads
> 1 teaspoon ground turmeric
> 1 teaspoon ground cinnamon
> 1 teaspoon hot-pepper flakes
> 10 cups Fish Stock (see page 57) or water
> 5 ripe tomatoes or 1 can (15 oz) plum tomatoes, chopped
> 2 cups coconut milk
> 2 cups fresh mint (leaves and thin stems), chopped
> 2 pounds clams or mussels, scrubbed
> 1 pound scallops
> 3 pounds red snapper fillets, cut into cubes

1. Shell prawns (do not discard shells) and reserve meat in refrigerator until serving time. In a large stockpot heat the butter and oil. Sauté prawn shells in butter-oil mixture until shells turn pink (5 to 10 minutes). Remove and discard.

2. Add onions, carrots, and garlic. Sauté 5 minutes and add ginger, lemongrass (if used), salt, pepper, cayenne, saffron, turmeric, cinnamon, hot-pepper flakes, stock, tomatoes, coconut milk, and mint. Bring to a boil, reduce heat to simmer, and cook 20 to 25 minutes. Refrigerate if not serving immediately.

3. To serve, bring soup to a boil and reduce heat to simmer. Add clams and cook for 2 minutes; reduce heat and add prawn meat, scallops, and red snapper cubes. Simmer until prawns turn bright pink and snapper cubes are translucent (5 to 6 minutes). Discard any unopened clams.

Serves 12 as a main course, 20 as a first course.

DELHI INDIAN CURRY

A curry buffet is not only easy on the cook but beautiful on the table. The traditional condiments—cilantro raita, cucumbers in yogurt, tomato chutney, mango chutney, cooked bacon, minced green onions, coarsely chopped peanuts, shredded coconut, deep-fried garlic chips, diced green bell pepper, dried currants, and steamed basmati rice—can be arranged in bowls circling the chafing dish of curry.

> 6 boneless chicken breast halves
> 2 tablespoons vegetable oil
> 3 tablespoons unsalted butter
> 1 medium onion, diced
> 2 cloves garlic, minced
> 1 apple, diced
> 1 green bell pepper, diced
> 1 jalapeño chile, minced
> 2 tablespoons curry powder
> ½ teaspoon salt
> ¼ cup flour
> 1½ to 2 cups Chicken Stock (see page 56)

1. Cut chicken breasts into 2-inch cubes. In a 14-inch skillet over medium heat, sauté chicken pieces in oil until lightly brown (about 12 minutes). Remove and reserve.

2. In same skillet over medium heat, melt butter. Stir in onion and garlic and sauté until lightly browned (6 to 8 minutes). Stir in chicken pieces, apple, bell pepper, chile, curry powder, salt, and flour. Cook, stirring, for 15 minutes. Stir in Chicken Stock and simmer 20 minutes to meld flavors.

3. Serve from a chafing dish or placed on a warming tray surrounded by condiments of choice.

Serves 8.

SALT-BAKED PRIME RIB OF BEEF

Moist and flavorful prime rib of beef is guaranteed with this simple recipe. Serve with Turnip and Leek Purée (see page 116) and Nora's Potato Gratin (see page 30).

> 3 pounds kosher or coarse salt
> 5 cloves garlic, minced
> ½ cup minced parsley
> 1 tablespoon dried basil
> 1 teaspoon dried oregano
> 4½ pounds prime rib of beef, boned and tied

1. Preheat oven to 425° F. In a 3-quart bowl combine salt, garlic, parsley, basil, and oregano. Place one third of the mixture in a 4-quart Dutch oven. Lay beef on salt mixture. Distribute remaining salt mixture around beef to cover completely.

2. Cook to desired doneness (125° F for rare, 130° F for medium, and 135° F for well-done on an instant-read thermometer; 1 hour and 20 minutes of cooking will produce a roast that is medium at each end and rare in the center). Remove from oven and let rest for 10 minutes. Slice ½ to ¾ inch thick. Serve warm.

Serves 6 to 8.

BARBARA'S SOUTHWEST TORTA

If it is more convenient, prepare this colorful and simple *torta* ahead and warm in a 350° F oven for 20 minutes before serving.

        5 tablespoons butter, melted
        7 flour tortillas
          (10-in. diameter)
        1 pound ground sausage
        1 onion, diced
        1 red bell pepper, diced
        1 jalapeño chile, diced
        1 teaspoon chili powder
     1¼ teaspoons salt
        ¼ teaspoon dried oregano
        1 tablespoon toasted cumin seed
        1 can (15 oz) cooked
          black beans
        ¾ cup (6 oz) grated Monterey
          jack cheese
        8 eggs, beaten
        ¼ teaspoon freshly ground
          pepper
        3 green onions, diced

1. Preheat oven to 350° F. Line a 9-inch springform pan with aluminum foil. Brush foil with 1 tablespoon melted butter. Place 5 tortillas around perimeter of foil-lined pan. Place 1 tortilla in center of pan to cover bottom entirely. Brush tortillas with 2 tablespoons butter.

2. In a 12-inch skillet over medium heat, sauté sausage until browned and crumbly (about 10 minutes). Add onion, bell pepper, chile, chili powder, ¼ teaspoon salt, oregano, and cumin seed, and cook until onion is tender (about 10 minutes).

3. Place sausage mixture in tortilla-lined baking dish; reserve cooking pan. Cover sausage with beans and Monterey jack.

4. In reserved skillet over medium heat, add remaining 2 tablespoons butter and scramble eggs. Stir in remaining salt, pepper, and green onions, undercooking eggs slightly. Press eggs over beans and cheese. Place remaining tortilla over eggs and brush with remaining butter. Place in oven and bake 25 minutes.

Cool 5 minutes before serving. To unmold, loosen edges with a knife; remove pan sides. Loosen bottom, then remove pan bottom. Peel away foil. Cut into 8 wedges and serve.

Serves 8.

ROAST BEEF HASH

Hash is one of the best ways to use leftover roast beef or corned beef.

        ½ cup butter
        2 large onions, finely chopped
        1 clove garlic, minced
        2 medium potatoes, cooked
          and diced
        4 cups cooked, diced prime
          rib of beef
        2 teaspoons dried basil
        ½ cup minced parsley
        1 teaspoon salt
        ¼ teaspoon freshly ground
          pepper
        2 ripe tomatoes, thickly
          sliced, for garnish

1. In a large, heavy frying pan over medium heat, melt 2 tablespoons butter until foamy. Add onions and garlic and cook, stirring occasionally, until onions are soft and golden (about 20 minutes).

2. Swirl in 2 tablespoons more butter, then lightly mix in potatoes, beef, basil, parsley, salt, and pepper. Press mixture down lightly with a spatula. Cook over medium heat until bottom of hash is golden brown (about 10 minutes). Loosen hash with spatula. Cover pan with a large plate and invert hash onto plate.

3. Add 2 more tablespoons butter to pan and slide hash from plate back into frying pan. Continue cooking slowly until bottom is golden brown (10 to 15 minutes). Once again, cover pan with a large plate and invert hash onto plate.

4. Working quickly, add remaining butter to pan and swirl until melted. Add sliced tomatoes to pan and sauté briefly to warm through (about 1 minute). Using a spatula, place tomatoes on Roast Beef Hash and serve immediately.

Serves 4 to 6.

GROUND BEEF ROULADE PIZZAIOLA

This simple roulade is half the work of pizza but has the same spicy flavors. It can be doubled or tripled for big parties and stored in the freezer until needed. To cook frozen roulade, just add an extra 30 minutes to the baking time.

     1½ pounds ground beef
     1½ pounds ground pork
        1 onion, minced
        4 cloves garlic, minced
        1 green bell pepper, diced
        1 egg
        2 tablespoons tomato paste
        1 tablespoon dried oregano
        1 tablespoon dried basil
     1½ teaspoon salt
        ½ pound mozzarella cheese,
          sliced thinly
        ¼ pound salami, sliced thinly
        3 tablespoons freshly grated
          Parmesan cheese
          Fresh Tomato Sauce (see page
          47), for accompaniment

1. Preheat oven to 350° F. In a 3-quart bowl place beef, pork, onion, garlic, bell pepper, egg, tomato paste, oregano, basil, and salt, and stir well to combine thoroughly.

2. Cut a piece of aluminum foil about 16 inches long. Pat ground meat mixture onto aluminum foil, covering foil (mixture will be about ¼ to ½ inch thick). Place mozzarella on meat mixture to cover. Next, place salami over cheese, also to cover. Roll up ground meat mixture jelly-roll fashion, peeling mixture from foil as it is rolled.

3. Press ends together to seal in filling. Place ground meat roll on a baking sheet with sides and sprinkle with Parmesan. Bake until browned (55 minutes). Let rest 5 minutes before cutting. To serve, slice about ¾ inch thick. Accompany with Fresh Tomato Sauce.

Serves 10 to 12.

ACCOMPANIMENTS

Crisp and varied side dishes are often the most difficult to prepare ahead. The best side dishes are frequently simple: steamed broccoli, sautéed green beans, or baked winter squash. These foods can be prepared at the last minute by a relaxed cook who has planned thoughtfully. Other side dishes in this chapter, such as Ratatouille Mille-Feuilles (see below), have components that can be assembled in advance and frozen, ready to bake and serve. The puff pastry awaits in the freezer, and the ratatouille can be made several days before the party. Vegetable purées, such as the turnip and leek version on page 116, can be successfully frozen and reheated in a double boiler.

RATATOUILLE MILLE-FEUILLES

Small squares, diamonds, or circles of airy puff pastry can become the base for all sorts of vegetable *mille-feuilles*. This recipe calls for a ratatouille filling.

> 1 medium eggplant, diced
> 1 tablespoon salt
> 8 tablespoons olive oil
> 1 onion, diced
> 2 cloves garlic, minced
> 2 zucchini, diced
> 1 yellow bell pepper, diced
> 8 medium tomatoes, peeled, seeded, and quartered
> 1 tablespoon dried basil
> 1 teaspoon dried oregano
> 1 teaspoon dried thyme
> Freshly ground black pepper
> 12 rectangles (4- by 3-in.) Quick Puff Pastry (see page 105)
> 1 egg, beaten
> ¼ cup freshly grated Parmesan cheese

1. Place eggplant in a colander and sprinkle with 2 teaspoons salt. Let sit 30 minutes. Rinse and pat dry.

2. In a 14-inch skillet over medium heat, add 3 tablespoons olive oil; cook half the eggplant cubes until lightly browned (about 5 minutes). Remove to a platter and reserve. Add 3 more tablespoons olive oil to skillet and cook remaining eggplant until lightly browned (about 5 minutes). Remove to a platter and reserve.

3. Add remaining olive oil to skillet; cook onion and garlic until translucent (about 5 minutes). Return eggplant to skillet. Stir in zucchini, bell pepper, tomatoes, basil, oregano, thyme, remaining salt, and pepper. Simmer, stirring occasionally, 20 minutes; reduce heat to low and then keep warm.

4. While eggplant mixture is simmering, preheat oven to 425° F. Line a baking sheet with parchment paper. Place Quick Puff Pastry rectangles on baking sheet. Brush tops of rectangles with beaten egg, taking care not to let egg drip over sides of pastry. Sprinkle each rectangle with 1 teaspoon Parmesan cheese. Bake until brown and crisp (about 24 minutes).

5. Remove from oven and halve each rectangle horizontally. Place about ½ cup ratatouille on bottom half of each rectangle, top with remaining rectangle, and serve immediately.

Serves 12.

Flaky puff pastry rectangles form edible cases for ratatouille, the French herb-flavored vegetable stew.

TURNIP AND LEEK PURÉE

Vegetable purées keep well in the refrigerator for up to three days or in the freezer for up to one month. Reheat in the top of a double boiler over low heat. If your double boiler is too small, create one by placing a large stainless steel mixing bowl in a shallow pan of simmering water.

    4   medium leeks, cleaned
        and chopped
    3   tablespoons butter
    8   small turnips, peeled
        and diced
    2   cups water
 1½   teaspoons salt
    ½   teaspoon freshly grated
        nutmeg
    ¼   teaspoon ground white pepper

1. In a 3-quart saucepan over low heat, cook leeks in butter until translucent and softened (about 20 minutes).

2. Stir in turnips, the water, and salt. Simmer over low heat until tender (about 25 minutes).

3. When turnips are easily pierced with a knife, remove vegetables and purée in a food processor or blender until smooth. Season with nutmeg and pepper.

Serves 12 to 16.

QUICK CORN BREAD

Use this wonderful corn bread as a base for stuffing turkey or pork chops, or serve straight from the oven with Green Onion–Dill Butter (see page 75).

    4   tablespoons butter, plus butter
        for greasing pan (optional)
    1   cup milk
    2   eggs
    1   cup flour
 1½   teaspoons baking powder
    2   teaspoons salt
 1½   teaspoons sugar
    1   cup cornmeal

1. Preheat oven to 400° F. Butter an 8-inch-square baking pan, or line pan with parchment paper.

2. In a small bowl combine the 4 tablespoons butter, milk, and eggs. In a 3-quart bowl, sift together flour, baking powder, salt, and sugar; stir in cornmeal, and make a well in center. Gradually stir milk mixture into dry ingredients until just combined and slightly lumpy. Do not overmix or corn bread will be tough.

3. Place mixture in prepared pan. Bake until top is golden brown (about 35 minutes).

Serves 8.

CHIVE AND CHEDDAR SPOON PUDDING

An old-fashioned side dish updated with Cheddar and chives makes a heartwarming, mouth-watering accompaniment to roast chicken, beef, or pork. This recipe is easily doubled or tripled for larger parties and will hold in a warm oven for about one hour. It is easily sliced and panfried the next morning for a delicious and unusual breakfast treat.

    5   tablespoons butter
    5   eggs
    ¾   cup buttermilk
 2¾   cups water
    1   teaspoon salt
    1   cup cornmeal
    ⅓   cup whipping cream
    ⅓   cup grated Cheddar cheese
    ¼   cup minced chives

1. Preheat oven to 425° F. Using 2 tablespoons of the butter, grease an 8-inch-diameter baking dish. Beat together eggs and buttermilk.

2. In a 3-quart saucepan bring remaining butter, the water, and salt to a boil. Slowly stir in cornmeal. Continue stirring mixture until it is smooth and pulls away from sides of pan (15 to 20 minutes). Stir in cream, cheese, chives, and the egg-buttermilk mixture. Pour into prepared baking dish and bake until firm and dry on top (20 to 25 minutes). Serve hot.

Serves 8.

BROCCOLI WITH HOLLANDAISE SAUCE

Steamed vegetables such as broccoli, asparagus, green beans, and Brussels sprouts can be dressed up with a spoonful of Hollandaise Sauce. Place the broccoli in the steamer basket when the butter for the Hollandaise is melted and hot. Both will be ready at the same time. This recipe can also be prepared as a variation of Ratatouille Mille-Feuilles (see page 115). Split a baked puff pastry rectangle in half horizontally; place the steamed broccoli on the bottom half, cover with the top half, and drizzle with Hollandaise Sauce.

    2   heads broccoli, cut in florets

Hollandaise Sauce
    ½   cup unsalted butter
    3   egg yolks
    ½   teaspoon salt
        Juice of 1 lemon

1. Fill a 4½-quart saucepan with water to a depth of 2 inches. Place a steamer basket or steamer insert into pan. Over medium heat bring the water to a boil.

2. Place broccoli in steamer basket and simmer until florets are easily pierced with a knife and bright green in color (about 4 minutes). Drizzle with Hollandaise Sauce and serve immediately.

Serves 12.

Hollandaise Sauce   In a small saucepan over high heat, melt butter. Place egg yolks, salt, and lemon juice in a blender or food processor and blend at high speed to thoroughly combine. With blender on high speed, pour hot butter into blender jar and blend until thickened.

Makes ⅔ cup.

DESSERTS

Pastries are often the easiest recipes to prepare ahead, but the most difficult to make in large batches. Crowded ovens and inaccurate measurements can create problems. When baking in quantity, always leave space in the oven for the hot air to circulate. To become familiar with the proper texture, cooking time, and appearance of a dessert, first prepare the recipe as written before increasing the yield. For greater accuracy, when possible weigh ingredients rather than using volume measurements; record the weight for future reference. If in doubt about whether a recipe will double or triple successfully, prepare it in several single batches. To shorten preparation time, measure all the ingredients at once, storing dry ingredients in clean plastic bags.

COFFEE SEMIFREDDO

Semifreddo means *half-chilled* in Italian. This lovely dessert multiplies readily and stores well in the freezer. It is customarily served just slightly melting.

- 1 *Milk Sponge Roll
  (see page 36)*
- 3 *tablespoons rum*
- ¼ *cup unsweetened cocoa*
- 1 *pint coffee ice cream, softened
  Chocolate Fudge Sauce
  (see page 37), for
  accompaniment*

1. Cut Milk Sponge Roll into 3 equal rectangles, each 5¼ inches by 11 inches. Sprinkle cake layers with rum; dust with some of the cocoa.

2. Place one cake layer on a serving tray. Cover with about 1 cup softened ice cream. Top with second layer and cover with 1 cup more ice cream; cover with third layer and freeze.

3. Twenty minutes before serving, remove cake from freezer and let rest at room temperature. Dust with remaining cocoa. Slice about 1 inch thick and place each slice on a chilled dessert plate. Drizzle with Chocolate Fudge Sauce. Serve immediately.

Serves 8 to 10.

Basics

DO AHEAD, DO NOW

Learning to organize cooking tasks into manageable segments will help you become more efficient in the kitchen. The following tasks are examples of how to divide the preparation of some common dishes into jobs that are "do ahead"—done in advance—and "do now"—done close to serving time.

Do Ahead

☐ Prepare and freeze muffins, bread, and unbaked fruit pies and tart shells up to 1 month ahead.

☐ Freeze baked, unfrosted cake layers up to 4 months.

☐ Assemble and freeze unbaked casseroles, meat pies, and filo pastries up to 1 month ahead.

☐ Wash salad greens and pat dry; wrap in a tea towel, place in a plastic storage bag, and refrigerate for up to 24 hours.

☐ Wash, trim, and blanch vegetables up to 24 hours ahead.

☐ Marinate meat, poultry or fish; refrigerate 1 to 24 hours.

☐ Make stocks and sauces ahead and freeze up to 1 month, or refrigerate up to 3 days.

☐ Prepare soups, stews, and vegetable purées; refrigerate up to 3 days or freeze up to 2 weeks.

☐ Cakes can be assembled and frosted about 24 hours before serving.

Do Now

☐ Bake muffin batters, fruit pies, and tart shells just before serving.

☐ Bake casseroles, meat pies, and filo pastries from the freezer.

☐ Tear washed greens and toss with dressing.

☐ Reheat blanched vegetables in boiling water or a steamer basket, or sauté them in butter and oil.

☐ Cook marinated meat, poultry, or fish.

☐ Pull stocks and sauces from the freezer and reheat without defrosting.

☐ Reheat refrigerated or frozen soups, stews, and vegetable purées.

When ripe, juicy peaches are in season, double this bread pudding recipe and freeze some for busy days or unexpected guests. Everyone will enjoy this sublime and simple dessert.

PEACH AND PECAN BREAD PUDDING

Assemble this dessert early in the day and relax. The bread will absorb the custard while the dish rests in the refrigerator.

    12 slices (each about ¾ in. thick)
        French bread
     ½ cup butter, melted
     4 cups half-and-half
    1¼ cups sugar
    10 egg yolks
     1 teaspoon vanilla extract
        Pinch salt
     4 large peaches, peeled, pitted,
        and thinly sliced
     1 cup toasted pecan halves
        Vanilla ice cream or whipped
        cream, for accompaniment

1. Preheat oven to 425° F. Brush bread with some of the melted butter. Put bread slices on a baking sheet and bake until golden brown (about 10 minutes).

2. In a 2-quart saucepan over medium-low heat, bring half-and-half to a simmer (bubbles will appear at edge of pan). In a 3-quart bowl beat sugar with egg yolks; whisk hot half-and-half into egg-sugar mixture. Stir in vanilla and salt; set aside.

3. Pour remaining butter into a 9-by 12-inch baking dish. Place 6 bread slices in dish; strain half of egg-custard mixture through a wire mesh strainer over bread. Distribute sliced peaches over bread-custard mixture; top with pecans. Arrange remaining bread over fruit and strain remaining egg-custard mixture over bread. Let stand 1 hour, covered with plastic wrap, or refrigerate up to 6 hours.

4. If refrigerated, remove from refrigerator about 2 hours before serving. Preheat oven to 325° F. Bake, uncovered, until golden brown and slightly crusty (about 1¾ hours). Serve warm, cut into squares and topped with vanilla ice cream or whipped cream.

Serves 8 to 10.

118

MOM'S DOUBLE DUTCH CHOCOLATE CAKE

This cake is easier to make than a packaged mix and just as foolproof. The chocolate frosting is a snap as well if you follow the simple steps for melting chocolate described in the recipe. This technique works especially well for white chocolate, which tends to scorch very easily.

2¼ cups flour
1¼ teaspoons baking soda
1 teaspoon salt
2¼ cups firmly packed brown sugar
1 cup butter, melted
½ cup unsweetened cocoa
1 cup water
2 eggs
1 tablespoon vanilla extract
⅔ cup sour cream

Chocolate Frosting

14 ounces semisweet chocolate
1⅓ cups sour cream, at room temperature
½ teaspoon vanilla extract
½ cup unsalted butter

1. Preheat oven to 350° F. Line bottoms of two 8-inch-diameter cake pans with parchment paper, or butter and flour bottoms and sides.

2. Sift together flour, baking soda, and salt; set aside. In a 1-quart saucepan melt brown sugar, butter, and cocoa in the water; cool slightly. In a 3-quart bowl stir together eggs, vanilla, and sour cream. Add cocoa mixture to egg mixture, then stir in sifted flour mixture. Divide evenly between prepared cake pans.

3. Bake until cake is dry on top and a skewer inserted 2 inches from edge comes out clean (30 to 35 minutes). Cool 10 minutes. Slip a knife around edge of each cake pan, invert cakes onto a cooling rack, and cool completely.

4. Place one cake layer on an 8-inch cardboard cake round or serving dish. Spread layer with ¾ cup frosting. Top with second layer and frost top and sides of cake.

Serves 8 to 10.

Chocolate Frosting Fill a 12-inch skillet with water to a depth of 1½ inches and bring to a boil. Chop semisweet chocolate into pea-sized pieces and place in a metal mixing bowl. Turn off heat under skillet, place mixing bowl of chocolate in hot water, and stir until chocolate is melted. Stir in sour cream, vanilla, and butter until smooth. Let rest at room temperature until spreading consistency (15 to 30 minutes), stirring occasionally.

Makes about 2½ cups.

APPLE AND WALNUT STRUDEL

Although apples are the classic filling for this Hungarian dessert, fresh peaches, cherries, or mixed berries will also be delicious. Add 2 tablespoons flour to these juicier fruit mixtures so they will thicken sufficiently.

¾ cup butter, melted
1 cup walnuts, coarsely chopped
4 tart green apples, peeled and chopped
1 cup golden raisins
3 tablespoons dark rum
½ cup sugar
1½ tablespoons cinnamon
1 teaspoon nutmeg
8 sheets filo dough
4 tablespoons bread crumbs

1. Preheat oven to 350° F. Brush a rimless baking sheet with 1 tablespoon of the melted butter. Place walnuts on baking sheet and toast 8 to 10 minutes; reserve.

2. In a 2-quart bowl toss together apples, golden raisins, and rum; let sit 15 minutes.

3. To apple mixture add sugar, cinnamon, nutmeg, and nuts. Toss with 4 tablespoons of the melted butter.

4. Place 1 sheet filo dough on work surface; brush with melted butter. Cover with a second sheet of dough and brush with butter. Repeat with 2 more sheets filo dough. Sprinkle

half the bread crumbs in a 2-inch-wide strip along narrow edge of dough. Place one half of apple mixture on bread crumbs. Roll up into a cylinder, tucking outer edges into cylinder as you roll. Place, crumb side down, on baking sheet. Repeat with remaining filo sheets and filling.

5. Bake strudels until golden brown (about 55 minutes). Serve warm.

Serves 8 to 10.

BLACKBERRY RICE PUDDING

Blackberries add a bright, elegant touch to a favorite homespun recipe. Prepare the mixture and store in the refrigerator, covered with aluminum foil, for up to 36 hours before baking. Or, after baking, reduce oven heat to 200° F, cover with aluminum foil, and hold in oven for up to 1 hour.

2 tablespoons butter, for greasing
6 cups cooked long-grain white rice
4 cups half-and-half
1¼ cups sugar
10 egg yolks
1 teaspoon vanilla extract
1 teaspoon ground cinnamon
Pinch salt
1 pint blackberries or 8 ounces frozen whole blackberries (without syrup)

1. Grease a 9- by 12-inch baking dish with the 2 tablespoons butter. Spoon rice into prepared dish. Preheat oven to 350° F. In a 2-quart saucepan bring half-and-half to a simmer (bubbles will appear on edges of pan).

2. In a 3-quart bowl beat sugar with egg yolks; pour hot half-and-half into eggs and sugar; stir to mix well. Stir in vanilla, cinnamon, and salt. Strain egg custard mixture over rice. Gently toss half the blackberries with rice mixture. Place in prepared dish.

3. Bake until lightly browned on top (45 minutes). Serve immediately while still warm, garnished with remaining blackberries.

Serves 12.

Served in a crystal goblet and dressed up with vanilla ice cream and your own fudge sauce, the humble, homey brownie gets uptown treatment.

BROWNIE À LA MODE

When eaten alone this rich, gooey brownie is a terrific snack, but layered in a shallow bowl with vanilla ice cream and fudge sauce, it is transformed into a chocolate lover's fantasy.

> 4 ounces unsweetened chocolate, coarsely chopped
> ½ cup unsalted butter
> 1½ cups sugar
> 3 eggs
> 1½ teaspoons vanilla extract
> ¾ cup flour
> ¼ teaspoon salt
> 1 cup toasted pecans (optional)
> 1 pint vanilla ice cream
> Chocolate Fudge Sauce (see page 37)

1. Preheat oven to 350° F. Line an 8- by 8-inch baking pan with parchment paper, or generously butter and flour.

2. In a 3-quart metal bowl, combine chocolate and butter. Place bowl in a shallow pan of water over low heat. Stir, while chocolate and butter are melting, for about 5 minutes.

3. Stir sugar into chocolate mixture while still warm. Add eggs and vanilla, mixing to combine. Sift together flour and salt; fold into chocolate mixture along with pecans (if used). Place in prepared pan and bake until a bamboo skewer inserted 2 inches from edge comes out with small moist crumbs clinging to it (about 30 minutes; brownies should be slightly underdone). Cool 20 minutes in pan on wire rack before serving.

4. Cut brownie into 16 squares. Place one square in a stemmed serving dish, top with one scoop vanilla ice cream, place a second brownie on the vanilla ice cream, top with another small scoop of vanilla ice cream, and drizzle with Chocolate Fudge Sauce. Repeat with remaining brownies, ice cream, and sauce.

Serves 8.

SPEEDY THANKSGIVING FEAST

*Rapid Roast Turkey
With Cream Gravy*

Cranberry and Corn Bread Stuffing

Old-fashioned Mashed Potatoes

*Steamed Broccoli With
Toasted Hazelnuts*

Fresh Fruit Salad

*Sweet Potato and
Cinnamon Muffins
(see page 94)*

Chris's Pumpkin Pecan Pie

*Zinfandel and
Sparkling Apple Cider*

Holiday dinners are always easier when preparation is shared by many willing hands. Once in a while, though, either because of an emergency or a last-minute change, you may find that you are responsible for the entire meal. Make the best of it, and ensure success by simplifying as much of the meal as possible and by being well organized (see Working From Lists, page 7). The only appetizers you need are olives, carrot sticks, celery, and Spicy Pecans (see page 46). This menu serves 12 to 16 people.

Preparation Plan

If necessary, this menu can be prepared and served in one day. Naturally it will take meticulous shopping and organization. For this menu, which serves 12 to 16 people, prepare a double recipe of pie dough and pie filling. Simmer the sweet potato and potatoes in separate pans. Make corn bread for the Cranberry and Corn Bread Stuffing, cook and cool remaining ingredients, and combine. Bake Chris's Pumpkin Pecan Pie. Increase oven temperature for muffins. Purée sweet potato and assemble muffin mixture. Bake and reserve until dinner. Roast turkey as directed. Start turkey stock for Cream Gravy while turkey roasts. Mash potatoes and reserve in a casserole to warm at serving time. Prepare your favorite fruit for a salad. Remove turkey from oven and set aside. Warm corn bread stuffing and mashed potatoes. At serving time, steam broccoli and toss with toasted hazelnuts.

RAPID ROAST TURKEY WITH CREAM GRAVY

Removing the backbone of the turkey and pressing bird as flat as possible in the pan halves roasting time. Purchase a fresh turkey to avoid thawing time.

> 1 turkey (16 lb)
> ½ cup butter, melted
> 2 cloves garlic, minced

Cream Gravy

> Turkey backbone, wing tips, and giblets
> 1 onion, quartered
> 1 carrot, coarsely chopped
> 1 bay leaf
> 1 sprig parsley
> 1 teaspoon dried thyme
> 6 tablespoons butter
> 6 tablespoons flour
> 2 cups whipping cream
> 2 teaspoons salt
> ½ teaspoon ground white pepper
> ¼ teaspoon ground nutmeg

1. Preheat oven to 400° F. Place turkey, breast side down, on a cutting surface. Using poultry shears or sturdy kitchen scissors, remove backbone from turkey by cutting along each side of backbone. Cut off wing tips. Reserve backbone, wing tips, and giblets for Cream Gravy.

2. Place turkey in roasting pan. Push legs down slightly so that they are flat in pan. Stir butter and garlic together in a small bowl; pour over turkey.

3. Roast turkey 15 minutes; reduce heat to 375° F and roast until 170° F on an instant-read thermometer and exterior of bird is a rich dark brown and juices run clear when joint is moved (about 2 hours and 20 minutes). After first hour baste turkey with pan juices from roasting pan. While turkey is roasting begin gravy.

4. Place roast turkey on carving board. Loosely cover with aluminum foil and let rest for 15 to 20 minutes before carving to maintain moisture of turkey and make it easier to carve. Strain pan juices into turkey broth (see below).

5. Carve turkey and serve piping hot with Cream Gravy.

Serves 16 to 20.

Cream Gravy In a 3-quart saucepan place backbone, wing tips, and giblets, onion, carrot, bay leaf, parsley, and thyme, and cover with water. Bring to a boil, reduce heat, and simmer for 30 minutes. Remove from heat and strain turkey broth into a mixing bowl. Discard turkey pieces. Stir in strained pan juices from roasted turkey. In a 3-quart saucepan over medium heat, melt butter. Whisk in flour, mixing until well combined and cooked (about 2 minutes). Add reserved turkey broth mixture and whisk until smooth. Cook over medium heat until reduced slightly (10 minutes). Whisk in whipping cream and cook another 10 minutes. Season with salt, pepper, and nutmeg.

Makes about 6 cups.

CRANBERRY AND CORN BREAD STUFFING

Cranberries, walnuts, and corn bread mingle to make a superb stuffing for turkey, pork roast, Cranberry-Stuffed Pork Chops (see page 112), and roast chicken. This stuffing is particularly appropriate for Thanksgiving. Corn and cranberries are native American foods that were part of the Indian diet when the Pilgrims arrived in the New World. If desired, add 8 ounces chopped fresh oysters to the stuffing mixture.

   4 tablespoons butter
   1 carrot, minced
   1 stalk celery, minced
   1 medium onion, minced
      Quick Corn Bread
      (see page 116)
  ¼ cup minced parsley
   3 tablespoons dried whole
      sage leaves
   2 teaspoons salt
   1 teaspoon pepper
   1 cup cranberries
   1 cup toasted walnuts
   3 cups hot turkey broth,
      Chicken Stock (see page 56),
      or water

1. In a 12-inch skillet over medium heat, melt butter; add carrot, celery, and onion and sauté until softened and cooked thoroughly (10 minutes).

2. Cut corn bread in 1-inch cubes. In a 3-quart bowl toss corn bread cubes with cooked carrot, celery, and onion, and parsley, sage, salt, and pepper. Add cranberries and walnuts. Mix in turkey broth.

3. Preheat oven to 350° F (or turn heat down to 350° F while turkey rests). Place stuffing in a 3-quart casserole and cover loosely with aluminum foil. Bake until hot (about 30 minutes).

Makes 10 cups stuffing, 12 to 16 servings.

OLD-FASHIONED MASHED POTATOES

These wonderfully simple potatoes are easily assembled, but can also be prepared a week or two ahead of the big day if you have the time; store in freezer and reheat at serving time. If used from refrigerator or if defrosting first, warm potatoes in a 350° F oven for 30 minutes. Frozen potatoes need to bake at 350° F for about 1¼ hours. If you don't have two ovens, you may want to defrost the casserole in the refrigerator to shorten the baking time or partially bake it before the turkey goes into the oven, rewarming at serving time. Serve with Cream Gravy (see page 121).

  10 potatoes, peeled and cut
      in 1-inch cubes
   6 cloves garlic, peeled
   8 tablespoons butter
  ⅔ cup milk or whipping cream
   3 ounces cream cheese, at room
      temperature
   2 eggs
  ½ cup (about 2 small bunches)
      minced chives
  1½ tablespoons salt
  ½ teaspoon ground white pepper

1. In a 4-quart saucepan cover potato cubes and garlic with water. Bring to a boil over medium heat, reduce heat to low, then simmer until tender and easily pierced with a sharp knife (30 minutes).

2. When potatoes are cooked, drain water. Press potatoes and garlic through a potato ricer or mash in their cooking pan. Stir in butter, milk, cream cheese, eggs, chives, salt, and pepper. Serve immediately or store in an ovenproof casserole.

Serves 12 to 16.

CHRIS'S PUMPKIN PECAN PIE

Partially baked tart shells and pie crusts keep in the freezer, well wrapped, for several months. Making the easy filling and doing the final baking before serving give the pie a fresher flavor, although you can bake the pie a day or two ahead and refrigerate it. Then, while enjoying the rest of the dinner, refresh the pie in a 350° F oven for 15 to 20 minutes. To serve 12 to 16 people, prepare two pies.

   1 cup firmly packed
      brown sugar
   2 tablespoons butter, softened
  ⅔ cup pecan halves
   1 eight-inch unbaked Butter
      Pastry tart shell (see page 12)
   3 eggs
   2 egg yolks
   1 cup pumpkin purée
   1 tablespoon flour
  ¼ teaspoon ground cloves
  ¼ teaspoon ground cinnamon
  ½ teaspoon salt
   2 cups whipping cream
   6 tablespoons confectioners'
      sugar, for garnish

1. Preheat oven to 400° F. Line unbaked tart shell with aluminum foil and fill with dried beans or metal pie weights. Bake 12 minutes; remove foil and beans. Set aside to cool completely. Mix ⅓ cup brown sugar and butter. Spread mixture in bottom of cooled tart shell. Dot with pecans and bake 10 minutes; set aside.

2. While pastry bakes, mix eggs, egg yolks, pumpkin purée, flour, remaining brown sugar, cloves, cinnamon, salt, and 1 cup whipping cream.

3. Reduce oven to 325° F. Place filling in pastry shell; bake until a knife inserted into pie is dry when removed (about 45 minutes). Cool.

4. Beat remaining cream with confectioners' sugar and pipe onto pie at serving time.

Serves 8.

It is possible for one cook to assemble a marvelous Thanksgiving menu such as this one on short notice and in one day.

INDEX

Note: Page numbers in italics refer to photos separated from recipe text.

U.S. MEASURE AND METRIC MEASURE CONVERSION CHART

		Formulas for Exact Measures			Rounded Measures for Quick Reference		
	Symbol	When you know:	Multiply by:	To find:			
Mass (Weight)	oz	ounces	28.35	grams	1 oz		= 30 g
	lb	pounds	0.45	kilograms	4 oz		= 115 g
	g	grams	0.035	ounces	8 oz		= 225 g
	kg	kilograms	2.2	pounds	16 oz	= 1 lb	= 450 g
					32 oz	= 2 lb	= 900 g
					36 oz	= 2¼ lb	= 1,000g (1 kg)
Volume	tsp	teaspoons	5.0	milliliters	¼ tsp	= ¹⁄₂₄ oz	= 1 ml
	tbsp	tablespoons	15.0	milliliters	½ tsp	= ¹⁄₁₂ oz	= 2 ml
	fl oz	fluid ounces	29.57	milliliters	1 tsp	= ⅙ oz	= 5 ml
	c	cups	0.24	liters	1 tbsp	= ½ oz	= 15 ml
	pt	pints	0.47	liters	1 c	= 8 oz	= 250 ml
	qt	quarts	0.95	liters	2 c (1 pt)	= 16 oz	= 500 ml
	gal	gallons	3.785	liters	4 c (1 qt)	= 32 oz	= 1 liter
	ml	milliliters	0.034	fluid ounces	4 qt (1 gal)	= 128 oz	= 3¾ liter
Length	in.	inches	2.54	centimeters	⅜ in.		= 1 cm
	ft	feet	30.48	centimeters	1 in.		= 2.5 cm
	yd	yards	0.9144	meters	2 in.		= 5 cm
	mi	miles	1.609	kilometers	2½ in.		= 6.5 cm
	km	kilometers	0.621	miles	12 in. (1 ft)		= 30 cm
	m	meters	1.094	yards	1 yd		= 90 cm
	cm	centimeters	0.39	inches	100 ft		= 30 m
					1 mi		= 1.6 km
Temperature	°F	Fahrenheit	⁵⁄₉ (after subtracting 32)	Celsius	32°F		= 0°C
					68°F		= 20°C
	°C	Celsius	⁹⁄₅ (then add 32)	Fahrenheit	212°F		= 100°C
Area	in.²	square inches	6.452	square centimeters	1 in.²		= 6.5 cm²
	ft²	square feet	929.0	square centimeters	1 ft²		= 930 cm²
	yd²	square yards	8361.0	square centimeters	1 yd²		= 8360 cm²
	a.	acres	0.4047	hectares	1 a.		= 4050 m²